Divestment and Strategic Change

Edited by

JOHN COYNE AND MIKE WRIGHT
University of Nottingham

Philip Allan/Barnes & Noble Books

First published 1986 by
PHILIP ALLAN PUBLISHERS LIMITED
MARKET PLACE
DEDDINGTON
OXFORD OX5 4SE

and in the USA by
BARNES & NOBLE BOOKS
81 ADAMS DRIVE
TOTOWA
NEW JERSEY 07512

British Library Cataloguing in Publication Data

Divestment and strategic change.
1. Corporate divestiture
I. Coyne, John, *1951–* II. Wright, Michael, *1952–*
658.1'6 HD2746.6

ISBN 0-86003-538-7
ISBN 0-86003-641-3 Pbk

Library of Congress Cataloging in Publication Data
Main entry under title:

Divestment and strategic change.

Includes index.
1. Corporate divestiture – Addresses, essays, lectures.
2. Corporate divestiture – United States – Addresses, essays, lectures. 3. Corporate divestiture – Great Britain – Addresses, essays, lectures. I. Coyne, John, 1951– II. Wright, Mike.
HD2746.6.D58 1985 658.1'6 84-24456
ISBN 0-389-20547-8 (hbk.)

Typeset by MHL Typesetting Ltd., Coventry
Printed and bound in Great Britain by
The Camelot Press, Southampton

Contents

About the Contributors

John Coyne BA, a graduate of Nottingham University, is currently Lecturer in Industrial Economics at the University of Nottingham and Warden of the Cripps Hall of Residence. He has published widely in such diverse areas as the Economics of National Heritage, Shop Stewards and Industrial Democracy. Recently he has been researching in the general area of small- and medium-sized enterprises and their role in the economy, and corporate change. His publications include *Can Workers Manage*? (with B. Chiplin and L. Sirc), *The Birth of Enterprise* (with M.R. Binks) and *Management Buyouts* (with M. Wright), and he has been a contributor to several other books. He has written for Bank Reviews and in the national press and has published articles in the *Journal of Economic Studies, Industrial Relations Journal*, and *Regional Studies* as well as a wide range of professional journals.

Mike Wright BA, MA, AIL, is Lecturer in Industrial Economics with special reference to Accounting at the University of Nottingham. He has published several books and numerous articles in academic and professional journals reflecting his wide research interests in management control systems, management buy-outs, competition policy, nationalised industry performance and control, divestment, small firm finance, inflation accounting, the determination of audit fees, and trade credit. His publications include *Competition Policy, Profitability and Growth* (with D.P. O'Brien, W.S. Howe and R.J. O'Brien), *Management Buyouts: Corporate Trend for the 80s* (with R.V. Arnfield, B. Chiplin and M. Jarrett), *Computers, Information and Manufacturing Systems* (with D.J. Rhodes), *Management Buyouts* (with J. Coyne) and *Manage I.T.* (with D.J. Rhodes). He has published articles in *Accounting and Business Research, Journal of Business Finance and Accounting, Antitrust Bulletin, European Journal of Operations Research, Journal of Management Studies, Journal of Applied Systems Analysis, Long-Range Planning* and other journals.

Professor Ray Thomas B Com, M Com, LlD, is currently Professor of Business Administration at the University of Bath where he has also been Head of the School of Management and a Pro-Vice-Chancellor. He has had a distinguished career as teacher, researcher and consultant. He is Chairman of a little Neddy and the Avon Area Manpower Board, and is much involved in the encouragement of new business, serving on committees of both the ESRC and the SERC. In 1982 he was the Chairman of the Committee to investigate the implications of the Laker Collapse. It is mainly in the area of management and corporate policy making that Professor Thomas has made his mark and he is the author of two major texts now in their second editions: *The Government of Business* and *Business Policy*. He was awarded the OBE in 1978, is a recipient of the BIM's Burnham Medal, and is a Companion of the BIM. He was awarded his LlD (honoris causa) by the CNAA in 1980.

Gary Davis, who has a degree in Mathematics from the University of New Brunswick, and a Master of Business Administration from the University of Western Ontario, is Associate Professor at the University of New Brunswick where he has taught Business Policy and related subjects since 1977. He previously worked on planning studies for a provincial government and for a large telecommunications company. He has also spent several years in an organisation promoting the development of new businesses in one of Canada's less developed regions. He has recently presented a number of papers on the development of strategic trading at international conferences and is currently completing his PhD on this topic.

Professor Mark Casson is Professor of Economics at the University of Reading where he has taught since 1969. An acknowledged expert on multinational enterprises, he is also well respected for his work on economic theory and the development of economic thought. He is a prolific author whose publications include *Introduction to Mathematical Economics, The Future of the Multinational Enterprise* (with P.J. Buckley), *Alternatives to the Multinational Enterprise, The Entrepreneur: An Economic Theory, The Growth of International Business, The Theory of the Multinational Enterprise: Selected Papers* (with P.J. Buckley) and *Multinations and World Trade* (with associates) as well as a number of books on unemployment. He has written widely in academic journals including the *Economic Journal, Econometrica*, and the *Review of Economic Studies*, and has contributed to a large number of edited volumes on multinationals, international trade and unemployment.

Professor Denis O'Brien BSc, PhD graduated from University College, London and took his PhD at Queen's University, Belfast. He was Assistant Lecturer, Lecturer, and Reader at Queen's University, Belfast from 1963 to 1972, and since 1972 has been Professor of Economics at the University of Durham. His research interests include the history of economic thought and competition policy. His publications include *Information Agreements, Competition and Efficiency* (with D. Swann), *J R McCulloch: A Study in Classical Economics, The Correspondence of Lord Overstone, Competition in British Industry* (with D. Swann *et al.*), *J R McCulloch: Treatise on Taxation, The Classical Economists, Competition Policy, Profitability and Growth* (with W.S. Howe, D.M. Wright and R.J. O'Brien), *Pioneers of Modern Economics in Britain* ((ed) with J.R. Presley), *Authorship Puzzles in the History of Economics* (with A.C. Darnell) and *Economic Theory in Historical Perspective* ((ed) with J. Creedy). He has published articles in *Economica, Scottish Journal of Political Economy, History of Political Economy, Manchester School, Journal of Industrial Economics* and other journals.

Alistair Bruce MA, PhD is Lecturer in Industrial Economics at the University of Nottingham. He graduated from St Andrews and took his PhD at Heriot-Watt University. His research has focused on the areas of Public Sector Economics and Political Economy as well as Energy Economics on which he has published in *Managerial and Decision Economics*.

Preface

Our principal aim in drawing together this particular collection of contributions is to help establish a balance in the literature on corporate change and perhaps even turn the tide against the prevalent belief in the inevitability of increased concentration and all that it entails. The process of divestment is in our view as worthy of close attention as the process of acquisition: the decision to sell is as vital as the decision to buy. In its various forms divestment helps to identify and highlight the boundaries of an organisation. Moreover, it serves to emphasise the limits to central organisational control, particularly in a rapidly changing commercial environment. Where trading relationships exist between a parent and subsidiary, the process of divestment also brings into focus the circumstances under which the introduction of a market transaction may be preferable to continued control through an internal hierarchy. It is to be hoped that increased awareness and acceptability of divestment as a corporate strategic option will provide both senior management and policy makers alike with a powerful tool for dealing with organisational and industrial restructuring as a means of adapting to change. Without such adaptation, there can be little prospect of long-run survival.

In acknowledging the efforts of those who have helped bring this work to fruition, our most grateful thanks go to the five authors who contributed chapters. We must record our particular satisfaction with the quality of the papers they have prepared, leaving us with a rather more pleasurable editorial task than might have been expected. We hope that our editorial efforts have done justice to their work. Each piece has been written specifically for this volume and designed to complement the other contributions. We are most pleased that our distinguished contributors have found the time in their busy schedules to orientate their work so sympathetically to the needs of this collection.

Each author has made his own acknowledgements to those who provided assistance in their research and who commented on drafts of their papers. We wish to add our thanks to them for their valuable assistance. In addition, we would like to thank the many typists who have prepared, amended and re-typed (not to say laboured over) the various drafts which have gone into producing this manuscript. We can only speak for ourselves when we say that they have regularly produced the goods out of adversity.

1

An Introduction to Divestment: The Conceptual Issues

John Coyne and Mike Wright

Introduction

Until the 1980s a disproportionate amount of attention was given to the growth and development of companies by merger and acquisition. Whilst many acquisitions were part of other groups, little attention was given to the decision to sell and almost exclusive focus was brought to bear on the decision to buy. The performance of companies post-acquisition has been the subject of enquiry and there has been some dissatisfaction that the doctrine of 'big is best' has not been proven and the anticipated economies of scale not realised (Meeks 1977; O'Brien 1978; Utton 1974).

Nevertheless the focus on the divorce between ownership and control is understandable within the framework of theories of the firm which place emphasis on the discretionary power of management. Acquisitive behaviour fits well with the emphasis on empire building and the extension of authority (Mueller 1972; Marris and Mueller 1980). The decision to sell, however, is an equally important decision in the realisation of company or managerial corporate objectives, and it may well be the case that something has to be sold before something else can be bought. It seems only logical, therefore, that attention should be focused on the decisions to sell and the attainment of corporate objectives through a realignment of subsidiaries within large groups.

The future of divestment, and the way companies adapt to their changing commercial environment, is the subject of this chapter and provides the groundwork for the additional contributions which follow. As divestment is so little examined, the chapter spells out quite carefully the adjustment process and the way in which divestments can occur, and the different forms they can take from partial to complete severance, and by various routes.

The stages through which a company progresses which precede the divestment are outlined, and the limited literature on post-divestment performance of both the former parent and the divestee is reviewed. In particular the effects on both efficiency and share price performance are examined.

From this general discussion a number of issues are taken up in later chapters and particular types of divestment (of the 'clean break' type) are examined in detail to marry the conceptual and practical matters.

The Divestment Spectrum

Divestment may be described in simple terms as the sale by an organisation of one part of itself to another party. The impression given by such a definition is that the severance of ownership is always complete and final. Whilst this is very often the case, it is clear from Figure 1.1 that such an approach does not provide a complete description of the process. It is useful to classify the various types of divestment by the nature of the ownership severance involved, the relative frequency with which it takes place and the post-divestment ownership form for the part disposed of. Although the focus of this volume is the complete severance type, it is vital to point out the alternatives as they may well alter the corporate strategy decision process.

For some types of product or service, franchising is the means by which trade can take place. The precise form varies, but normally involves some kind of competition for the exclusive right to produce a firm's product or service in a particular area for a given period. Contracting-out has similarities with franchising, in that firms

Type	*Ownership severance*	*Relative frequency*	*New ownership form*
(1) Franchising	Complete; limited period	Frequent	Subsidiary or independent
(2) Contracting-out	Complete, but trading relationship remains	Frequent	Subsidiary
(3) Sell-off	Complete; usually permanent	Small sell-offs frequent; part of a series Large sell-offs – function of crisis	Subsidiary
(4) Management/ leverage buy-out	Usually complete & permanent; parent may retain equity interest	Small – frequent Large – becoming more frequent in UK; frequent in US	Independent
(5) Spin off/ demerger	Split rather than severance; may involve dilution of ownership; usually permanent	Small – frequent, especially in high technology, where management takes equity stake	Quasi-independent
(6) Asset-swap/ strategic trade	Complete, but exchange involved so size of parent maintained	Unusual; small asset-swaps may arise in anti-trust divestitures; large asset-swaps voluntary	Subsidiary

Figure 1.1 Spectrum of Divestment

engage in tenders for the production of a service. However, the distinction may be made that contracting-out involves the provision of a specific good or service to the parent company. To all intents and purposes, the contractor obtains a monopoly position for the period of the contract, and the service or good will normally be provided by a contractor who is a specialist in that area. Thus the benefits of economies of scale may be obtained (not least by the contractee through the payment for lower cost services) which the contractee, who is a non-specialist in that area, could not enjoy. In this way a company may 'dispose' of part of the operation which it does not wish to exploit internally but maintain an ownership interest.

A sell-off is likely to be a permanent arrangement involving an identifiable business unit rather than the provision of a good or service. For the reasons elaborated below, a sell-off may involve units that are small in relation to the parent either in a series of divestments, a one-off divestment or a large sell-off, but in all cases the subsidiary either becomes independent or part of another organisation. In the case of management or leverage buy-outs, for example, where a part of a large company is sold to its management or a consortium of institutions, it becomes an independent entity. In some cases, especially in the US, the parent may retain a short- or medium-term equity interest which effectively amounts to a deferral of payment.

Where spin-offs occur, the question of immediate and complete ownership severance does not arise. Rather, part of the parent company becomes a separate legal entity but remains substantially owned by the same shareholders as the parent (Burgelman 1984). Some dilution of ownership may occur in the short-term if managers are given a significant equity stake, as in spin-offs of new high-technology developments (Garvin 1983) or where the shares of both parts are traded on separate stock exchanges, as is the case with the recent demerger at Bowater which is discussed in detail in Chapter 3. The part which is spun off may be regarded as quasi-independent since it can decide its own management structure and raise finance in its own right.

The case of asset-swaps or strategic trades are treated separately because, strictly speaking, little if any funds change hands. Transfer of ownership is effected by exchanging some of the assets of one firm for some of those of another. A match is required, but this is not between what one company has to sell and what another is prepared to pay; it is, rather, between what one company has which it wishes to dispose of and what part of another company is prepared to accept, and vice versa. It might thus be expected that the available market is considerably narrowed.

In all the cases of divestment just described, the part of the organisation disposed of may be small (say 10 per cent) or large (greater than 10 per cent) in relation to the parent. Having outlined the types of divestment, attention is now turned to a consideration of how the need for divestment might arise and the circumstances under which each of the above might be appropriate.

The Growth of Firms and Adaptation of the Organisation

Firms may seek to grow in order to satisfy a number of objectives, the major ones of which are likely to be the maximisation of shareholder wealth or managerial welfare. In both cases the avoidance of takeover and the maintenance of the firm as an independent entity are likely to weigh heavily in determining managements' behaviour.

In order to obtain growth, a company has seven broad policy options available to it: the expansion of existing activities and markets; vertical integration; diversification; innovation; international operations; defence of an existing market; or divestment and restructuring (Chiplin 1982). The individual options are not mutually exclusive and the last two named may require some degree of marking-time or contraction before longer-term growth is possible. International operations may involve elements of the other options as a company may integrate backwards by securing essential raw material supplies overseas or seek to exploit some technical superiority in widening its sales into an international context (Franco 1976; Dunning in Casson 1983; Caves 1982). Growth may be achieved through any of these options by internal (organic) or by external (acquisition) means.

Before embarking upon any action designed to achieve growth, a company determines its corporate strategy, which compares where the firm is at present with where it wants to be, to indicate what needs to be done to meet its objectives. The assessment of the company's current position will include an examination of its markets, its financial resources and its other resources in general. Strategic search is undertaken so as to identify feasible courses of action that will close the gap between the company's current and desired future positions. The procedure will need to take account of the competitive environment in which both the company and possible new ventures are operating. It will be necessary to establish investment criteria which new projects must meet in order to be acceptable, and to ensure that adequate managerial expertise is available to put plans into action.

The benefits to the company as a whole from the successful implementation of the above growth strategy may accrue from technical economies of scale or by the synergy released as two or more separate entities are forced together. It has increasingly come to be argued in recent years that benefits may also accrue to the company from the reduction in transactions costs which are derived from the internalisation of transactions previously carried out through market contracts (see Williamson 1981). Such internalisation of transactions is considered to reduce opportunistic behaviour on the part of customers or suppliers. However, in order to be successful it may be necessary for the management hierarchy in the company to become divisionalised so that opportunistic behaviour by managers within the company may be minimised (Teece 1984). The divisionalised management organisation may be accompanied by a centralisation of the finance function, and in particular an internal capital market may be set up so as to allocate investment funds between competing divisions according to the firm's own investment criteria. It has been argued that as greater information is likely to be available internally, such allocations of investment funds should be more efficiently carried out than if recourse was made to the external capital market (Williamson 1975).

The above brief discussion has set out the basic ground rules for how firms may plan, undertake and manage their growth. The points that have been raised are likely to be appropriate to many firms. The next section examines how the above strategies and management structures may begin to break down and provide the circumstances under which divestment may be considered.

The Emergence of a Need to Change

The corporate strategy adopted by a firm and the consequent direc-

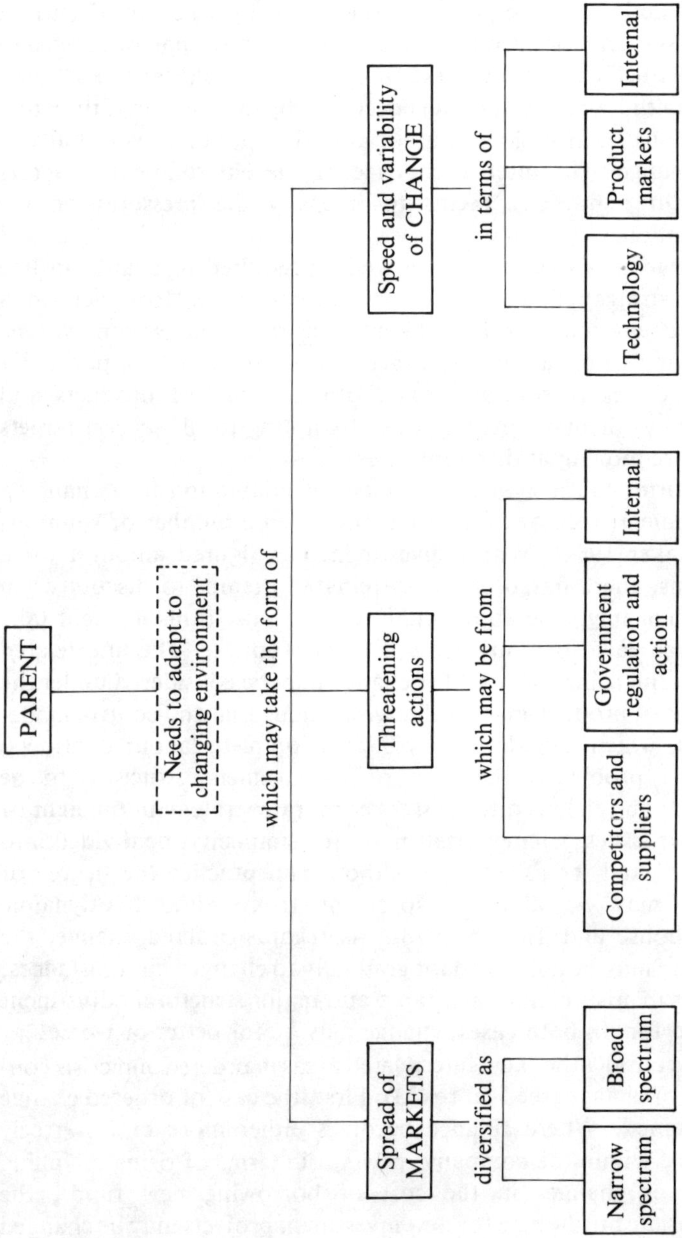

Figure 1.2 The Parent and the Need for Strategic Change

tion of action is a response to the company's perceived current weaknesses and the current environment and how that is expected to change. Such change may take three main forms (Figure 1.2), arising from the spread of markets occupied by the company, threatening actions from various sources, and the speed and variability of such change. The interdependence of the environmental factors shown in Figure 1.2 seems to intensify the pressures on the organisation.

Management structures may well be required to change in line with a strategy designed to cope with change. However, in a dynamic environment it is likely that the organisation will be attempting to hit a moving target. More precisely, if a particular firm operates in several areas (both in terms of products and geography), it may be viewed as attempting to hit several targets which are moving at different rates.

For firms faced with the problem of adaptation to a changing environment, recent research has proposed a number of solutions (e.g. Aaker 1984). Whilst divestment has figured amongst these solutions, there has been no systematic attempt to discuss when divestment might be appropriate, the various forms it might take and when each form might itself be appropriate. The interrelated issues influencing the need for change may be considered under the headings of product-market changes; managerial and control inadequacies, which include the issue of incomplete labour contracts; financial problems; the type of management structure to be adopted; and the need to reassess corporate strategy in the light of the other issues. Change itself may, for simplicity, be divided into 'ordered' and 'crisis' change, although in practice the degree of change may lie along a spectrum from static to dynamic (Waterhouse and Tiessen 1978). As regards ordered change, the company may be able to adapt gradually to changed circumstances, whereas in crisis conditions, rapid and major structural adjustment is called for. In both cases, change may be for better or worse!

Now consider the 'key' interrelated areas in ordered and crisis conditions of change (see Figure 1.3). First, the case of ordered change is examined. Where finance becomes either more or less freely available within the company, perhaps in terms of rising or falling profits or changes in the cost of borrowing new funds, the appropriate hurdle rate for new investment projects may be changed accordingly. As jobs develop with growth of the company or change

	Finance	*Labour contracts*	*Product markets*	*Management structure*	*Corporate strategy*
Normal/ ordered change	Adjust hurdle rates for new investment	Change payment & incentive structures	Rideout cyclical falls; encourage product differentiation; excess capacity, greater expenditure to deter entry	Extend existing structure	Absorb incremental changes
'Crisis' conditions	Severe funding constraint; internal capital market fails	Insufficient incentives; inability to monitor; divisional employees require parity with co-workers; inability to change pay & incentive structure	Long-term decline in market; affinities with other product areas breakdown; entry deterrence requires ownership change	Change structure (monitoring system U→M)	Structural shift

Figure 1.3 Divestment, Change and Breakdown in Key Areas

in the nature of its products, an extension of payments and incentive structures may be required to monitor and control opportunism on the part of management. In terms of gradual changes in the product market, the company may most obviously adapt by riding out cyclical falls in demand or by developing product differentiation. Alternatively, the established dominant firm may engage in expenditure to maintain excess capacity and so deter the entry of new firms into the market. The existing management structure itself does not require major change at this stage but is able to deal with change either through supervision of the existing managers, recruitment of further managers or the non-replacement of those who leave. Overall corporate strategy may well have been set in terms of aiming for an annual substantial increase in profits within which incremental changes may be comfortably accommodated.

As far as divestment is concerned at this stage, though it may take place it would probably be limited. The most likely form that this might take is for small subsidiaries to be sold off to new parents or to the managers. The conditions under which these types of divestment might occur may be when the parent has made an acquisition of a group which includes parts that are of no interest to it or in which it has no expertise. Considerations of the failure of the subsidiary leading to divestment may arise where it does not achieve its target return on investment but nevertheless earns some profits. Divestments might also occur through the spinning-off of companies to exploit new developments which are insignificant for the parent to deal with itself.

In crisis conditions the possibilities for divestment are greatly enhanced. Consider the key areas shown in Figure 1.3. Crisis conditions may be manifested in poor performance of an organisation, though this may be relative to what could be achieved and not necessarily an absolute position. However, structural changes may be necessary to deal with these conditions as change cannot be accommodated by incremental adjustment in the organisation (Miller 1982).

Initially, as we have seen, a move from a unitary style of management to a divisionalised form may be appropriate. But a divisionalised form or organisation may also reach its own limits for a number of reasons. Firstly, as Dugger (1983) has pointed out, the divisionalised form of organisation, with its central office acting as a monitor, may prevent opportunism in the subsidiaries but the gains may be appropriated to the head office managers in the form of increased salaries rather than being passed on to shareholders. Opportunism is generally understood to refer to behaviour by the managers of the subsidiary which is not compatible with the objectives of the organisation as a whole and hence is detrimental to its performance.

Secondly, the organisation may become too diverse and large so that the central office is unable to prevent opportunism occurring in the divisions, as it cannot enforce incomplete contracts of the management (Klein 1983). This position may occur regardless of whether or not a trading relationship exists between the subsidiaries (Wright 1986).

The third reason concerns the whole question of the meaning of 'opportunism'. Where the possibility for opportunism exists, monitoring is required to ensure that subsidiary managers follow the organisation's goals. Such a view is acceptable if the organisation's goals are optimal, but this may not necessarily be true in a dynamic or turbulent environment. A rapidly changing environment may hinder the subsidiary management's ability to adapt to changed circumstances, and hence poor performance results through control loss (Wright *et al.* 1983).

Alternatively, subsidiary entrepreneurship ('intrapreneurship') may be stifled such that new opportunities which would benefit the organisation are missed. Burgelman (1984) has suggested a framework by which senior management should encourage corporate 'intrapreneurship' and find ways of integrating it into the organisation for the benefit of the company as a whole. Senior management should assess both the strategic importance and operational relatedness of each new entrepreneurial initiative. Actions can then be determined as to how best to deal with such opportunities. Depending upon the importance of the new opportunity, actions may range from direct integration, through setting up new business departments/units/divisions, to contracting out or even complete spinning off of the activity.

Initially, then, enabling subsidiary management to pursue their own goals may have feedback benefits to the organisation where it involves new opportunities which have strategic and operational importance for the company as a whole. However, there may be circumstances under which it is not possible to change labour contracts to provide the necessary incentives to managers. Such a position might occur because of the dangers, from the parent's point of view, that paying large incentive-based wages to certain sections of the company may have. It could have a ripple effect across the whole organisation, since employees in various divisions are not oblivious to what is happening in other parts of the company. This goes some way to explaining why a company may not internalise expensive consultancy services and why some of the companies providing such services have been set up by managers leaving parent organisations.

Alternatively, and of more relevance for divestment, there may be the incentive for some managers to leave the organisation and set up in direct competition to the parent company (Frank 1984). However, the pushing may come from the other side. That is, if managers engage in opportunistic behaviour which cannot be resolved internally by improved incentives so that monitoring is imperfect, the parent itself may encourage managers to buy out the company (a point which is taken up in Chapter 6). The divestment of the company in this way may have an effect on performance, which the parent can benefit from, in its trading relationships with the former subsidiary. The threat, however, must exist for other competitors in the market place to take over the trading relationship with the former parent, and the former subsidiary must to some extent remain dependent on the parent for some time. Effective competition may have been prevented previously as the subsidiary was protected by being part of the parent's organisation.

The problem of employees being aware of what employees in other divisions are earning may make it difficult to alter remuneration packages in an ailing subsidiary so as to make it viable. Spinning off the subsidiary and retaining an equity stake may make it easier to effect the required changes and obtain rewards from continued ownership.

Where reliance has to be placed on the workings of a capital market internal to the firm, problems may arise for newer opportunities either because the project may only exceed the organisation's required rate of return in the longer term, and is hence subject to risk and uncertainty, or because it may lose out to the political bargaining processes which exist between divisions. Such a position may be difficult but not fatal where sufficient funds are available in the firm as a whole. As the majority of investment funds of UK firms are generated internally (e.g. in 1983 the figure was 56.3 per cent), severe problems may arise where performance of the firm is weak. Alternatively, a part of the business may demand large injections of funds to finance major investment which is required if it is to remain competitive. The parent may be quite profitable but unable to generate internally the level of funds required, so that the internal capital market breaks down. Recourse may then be made to the external capital market in order to raise the additional funds. But the effectiveness of the capital market in this regard, particularly in the UK, has been subject to much criticism (e.g. Briston 1977; Wilson 1980). The recent dominance of the UK capital market by pension funds is said to have led to over-emphasis on the secondary rather than the primary (new issue) market and to investment funds being diverted away from areas where substantial returns may only be forthcoming some way into the future. This is less of a problem in the US stock market.

A further substantial impediment to the raising of new funds may be the normal requirement on the UK stock exchange that such finance should be raised by way of a rights issue to *existing* shareholders. In the US, in contrast, additional funds may be raised through offer to the general public as well as to existing shareholders. However, in some cases the market may be reluctant to provide sufficient funds at an acceptable price where it feels unable to identify the precise nature of the company's activities. This reason figures highly in Bowater's decision to separate itself into US and rest of the world businesses, as will be seen in Chapter 3.

The ability to raise extra finance externally may therefore be highly restricted for the firm as a whole. It can be even more restricted for a division which usually would have no independent means of raising funds. Possibilities may exist for foreign subsidiaries to raise some debt-funding on overseas capital markets, which could be more sympathetic than the parent's home capital market, but in general the options available are likely to be severely limited.

Where the lack of finance is absolute, parents may sell off subsidiaries which are the greatest drain on resources or, in some severe cases, those which provide the easiest means of raising funds quickly. In a deep recession the size of the divestments may be expected to rise steeply, as was certainly the case in the UK during the early 1980s (Coyne and Wright 1982).

Long-term decline or serious poor performance in a market area in which the organisation operates may lead it to consider divestment as a means of adjustment (Harrigan 1980). The extent to which this route is possible is a function of the barriers to exit faced by the organisation (Porter 1976). The price that may be obtained by the vendor is closely related to the extent to which asymmetry of information exists between the parties to the transaction (Chiplin and Wright 1980). Where buyers are available, barriers to exit for the parent may be reduced even though the assets being transferred are specific to a particular industry. Buyers may arise from either inside or outside the firm, both believing that the subsidiary to be disposed of may be made to perform better under new ownership. The question of sale to the current managers may be a vexed one where they are in a bargaining position which enables them to obtain the subsidiary at a discount by the threat of vetoing external purchasers. This problem may be particularly acute where the parent is desperate to sell, where the incumbent management constitute a substantial part of the worth of the subsidiary and where few alternative purchasers exist. In the UK, where such management buy-outs have occurred, discounts on the book value of assets was a common feature of transactions in the early 1980s (Coyne and Wright 1982). However, more recently the *offensive* strategy of parents to remove subsidiaries has been counter-balanced in a number of cases by a *defensive* strategy to prevent management seeking to buy out (since they are now more aware of the possibilities), especially where this is not in accord with corporate policy. One result of this shift has been for the discounts on management buy-outs to disappear (Wright and Coyne 1985).

A long-term decline in a product market may accompany breakdowns in the traditional affinities with other product areas that the organisation has been associated with (Rumelt 1982). The economic rationale for affinities with other areas may be related to vertical integration, horizontal integration or risk-spreading conglomerate behaviour. Where rapid change makes integration a less attractive option (e.g. it may be difficult to control across integrated processes, or integration in different markets may now be required) or where a change of markets to achieve effective conglomerate risk spreading is required, affinities may break down and accelerate the need for divestment.

For a firm faced with a threat to its dominant market position, entry-deterring pre-emptive action may usually take the form of investment in excess capacity (Spence 1977). However, in some circumstances capacity reduction through divestment may be warranted (Lewis 1983). By following this route a firm may reduce the cost to itself of future entry-deterring behaviour since by selling capacity it will depress prices. This route to divestment may be dangerous, though, if capacity is sold to a competitor or a parent who is able to engage in cross-subsidisation. As a result, firms may prefer to close down capacity rather than divest in order to gain strength from the profitable use of remaining capacity.

The above discussion may be extended to the case of multinational organisations. Multinational companies may, it is true, gain benefits from economising on transactions costs, but a major question arises as to the appropriate form of organisation to be adopted. In essence, the major problem concerns which form of divisionalisation to implement. Three main options are available. First, the company may choose to organise domestic divisions on a product basis, with international activities being grouped together under one heading. However, problems may arise here from a lack of co-ordination between international and domestic aspects of the same products. The second option is then to adopt a geographical divisionalisation along product lines. But this form ignores the benefits to be derived from solving common problems which arise in a particular geographical area of operation. The third option is to adjust the organisation to what is appropriate given the types of products produced or traded internationally (Caves 1982). In a developing multinational company, particularly one having to cope with restructuring, achievement of the appropriate form of organisation may be problematical. Moreover, the question of finance may become particularly difficult for this type of company. It has been argued that centralisation of the finance function is a common feature of multinational companies as financial decisions affect the profitability of the whole enterprise in an interdependent way (Caves op. cit.). Such an approach may be acceptable if the internal capital market functions adequately and there are adequate funds available in total. When the kind of conditions arise which serve to push the divisionalised firm to its limit, the necessity for co-ordination across national boundaries may exacerbate the problem.

The parent may still engage in simultaneous acquisition activity in the above circumstances where divestment has brought it within the optimal monitoring limit or where the characteristics of the acquisition are such that the possibilities for opportunistic behaviour on the part of managers do not arise (c.f. Frank op. cit.).

Stages of Divestment

The types and course of divestment discussed in the preceding sections need to be placed in the context of the development of an organisation's corporate strategy. A firm may, at a period of time, engage in all the types of divestment shown in Figure 1.3, but their appropriateness will depend on the circumstances facing it.

An approach to fitting divestment into the development of corporate strategy is shown in Figure 1.4. The organisation is assumed in Stage 1 to be in a state of fuzziness (Amey 1979). In other words, it is unclear about its objectives and as a consequence is engaged in a set of activities which display little underlying strategic logic. Arrival at this position may be the result of previous activities which have not been directed towards a coherent strategy or where the strategy has been inappropriate to the changing environment. At some point the need to reassess the position arises. This point may emerge because of a change in management, the new management reading early warning signs and deciding that change is required. In this type of case the degree of change undertaken may be quite minor. Alternatively, management's hand may eventually be forced as performance deteriorates sharply. Management may also have its hand forced in two other ways. Firstly, it could be compelled to sell off a part of the business as a requirement of competition policy. This has been less prevalent in the UK than in the US, and the relationship between divestment and anti-trust is examined in some detail in Chapter 7. The issue is also raised in the specific strategic trade in the US brewing industry examined in Chapter 4. Secondly, as has been the case recently in the UK, governmental privatisation policy may seek to break up large state-owned monopolies. This issue is dealt with in Chapter 8.

Initially consider that the company's environment is changing slowly so that the pressures faced, as outlined in Figure 1.3, are less severe. Management in Stage 2 of Figure 1.4 is able to reassess the organisation's corporate strategy by taking into account environmental uncertainties, deciding the direction to go and what is to be done to get there. The required action to achieve the reassessed strategy may involve a combination of organic growth, acquisition, divestment and a change in the management structure to ensure effective monitoring. At this point, Stage 3, changes in the management structure are likely to concern additions and extensions to the existing position. Divestments may involve franchising, contracting-out, the sell-off of small subsidiaries which are below the size at which parental control is deemed to be efficient, either to the management or another parent, and small spin-offs where, by

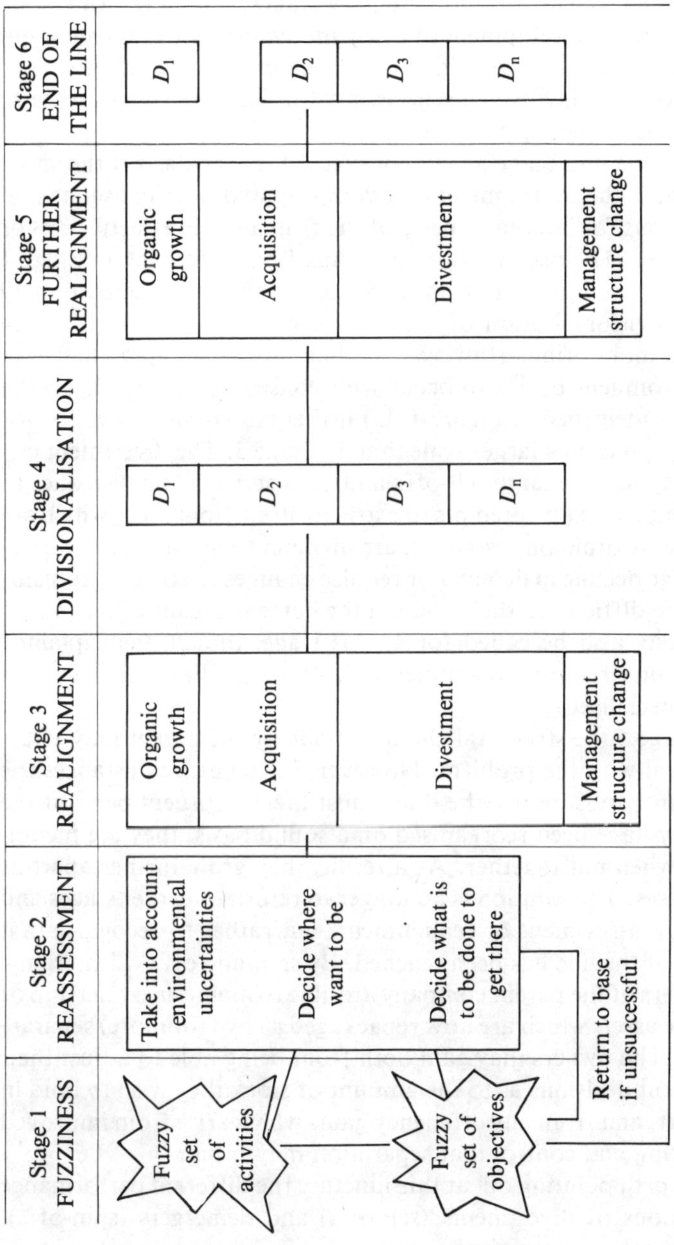

Figure 1.4 Route to Adaptation Through Ownership Change

giving management substantial equity stakes, a high return can be achieved in the development of a new innovation with which it is not worth the parent involving itself. In the cases where a high degree of independence is involved it is necessary for the divested part to be an identifiable, separate, viable entity.

Realignment in Stage 3 may not succeed, particularly if the speed of change in the environment is under-estimated, with consequential implications for internal aspects of the firm and the effectiveness of monitoring. The organisation may thus find itself back in Stage 1 and be required to start again. If Stage 3 is successful, growth may require divisionalisation of the organisational structure to secure effective monitoring. However, assume now that rapid change in the environment begins to occur with consequential effects on the key areas identified in Figure 1.3. Further realignment is called for in Stage 5, but on a larger scale than in Stage 3. The divestment element may involve large sell-offs and/or a series of smaller ones as the parent company attempts to extricate itself from areas which are an excessive drain on resources, are difficult to monitor, are suffering a large decline in demand or require changes to correct problems which are difficult to digest within the current organisation. Asset-swaps may also be called for at this stage, though, as explained earlier, the circumstances under which they are likely to occur are rather specialised.

At Stage 5 the structural changes made by the parent may effectively deal with the problem. However, in some circumstances the underlying pressure may be that whilst the constituent parts of the company have been reorganised on a sound basis, they are incompatible when put together. As a result, they grow further apart as time passes. The solution is no longer to return to earlier stages and attempt reassessment or realignment, but rather to recognise that the end of the line has been reached. By spinning off or demerging, the owners of the parent company are able to maintain ownership of the same assets which are now repackaged as two (or more) separate entities. The owners may gain both from being able to adjust their investment decisions as to the amount of stock they wish to hold in each part, and from any efficiency gains which arise from improved monitoring and control that separation may bring.

It is worth pointing out at this juncture the different performance implications of divestments (sell-offs) and demergers (spin-offs). Divestment may normally be regarded as involving some element of failure through either a misfit with the parent or unsatisfactory performance. To some extent in demergers the problem is one of success – there are difficulties from strategic and managerial points of view if the two parts remain within the same parental organisation, but there may well be shareholder gains to separation, i.e. demerger may release negative synergy in that the two parts on their own are greater than the whole. Maintaining ownership through the form afforded by demerger may produce a greater return to shareholders than would be available if one part was sold off completely and the resulting funds reinvested in new or existing ventures. As is shown in the next section, such benefits may, in practice, be quite substantial.

Studies of the Effects of Divestment on Performance

The effects of three main types of divestment have hitherto been examined in the literature, all of them relating to the United States. These types of divestment have been voluntary sell-offs, voluntary spin-offs/demergers and involuntary actions which are the result of competition policy.

The studies have focused on the effects on shareholder wealth, as an indicator of the change in performance of the firm, following divestment. As the reasons for divestment differ, the effects on shareholder wealth may also be expected to vary. In the case of enforced divestitures as part of competition policy, it is argued that if a monopoly has been enjoying its market power, the shareholders will lose by the removal of that power. Sell-offs may be undertaken as an investment decision by management. If management is interested in wealth creation, such a decision should have a positive NPV and accordingly this should provide a signal to investors which results in an upward movement in the share price. Upward movements in the share price of companies involved in spin-offs should be observed for four main reasons which may be viewed as changes in existing contracts.

First, demerger may improve the efficiency of the firm. Second, demerger may alter the contractual relations between shareholders and regulators. As a result, the manner in which rates are regulated may be relaxed to the overall benefit of shareholders. The third and fourth reasons result from transfers to the initial shareholders without the total value of the firm increasing. Either, following

Hakansson (1982) and Hite and Owers (1983), shareholders benefit from an increase in the opportunity set of securities available to them or, according to Galai and Masulis (1976), shareholders may benefit from an overall transfer from debtholders. The opportunity set of securities is increased as the initial shareholders can, following demerger, adjust the proportion of shares held in the two separate entities to suit their own risk-return preferences. A transfer from debtholders to shareholders may be said to occur when, upon demerger, shares are distributed solely to the shareholders of the parent corporation, resulting in them 'stealing away' a portion of debtholders' collateral as they no longer have any claim on the assets of the newly independent entity.

Empirical studies of the effects on shareholder wealth have essentially focused upon the measurement of abnormal returns which arise on the announcement of each particular form of divestment and relate to the USA. Studies of the effects of enforced divestitures have produced conflicting results which may be partly attributable to methodological weaknesses, particularly in the earlier studies (Brown and Warner 1980). Burns (1977, 1983), examining divestiture in the early part of the century, found positive increases in shareholder wealth, whilst studies of more recent cases by Kudla and McInish (1981) and Boudreaux (1975) have observed negative effects. Even where negative effects are recorded, it may well be that these are insufficient to outweigh the large positive abnormal returns that have been accumulated over a number of years leading up to the divestiture (Ellert 1976).

Tests on both spin-offs and sell-offs have indicated positive announcement effects on share prices. The early study by Boudreaux (1975) of 138 firms that made voluntary divestitures between 1965 and 1970 found positive effects, but he did not perform significance tests nor did he distinguish between sell-offs and spin-offs. Miles and Rosenfield (1983) analysed 55 voluntary spin-offs for the period 1963–80, Schipper and Smith (1983) examined 91 such cases for the period 1962–81 and Hite and Owers (1983) tested the effect on shareholder returns of 123 spin-offs for 1963–81. All three studies found significantly positive abnormal returns to shareholders. In examining the sources of these gains, it is interesting that both the Miles and Rosenfield and the Hite and Owers studies found that large spin-offs had a statistically significant greater positive impact on share prices. From the viewpoint of the improvement in efficiency of operation that demerger may bring, it is important to note the findings by both Schipper and Smith and Hite and Owers that there is little or no evidence to support the view that gains to shareholders arise because of transfer from bondholders. On the contrary, gains in shareholder wealth are found to be mainly attributable to the improvements in efficiency which derive from a reduction in the diversity of interests controlled by the parent company and from the increased ability provided by the new financial and operating structures for the two separate entities created on demerger to pursue their own investment opportunities.

The only recent study to date to focus solely on sell-offs is that by Alexander *et al.* (1984) which found slight positive announcement effects on shareholder returns. However, examination of the returns obtained in the period before divestment takes place reveals important differences between sell-offs and spin-offs. Sell-offs appear to be announced after a period of generally negative abnormal returns, whilst spin-offs are likely to be preceded by a period of generally positive abnormal returns. This finding seems to indicate that sell-offs are more likely to be associated with problems of failure whilst spin-offs are associated with problems of success. Overall, then, there seems to be a strong consensus in the empirical studies that demerging improves shareholder wealth. This increase in shareholder wealth appears to be derived from real efficiency gains resulting from the removal of control loss, rather than from changes in the opportunity set with which shareholders are presented.

The Issues in Practice

The process of divestment in its particular forms is developed in greater detail in the remainder of this volume. Each chapter takes a specific type of 'clean break' divestment and analyses the particular way in which the general issues on adaptation and change addressed in this chapter relate to the circumstances of the divestment form under discussion. The conceptual issues are thus taken up into a more specific context and married with the more mechanistic and practical aspects of effecting a sell-off. In all chapters the analysis is illustrated with case study material which is selected to best illustrate the process. In some instances that involves taking a case right through from beginning to end, and in others selecting material from a number of mini cases, or selecting the particular case which illustrates a point when a degree of breadth is required.

The chapters cover both voluntary and enforced divestments, the public sector as well as the private sector, and international in addition to UK and US domestic experience. The complexity and variety of issues therefore extends from the relatively straightforward to the exceptionally complex.

Chapter 2 looks at the straightforward, conventional divestment where a part of an organisation is sold off to another parent and it considers the extent of UK activity in this area. From the wide variety of divestments of this kind, Professor Thomas selects a number of cases which demonstrate the breadth of issues that this otherwise seemingly ordinary but neglected activity encompasses. He outlines not only the basic rationale, in a manner which has wide applicability across all sell-offs, but also illuminates the technical matters of ownership transfer and its wider implications.

In Chapter 3 the concept of demerger or spin-off, where an organisation is split into two quite separate legal entities, is examined with specific reference to the case of Bowater. The broad adaptation of companies to their changing environment which has been the subject of this chapter is adapted to demonstrate the precise route which may lead to demerger. The demerger itself is seen as a final stage in a process of corporate realignment, and one which is usually a last rather than a first resort in corporate development. It is no doubt a consequence of the complexity and the specific circumstances under which such a move would be a success that leads to this position.

The Bowater case provides a classic illustration of not only the technicalities of demerger but also the process of company development over time. Consequently, the chapter considers the corporate build up of the Bowater empire in order to set the scene for the demerger.

In Chapter 4, Professor Davis examines the use of an asset swap or strategic trade as a means by which two companies may simultaneously move closer to their individual corporate goals. The process requires the coincidence of objectives in two firms where one wishes to get out of an area just as another wishes to get into it and where the bundle of assets in question is of equal value. It may therefore be expected to be a relatively rare occurrence, but on the occasions when it does take place it can be seen to offer rapid adjustment at relatively low cost. The strategic trade between two major brewers in the United States, Pabst and Stroh, is analysed closely against the background of the corporate aims of the two companies and the process of realignment in the US brewing industry in general.

The major and spectacular divestment by Chrysler of its UK operation is the subject of Professor Casson's chapter in which he demonstrates the complexity and large-scale shifts involved in such a major decision by a multinational company. The case has political, economic, financial and managerial dimensions which are intertwined in the decision to divest.

Chapter 6 looks at an increasingly important part of the UK divestment scene, that of management buy-outs. The seller may be expected to be indifferent as to who he sells his company to, providing he gets the right price and does not intensify competition in markets in which he wishes to maintain an interest. However, the whole development of management buy-outs has added an extra dimension to the buyer–seller relationship. These issues are taken up in this chapter together with the practical aspects of effecting this still relatively new means of ownership transfer. Evidence from a recent survey of UK buy-outs is presented and the variety of arrangements illustrated with reference to a number of cases.

In Chapters 2 to 6 there is a presumption that the divestment is both private sector and voluntary. This need not be so and the final chapters concentrate on two dimensions where an element of compulsion may be involved.

Professor O'Brien places the divestment in the context of competition in general, and antitrust in particular. He shows how the break-up of an organisation has been held to be necessary under certain circumstances in order to generate competition in a particular industry. Although more common in the US, this enforced divestment has implications for competition policy in general. The structure–conduct–performance paradigm is used to analyse the case for enforced divestment. Emphasis is seen to be in using enforced divestment to correct problems of anti-competitive conduct rather than structure *per se*. The case of the enforced divestment at AT & T is outlined in some detail.

In the final chapter Alistair Bruce examines the second aspect where some compulsion is involved in his analysis of the privatisation of Sealink by the British Government. The wider ideological issues are outlined which supplement, and complicate, the already difficult commercial questions relating to divestments of this kind.

References

Aaker, D.A. (1984) 'How to select a business strategy', *California Management Review*, Vol. XXVI, Spring.

Alexander, G.J., Benson, P.G. and Kampmeyer, J.M. (1984) 'Investigating the valuation effects of announcement of voluntary corporate sell-offs', *Journal of Finance*, Vol. XXXIX, No. 2, June.

Amey, L.R. (1979) *Budget Planning and Control Systems*, Pitman.

Boudreaux, K.J. (1975) 'Divestiture and share price', *Journal of Financial and Quantitative Analysis*, November.

Briston, R. (1977) *The Stock Exchange and Investment Analysis*, George Allen and Unwin.

Brown, S.J. and Warner, J.B. (1980) 'Measuring security price performance', *Journal of Financial Economics*, Vol. 8.

Buckley, P. and Casson, M. (1976) '*The Future of the Multinational Enterprise*', Macmillan.

Burgelman, R.A. (1984) 'Designs for corporate entrepreneurship in established firms', *California Management Review*, Vol. XXVI, No. 3, Spring.

Burns, M.R. (1977) 'The competitive effects of trust-busting: portfolio analysis', *Journal of Political Economy*, Vol. 85.

Burns, M.R. (1983) 'An empirical analysis of stockholder injury under S.2 of The Sherman Act', *Journal of Industrial Economics*, Vol. 31.

Casson, M. (1983) *The Growth of International Business*, George Allen and Unwin.

Caves, R.E. (1982) *Multinational Enterprise and Economic Analysis*, McGraw-Hill.

Chiplin, B. (1982) 'Corporate strategy', Ch. 11, in J. Bates and J. Parkinson (eds), *Business Economics*, 3rd edn., Basil Blackwell.

Chiplin, B. and Wright, M. (1980) 'Divestment and structural change in UK industry', *National Westminster Bank Review*, February.

Coyne, J. and Wright, M. (1982) 'Buy-outs in British industry', *Lloyds Bank Review*, October.

Dugger, W.M. (1983) 'The transactions cost analysis of Oliver E. Williamson: a new synthesis?', *Journal of Economic Issues*, Vol. XVII, No. 1, March.

Ellert, J.C. (1976) 'Mergers, antitrust law enforcement and shareholder returns', *Journal of Finance*, Vol. 31.

Frank, R.H. (1984) 'Are workers paid their marginal products?', *American Economic Review*, Vol. 74, No. 4, September.

Franko, L.G. (1976) *The European Multinationals*, Harper and Row.

Galai, D. and Masulis, R.W. (1976) 'The option pricing model and the risk factor of stock', *Journal of Financial Economics*, Vol. 3, No. 1.

Garvin, D.A. (1983) 'Spin-offs and the new firm formation process', *California Management Review*, XXV, January.

Hakansson, N.H. (1982) 'Changes in the financial market: welfare and price effects', *Journal of Finance*, Vol. XXVIII, No. 3, September.

Harrigan, K.R. (1980) *Strategies for Declining Business*, Lexington Books.

Hite, G.L. and Owers, J.E. (1983) 'Security price reactions, around corporate spin-offs announcement', *Journal of Financial Economics*, Vol. 12, December.

Klein, B. (1983) 'Contracting costs and residual claims', *Journal of Law and Economics*, Vol. XXVI, No. 2.

Kudla, R.J. and McInish, R.S. (1981) 'The microeconomic consequences of an involuntary corporate spin-off', *Sloan Management Review*, Vol. 22, No. 2, Summer.

Kummer, D.R. (1978) 'Valuation consequences of forced divestiture announcements', *Journal of Economics and Business*, 30, pp. 130–36.

Lewis, T.R. (1983) 'Pre-emption, divestiture and forward contracting in a market dominated by a single firm', *American Economic Review*, Vol. 73, No. 5, December.

Marris, R. and Mueller, D.C. (1980) 'The corporation, competition and the invisible hand', *Journal of Economic Literature*, Vol. 18.

Meeks, G. (1977) *Disappointing Marriage; A Study of the Gains from Merger*, University of Cambridge, Dept. of Applied Economics, Occasional paper, CUP.

Miles, J.A. and Rosenfield, J.D. (1983) 'The effect of voluntary spin-off announcements on shareholder wealth', *Journal of Finance*, Vol. XXXVIII, No. 5, December.

Miller, D. (1982) 'Evolution and revolution: a quantum view of structural change in organisation', *Journal of Management Studies*, Vol. 19, No. 2.

Mueller, D.C. (1972) 'A life-cycle theory of the firm', *Journal of Industrial Economics*, Vol. 20.

O'Brien, D.P. (1978) 'Mergers – time to turn the tide', *Lloyds Bank Review*, October.

Panzar, J.C. and Willig, R.D. (1981) 'Economies of scope', *American Economic Review (Papers and Proceedings)*, May.

Porter, M. (1976) 'Please note location of nearest exit', *California Management Review*, Vol. XIX, No. 2, Winter.

Rumelt, R.P. (1982) 'Diversification strategy and profitability', *Strategic Management Journal*, Vol. 3.

Schipper, K. and Smith, A. (1983) 'Effects of recontracting on shareholder wealth: the case of voluntary spin-offs', *Journal of Financial Economics*, December.

Spence, M.A. (1977) 'Entry, capacity, investment and oligopolistic pricing, *Bell Journal of Economics*, Vol. 8, Autumn.

Teece, D.J. (1984) 'Economic analysis and strategic management', *California Management Review*, Vol. XXVI, No. 3, Spring.

Utton, M.A. (1974) 'On measuring the effects of industrial mergers', *Scottish Journal of Political Economy*, February.

Utton, M.A. (1977) 'Large firm diversification in British manufacturing industry', *Economic Journal*, Vol. 87.

Waterhouse, J.H. and Tiessen, P. (1978) 'A contingency framework for management accounting systems research', *Accounting, Organisations and Society*.

Williamson, O.E. (1975) *Markets and Hierarchies*, Free Press.

Williamson, O.E. (1981) 'The modern corporation: origins, evolution and attributes', *Journal of Economic Literature*, Vol. 19, December.

Wilson, Sir H. (1980) *Committee to Review the Functioning of Financial Institutions – Report*, Cmnd. 7937, HMSO.

Wright, M. (1986) 'The make-buy decision and managing markets: the case of management buy-outs', *Journal of Management Studies*, Vol. 23, July (forthcoming).

Wright, M. and Coyne, J. (1985) *Management Buy-Outs*, Croom Helm.

Wright, M., Rhodes, D. and Jarrett, M. (1983) 'Growth, survival and control in small manufacturing systems', *European Journal of Operational Research*, Vol. 9.

2

Parent-to-Parent Divestment

R.E. Thomas

Introduction

Firms survive and evolve by adapting to changing circumstances through adjustments, even fundamental switches of direction, among the activities in which they engage. To an earlier generation the broad movement from below, whereby new firms emerged to perform new tasks displacing those whose missions had been accomplished, was epitomised in Marshall's analogy of trees in a wood (Marshall 1890). New growths developed as saplings in the shade of older, more mature trees that eventually withered and died. This view breaks down when those mature firms continue as governing organisations of changing activities (Steindl 1945). Such persistence is not just a matter of their ability to hold off new rivals through their greater resources and bargaining power: it reflects their movement into, and out of, activities. In this process their shedding of activities can be as significant as their acquisition of new ones.

Today the chances of divestment are far more frequent for several reasons. The first two are the direct consequence of the spate of mergers and acquisitions of the past thirty years. As boards of directors face the consequences of such amalgamations, one problem is the sheer difficulty of managing diverse activities and enterprises; this may, in itself, lead to not just an internal regrouping but the disposal of unrelated, even incompatible, activities. A second is the consequence of the inflated prices paid, particularly in contested takeovers. In order to justify the expectations raised, quick action may be needed to release resources and cut costs. Either immediately or after a period of consolidation, specific units or activities may be disposed of. Such action ought to be distinguished from straight capital-stripping activities, although sometimes these may be difficult to differentiate.

The third reason is the combined impact of recession and accelerated structural change. This has led companies to reconsider their 'portfolios'. Where diversification has yet to yield hoped-for gains, perhaps against a now shortened period in which to prove its worth, companies may tend to 'stick to the knitting', to borrow a slogan from a popular American analysis (Peters and Waterman 1982). New or ancillary activities are therefore discarded in the interests of what are seen as the primary thrusts of a company.

This review of portfolios reaches its most critical phase for the company that is in such financial difficulties as to require drastic action. Such action may not be confined to the disposal of surplus assets (Slatter 1984) but may extend even to the disposal of a subsidiary that accounts for much of its total turnover. In January 1985 Redman Heenan International, an engineering group based at Worcester, announced plans to sell Froude Consine, a manufacturer of plant-testing equipment, to Babcock International. Froude Consine represents 80 per cent of Redman Heenan's turnover and its sale would leave the group without significant manufacturing interests.

This ability to move into, or out of, activities is not, of course, open to all private-sector, let alone public-sector, organisations. The activities of some undertakings are constrained by the very statutes that facilitate their present range of operations. Thus building societies have hitherto been constrained in the banking services that they were permitted to offer, although banks were not so constrained. The latter's earlier unwillingness to compete for home loans was a matter of custom and practice, not permitted activities. Similarly statutory bodies, such as nationalised industries, have been constrained both by their authorising statutes and through the attitudes of governments to their range of activities. Thus policies have ranged from the 'hiving-off' of parts of the steel industry, at various stages in nationalisation, to the more recent emphasis on partial or total privatisation.

Structural changes have intensified and are rarely just a question of continued acquisition or merger, particularly when complex groups are involved. An element of divestment is a possibility in any such acquisition. Thus the bid by the Bath building and property group C.H. Beazer in late 1984 for the Bath and Portland Group stimulated a successful counter-bid from Consolidated Goldfields in which Bath and Portland announced the projected disposal of their Agricultural Feeding subsidiary. The projected merger of Sterling Guarantee and P & O in 1985 was accompanied by the sale of P & O's continental car ferry operations to European Ferries (Townsend Thorensen).

Such divestment becomes very much more marked where, as in the P & O situation, we have in effect strategic trading in identifiable strategic business units. However, the latter situation is outside the scope of this chapter (see Chapter 4). Here our concern is with the disposal of business activities that are independent of such trade-offs, and also of the special circumstances of management buy-outs, whatever their composition. This still leaves us with a lot to explore.

The scale of this activity is substantial and appears to move roughly in line with the scale of acquisitions and mergers, as set out for the decade 1973–83 in the table below (Table 2.1). Whether measured by the number of firms acquired, the number of subsidiaries sold by one group to another or by the value of the transactions, there is a fluctuating but substantial scale of activity in even the quietest of years.

It is interesting to compare leading firms, both across industry generally and within each major sector, over longer periods, say 20–30 years, to see, firstly, which names survive and, secondly, of those that do, how far they have changed their scope of activities, for example through the subsidiaries that they are listed as owning and the activities in which those subsidiaries continue to trade (Whittington 1972). Taking the top 100 companies by profitability in 1972, as listed in *Management Today*, no fewer than 30 had ceased to exist as independent companies twelve years later in 1984. Of these, 8 had been absorbed or dissolved by 1978 and the rest by 1984 (Table 2.2). The great majority had been acquired or merged, with or without divestment, leaving only four to be broken up on dissolu-

Table 2.1 Acquisitions and Sales of Subsidiaries between Company Groups, 1973–83

	Acquisitions/mergers		*Sales of subsidiaries*	
	Number	*Value (£ million)*	*Number*	*Value (£ million)*
1973	1,205	1,304	254	247
1974	504	508	137	49
1975	315	219	115	70
1976	353	448	111	100
1977	481	824	109	94
1978	567	1,140	126	163
1979	534	1,656	117	186
1980	469	1,475	101	210
1981	452	1,144	125	262
1982	463	2,206	164	804
1983	447	2,343	142	436

Source: Business Monitor, 2nd Quarter, 1984.

Table 2.2 Survival of 'Top Companies by Profitability' 1972–84

	Top companies in 1971–72	*Still separate and operative 1984*
Top 100	100	70
Second 100	100	85
Top 200	200	155

Source: Management Today, October 1972, 1984.

tion. Successful survivors include some that have retained a continuity in their composition and outward appearance, particularly in industries having difficulties of entry – and perhaps egress. Rather more are present in name but with radically changed composition. Some have left their original sectors altogether, while others have so diversified that their portfolios are more analagous to investing institutions than trading concerns. Others have disappeared as separate entities or even been dissolved.

Divestment is as much a part of this process of evolution as merger and acquisition. It may be a dramatic withdrawal or a protracted affair. The readiness to dispose of an activity has to be matched by the opportunity to do so. At any time there are businesses for sale, or that could be put up for sale, if there were a buyer and the terms were right. Equally, there are potential buyers. Both suitors may have little or no knowledge of each other's interests or intentions, and the opportunities for engagement may be fleeting. But, as in human relationships, there may be a very rapid courtship and a sudden deal, just as there may be a very protracted withdrawal by one party and an equally slow matching interest by a new proprietor.

Our aim here is to review the rationale for such divestment, the conditions for its successful implementation, and some of its implications. The disposal of business units or activities is distinguished from that of specific physical assets, although the two are frequently inseparable in practice. Such disposal of business units involves the identification, even the creation, of new distinct entities, usually in the form of wholly-owned subsidiary companies. The latter may be previously independent concerns or newly created to facilitate the floating-off of particular activities.

There is, of course, a more general problem of identifying such units in the accounts and reports of groups. Indeed, it has been argued (Tricker 1984) that the whole matter of corporate accountability would be better served if performance could be identified on a strategic business unit basis rather than the current practice of the consolidation of accounts on a group basis. Such a separation would facilitate both the evaluation of performance and the identification of suitable candidates for acquisition or disposal.

The act of divestment involves the sale of a discrete business to another company and the ending of any direct managerial control of that activity by the company selling it. Subsequently there may be anything from a continued close association, as in a franchise operation, to a clean break, such as accompanies a total withdrawal from an industry or trade by the divesting company. Between these two there may be a variety of continued trading relationships between the companies involved. For our present purposes total separation, with no special continuing arrangements, is assumed to be the intended outcome. While our primary interest is in the rationale of the directors of the company disposing of an activity, their success in doing so depends upon the existence of a prospective purchaser, and therefore on their perception of the latter's rationale. To this may be added the interest of third parties who may appear to act as brokers. Their role becomes more apparent when consideration is given to the opportunities for such a transaction.

While the analysis which follows starts with the presumption of a deliberative rational process of choice, the reality is often one of highly opportunistic circumstances that may arise unexpectedly. If account is then taken of the influences at work in the corporate marriage and divorce market, it is essential that attention is given to those institutions or individuals that are in a position to act as brokers.

These must include those who have close knowledge of possible partners or parties to a sale. Financial institutions, consultants and others in the business information market place may not only spot possible links but arrange those chance encounters that may trigger off a deal. What is particularly difficult to establish is the nature and extent of any such broker's interest in any outcome! Clearly for some there are business possibilities in the execution of such a deal.

The Rationale of Divestment

Given the range of possible triggers to a strategic review of a company's activities, the situation of the potential divestor may vary from the urgency to release resources in a crisis to the more proactive position of the board that concludes that a particular activity is disposable in favour of other, perhaps as yet unspecified, uses of corporate resources. While the latter is evidently the happier scenario, one has to acknowledge the urgency, and frequency, of the crisis trigger to divestment. It is therefore appropriate to deal with it first.

To treat it in this sequence is not just expediency; the nature of the crisis may be very central to the general incidence of divestment. Thus the crisis may be in the activities that are now viewed as the main thrust of the group's interests, or it may be in the specific business that is subsequently proposed for divestment.

The presumption in what follows is that the board is still in control and that the position has not deteriorated to the point at which a receiver has been injected into the company, let alone a liquidator appointed. The basic questions are present even more starkly where a receiver has been appointed, and he has the task of recovering funds owed to those who installed him. His position is adequately described elsewhere (Slatter 1984, p. 17).

Taking the former case, the continuation of the main thrust may call for the release of resources through the disposal of assets and activities that are regarded as both expendable and cash-generating. Thus the developing cash crisis of the RB211 engine at Rolls-Royce in 1970–71 led to a number of disposals prior to the decision to call in the receiver. A number of subsidiary businesses were sold off to other companies that were seeking new openings and possibly resources. Thus what started, on the one hand, as a search for cash and, on the other, as a bid for skilled labour, thought to be surplus, led to the sale of two ancillary activities to a West Country group and the transfer of both the businesses and a number of engineering craftsmen from Derby to Barnstaple, with spin-off effects to other firms at the receiving end.

Such disposals may be of established subsidiary or supporting activities, or they may be of new developments which the group is prepared to part with. The rationale may be that, as new developments, they are divorced from the group's mainstream, or that they have yet to meet expectations. Recent studies of diversification reveal a somewhat alarming picture of new developments being dropped in favour of established activities through lack of internal backing within senior management. Political clout is in these instances concentrated on those representing the established mainstream activities, even though their future may be, at the very least, questionable. There could even be, as in the Rolls-Royce case, an example of the 'big-project' that Argenti (1976) has so clearly identified as a potential threat of 'corporate collapse'.

The kernel of the decision in cases like Redman Heenan, Rolls-Royce and Airfix, is the choice of what is to be retained as the firm's main thrust. Profitable activities may then have to be sold off in order to sustain the chosen core of continued activity. The presumption here is that a turnaround is feasible and that the resources so realised can help to achieve the necessary rescue of the group as a whole, or at least the chosen core.

The crisis, however, may be in a subsidiary activity, possibly a new venture, and the main issue is one of whether to continue with it or cut a firm's losses and quit, disposing where feasible of any business unit or assets that can be sold off. Unless the crisis is of a magnitude that threatens the group as a whole, then the decision to discontinue is likely to involve four main considerations, outlined below:

(i) the scale of the resources that would be required if the situation were to be corrected set alongside those available to the owning group;
(ii) the expectations as to the viability of the problem subsidiary, assuming an appropriate support can be mounted;
(iii) the strategic importance of the activity involved in relation to the current view of the group's longer-term aims;
(iv) the other options open to the group if it were now to pull out of the activity under consideration.

The term resources requires definition. It is not only finance that may be in short supply but also management and technical support. The corrective action may call for an injection of cash from the group or through its borrowing capacity. It may also require management time and support which may strain its limited resources. Can these be supplemented quickly enough?

Such a review embraces precisely the same issues as one would hope to cover in a regular ongoing strategic review but with the added pressure of the need to decide quickly on what rescue, if any, to attempt or, failing that, what emergency action to take to limit the damage as quickly as possible. However, the problem with both the mainstream activity and a subsidiary may not be that of impending collapse but of ability to sustain future growth, particularly where a new activity shows potential for fast growth if greater support is made available.

Such a problem affects the ability to sustain the momentum of growth and/or achieve proper payoff where this involves a long lead time and appropriate backing while in progress. One outcome could be the search for new backers for the whole enterprise, perhaps through an agreed takeover by a stronger group which undertakes to support present management to develop the business further. An example was the case of Solartron Electronics (Learned, Aguilar and Valtz 1963). This very fast-growing business was developed by

John Bolton to a point at which further progress on some of its products was beyond the group's resources. A takeover for the entire group was therefore sought and arranged. The management of Solartron remained largely intact and progress was sustained. Interestingly, the scale and pace were such as to prove, *inter alia*, not fully compatible with the 'parent' group that had acquired Solartron, and a second 'sponsor' was found to which the Solartron group was sold.

An example of this second situation is the case of Clares (Wells) Ltd, a firm of industrial clothing and related manufacturing, which moved into shopfitting equipment. This then took off on a much larger scale as systems were developed for the supply of supermarket trollies and racking. The original firm remained in its field of activity; the shopfitting equipment business was separated and became a part of the Guinness group of companies.

In each of the challenges discussed so far the common thread is a trigger to question an activity that has become a problem requiring a speedy, almost a crisis, decision. If, however, the pressures of an immediate crisis are dropped, and consideration is given to the more pro-active situation of a company where the board considers future prospects as part of a continuing review of its strategy and performance, even if the very fortunate outcome is that it has no prospective 'dogs', there may still be a choice as to whether to retain particular activities. Thus, highly successful companies may insist on much higher performance in any activity than other companies that would be only too happy to have the performance of the poorer parts of their more successful brethren. The reasons for divestment are then long-term strategic choices as to areas and types of activity.

Such a selection may follow consideration of longer-term scenarios as to prospective opportunities and threats. The latter may embrace political, social, environmental or other pressures that it is thought preferable to avoid or which imply value judgements as to the acceptability of particular courses of action. Thus, assessment of the political risks of operating in, or for, particular national markets may lead to a decision to distance a firm from them by subcontracting to local nationals well before any political pressure to do so is felt. A particular market could involve acceptance of practices which a company may refuse to countenance. Thus, some UK civil engineering companies have elected to pull out of areas where a Mafia presence has been found to be pervasive. Similarly, a product might involve such extensive risks of political exposure and public pressure that a company elects to pull out of an industry, as Distillers did with pharmaceuticals following the thalidomide tragedy. In the past there have been companies that have declined to be involved in alcoholic drinks, or some other 'controversial' activity as perceived by their directors.

The possible political risks of remaining in what is currently a highly attractive and profitable market are evident in the views taken by different companies of activities in South Africa. Competing political risks, such as those of the boycott office of the Arab League in its long campaign against Israel, can have similar consequences. But whatever the weight given to such political and social pressures, they are most commonly subsumed in an appreciation of market possibilities on an essentially commercial basis. Such an appreciation may be based on one or more of the now well-known analytical matrices of the SWOT (strengths/weaknesses, opportunities/threats) type of analysis (Thomas 1983).

By applying this approach at least three situations offering candidates for possible divestment can be identified. The most obvious first candidate for axing is that where the market is declining or with a limited future, where the firm is in a relatively weaker competitive position and there is the possibility of quitting the sector while being able to sell its present activity there as a going business. The fact that a market has poor, even negative, growth prospects does not mean that it is a total write-off (Harrigan 1980). There may be a continuing demand over a long period, perhaps for the foreseeable future, and there could be a role for a firm which can increase its market share, even be a market leader, simply as others pull out, for as long as the market continues.

However, our potential divestor may not only be less well placed to pursue such a role but also have alternatives open to it which are not available to others. In such a situation, disposal to a firm already having a larger share will appeal to the latter and release resources while, in the case of products with a major parts-replaceable business, it ensures that customers are assured of continued support.

The presence of a significant follow-up service of this kind could deter a company from leaving a product market as long as the replacements are a very significant element in overall profitability. However, the appearance of smaller specialist replacement suppliers might destroy the basis both for continued presence and for disposal, as has been illustrated in the UK car exhaust/silencer market. Here specialist suppliers and service outlets have made major inroads into the markets, and especially the profitability, of those supplying for initial installation in new vehicles.

The less obvious candidate for disposal is that where there is a potentially good market but a firm's ability to succeed in it is questionable. The doubts could centre on its ability to compete effectively on technical or commercial criteria, irrespective of the scale of any investment that would be needed, or there may be a need to invest significantly in order to have a chance to be competitive. In the latter situation the managerial judgement as to the relative prospects of particular options has to be set in the context of the scale of investment required and the alternative uses to which that investment may be put.

This is an apt opportunity to review future directions of its resources and the conclusion could well favour divestment, both where attractive alternatives beckon and in situations where other threats may be on the horizon for which anticipatory action might be thought necessary. The chance to sell out to an interested bidder, or even to collaborators in a joint venture, may appear too good to miss. Thus the Bristol group, Charles Hill & Sons, having interests in shipbuilding, shiprepairing, ship management, and building and contracting, elected to pull out of a North Atlantic container consortium in order to release resources for other developments. Subsequently, it wound up its shipbuilding activities when the City of Bristol proposed a comprehensive redevelopment of the central docks area in the city, and explored opportunities for new investment starting from the assumption – later dropped – of steering clear of all its existing activities.

The impression of some of the arguments so far advanced is of risk avoidance mixed with opportunistic realisation of a current activity on a going-concern basis. However, underlying the reasoning of a board may be a view that on commercial, technical and political grounds there are areas it wishes to be in, in preference to those where it is present today, and that to do so assets must be realised, if only to provide resources for as yet unspecified new ventures by whatever route.

Once again candidates for disposal appear both because they are less favoured, if not disfavoured, on strategic grounds, and because they appear most saleable on terms that are attractive on several counts: price, transferability of liabilities, including those to employees and customers, as well as creditors. The unit(s) selected is thus one that is also looked at in terms of its attraction to a possible purchaser. This therefore brings us to the question of finding such a prospect.

Effecting the Divestment

Since there are so many sensitive issues that are rightly raised by any divestment, its consideration and early implementation is likely to occur in secret. The repercussions among employees at all levels, both in the unit(s) affected and elsewhere in the organisation, are likely to be so depressing in terms of morale as to threaten the efficiency, and even the disposal value, of at least the unit(s) involved. There is the wider concern of financial standing, carrying with it the possible risk – in the case of quoted public-limited companies – of a counter-bid for whatever is involved, if not for the whole concern. While a counter-bid for a unit might be welcome as a price raiser, the more potent threat to the firm as a whole would defeat one of the aims of the whole exercise.

The board, including those senior managers who are directors, has now to determine its approach on three issues. The first is whether the scope of what is to be divested is negotiable and, if so, on what basis. The corollary is clearly what is not to be parted with. In resolving this, consideration has to be given to the scope of the assets and liabilities deemed to relate to the business for sale, the employees, including senior management, who are to go with it, and the patents or similar property rights associated with it. As for employees at the date of transfer, there is now an EEC Code of Conduct as to what is transferable. If redundancies are to follow, then the buyer may find itself faced with this problem as well as the seller. The disposal of P & O Continental ferry services to European Ferries in January 1985 demonstrated this: the selling company dismissed shore staff and the buying company announced plans to rationalise ship utilisation.

In such circumstances much must depend on the scale of reorganisation envisaged after the acquisition. The purchaser may intend to acquire the name, good will and other assets, but have no intention of continuing production in present premises or even location. The vendor may be interested only in disposing of the activity, or it may be so concerned about its likely fate and those of its current employees as to take such matters into consideration when negotiating, even to the point of their becoming a critical factor. An element here may be the pensions obligations where a private-company-based scheme is involved.

Equally, the likely or possible use of the business being sold, in terms of future competition with what the disposing company intends to pursue, is an important strategic issue. Clearly, there is no problem where a company is opting out of a product market, as in the Redman Heenan situation, but there may be one where the likely purchaser is in a closely related field to any which remains of interest to the prospective seller.

For the board and such few senior managers as are privy to the decision to divest, the next two important choices concern who is to lead the search and negotiation, usually the chairman, and who is to be left to manage the business, together with the question of when that management is to be informed of the board's intentions. The timing of such communication is vital for two reasons: firstly, a disposal may well have a depressing effect on morale and performance in both the unit concerned and across the group as a whole; secondly, it may be very difficult to keep secret once prospective buyers are seen 'casing the set-up' or advertisements appear that look strangely familiar – especially if a response is made which arouses maximum suspicion.

At the same time, some internal preparatory steps have to be taken. One of these is the clear identification in accounting terms of the unit, its assets and liabilities, and of those contracts that are assignable with it. There will then have to be a confidential valuation of the business involving the firm's accountants. This, in turn, suggests at least a bargaining position as to the terms to be sought. It is most likely that this has to be done very quickly as well as in secret and there is, therefore, a risk of incomplete data. But what is of most significance is not what the business or its assets are valued at, either in its books or the cherished hopes of its directors; what matters is its value to a potential buyer at the time of sale. This, in turn, depends upon the prospective purchasers.

Thus an American company with a relatively modern factory that it found surplus to its requirements following a rationalisation of its

European operations allowed it to lie idle in the hope of at least realising its 'revalued' book price. No buyers were forthcoming, however, and a company with which the writer is associated sought to acquire it for conversion into workshops for small firms, this being achieved for just over half the book value, whereas similar premises remain unsold because of failure to face the price attainable for fear of its repercussions on a firm's accounts.

This value to a prospective buyer, therefore, turns on who might want the business and its assets. As the latter, if very specialised, could be of interest to very few purchasers, the main interest is likely to be in the business, its technology and commercial contacts, as reflected in its turnover. However, valuable as its existing business may be, the potential to a buyer may eventually lie in a different use of its capabilities. The search has therefore to be much wider than its immediate competitors. It has to proceed discretely at several levels: a review of immediately adjacent firms in its product or process; a scan for possible purchasers of its capability for redeployment to meet another company's needs for capacity and/or capability; and a trawl of firms with funds looking for appropriate outlets, perhaps as additions to their current portfolios.

Normal trade intelligence should indicate which firms are in the first category, how they stand at present, which – if any – are on the lookout for new facilities or for increased market share, and which are thought to be in a position both to pay for the business on offer and be willing to offer an acceptable price. In assessing this group, one consideration has to be whether such a deal would be allowed to go through by the Office of Fair Trading or whether there would be indirect pressure from other interested government agencies or departments to either oppose or support it on some public-interest criteria.

For example, the British Oxygen Company was known to wish to dispose of its engineering subsidiary manufacturing the oxygen equipment installed in civil aircraft as a precaution against loss of pressure. One of the prospective purchasers was a manufacturer of life-support systems for use in civil and military aircraft. It was made clear to both that the Ministry of Defence, a major customer of both, would oppose such a transfer as reducing its potential range of choice of suppliers.

The wider scan of those interested in capabilities to whom present turnover is a welcome, but not a decisive, factor may require both normal trade intelligence and perhaps a trade advertisement without disclosure of identities. Thus the same concern that was unsuccessful on oxygen-set manufacture went ahead with acquiring a heat treatment company having a product in a totally unrelated market so as to obtain plant, capability, and the useful cushion of an established business to sustain it, as it moved to deploy that capability for its own very different products.

At any time there are businesses seeking acquisitions, owners seeking acquirers or buyers of parts of their activities, and institutions or individuals who are in a position to act as brokers. Those seeking acquisitions include firms running out of steam on established lines but well heeled enough to buy-in their next business activity. There are also those who have spotted their next desirable lines of development but for whom the quickest and easiest way forward is by acquisition of a firm already in the desired business, albeit on a smaller scale. Those seeking to be acquired may want to retire or to continue development but as part of a larger group that may have greater resources with which to back development.

Of most interest at this point, however, are those who have close knowledge of possible partners or parties to a sale. Such knowledge will be available from financial or other advisers acting as financiers or as consultants to one or other of the firms concerned. Anyone in such a role may find someone saying, 'we are on the lookout for an interesting firm in super-widgets', and perhaps even know of a super-widget supplier who is looking for a new partner or is part of a group that has lost its earlier enthusiasm for super-widgets. Chance meetings between the parties, and not so chance, even arranged 'spontaneous' encounters, may sow seeds which eventually lead to the exploration of a possible deal, and in a minority of such encounters the end result is a transfer of ownership.

Yet before this is accomplished at least three other factors have to be reckoned with. The first is the understandable suspicion of any prospective purchaser as to the reasons that lie behind any willingness to divest as much as of readiness to be taken over. What problems, as yet undisclosed, lie at the root of the wish to divest? Are there investment, solvency, or trading liability problems ahead which the seller seeks to pass on? The second is that prospective purchasers may include those groups that are well-known predators that watch closely for acquisition opportunities among companies in turnaround situations, particularly where the essential steps are being taken but the payoff is some way ahead. This leads directly to the third, the possibility of triggering a takeover for the group as a whole. This risk is not confined to the possible purchasers of the business for sale but to 'third parties' whose attention is drawn to the group as a potential acquisition once it becomes public knowledge that a divestment is being negotiated. Consequently, the board of any divesting company has to be sensitive to the wider risks of a challenge of this kind.

For all these reasons, both secrecy and negotiating skill are at a premium and both are related to the nature and extent of intermediaries or advisers who may be brought in. The firm may conventionally look to its accountants as natural allies in this matter, but they may well be ill-suited for such a task. There are other businessmen who specialise in disposal and turnaround negotiations and whose experience can be of immense value to smaller firms when selling off to larger companies.

Once agreement is reached and is ratified by the directors of the companies concerned, the aim is to give immediate effect to the transfer of ownership. As soon as the sale becomes public knowledge, there have to be negotiations with all directly interested parties and the implications of the understandable secrecy of the process become evident. Both parties have therefore to anticipate these implications as they affect suppliers, customers, employees and creditors when drawing up the detailed agreements for the divestment. Such implications are not, however, all that follow from the change of ownership, and we need to look briefly at the wider implications of such restructuring.

Wider Implications

Much of the argument and most of the illustrations cited relate to divestment as an integral part of (a) turnaround and recovery situations, and (b) longer-term strategy in terms of where the greatest opportunities lie and the strongest position can be sustained. The judgement of the latter is often more of a political process than a strictly economic appraisal. The strategic business planning of major companies has been likened to the conduct of planned economies (Eliasson 1976). The retention or disposal of strategic business units then becomes subject to such considerations as where a group seeks a presence, on what scale, and for what purpose.

That presence may be strictly regarded as a profitable investment in its own right, as a means of understanding what is going on in a market related to the firm's main interest or overall range of activities, or it may be designed to enable it to gain technical expertise which is primarily for use in its main field. Similarly, presence in particular geographic areas, notably specific international markets, may be seen as a wider market representation or even as a political step in the national political sense. Government is known to exert pressure to retain a British presence in particular markets or to interest companies in maintaining a UK capability in what is regarded as a sensitive industry, e.g. on matters of defence procurement.

Divestment fits into this scenario where, for example, there is a government-induced or government-led move to rationalise the number of suppliers from whom it wishes to continue to be able to purchase or whom it seeks to encourage as part of some wider industrial strategy. The regrouping among aerospace-industry firms at several periods in the past three decades illustrates the former; the similar movements in the UK computer industry exemplifies the latter. Although there is currently no overt restructuring policy of the sort associated with the Industrial Reconstruction Corporation (1967–70) or the National Enterprise Board from 1975 onwards, the issue is still far from dormant and has to be lurking in the pragmatic operations of the Office of Fair Trading when applying monopolies and mergers policy.

The principal justification for continued widespread divestment by companies is not just the retreat into doing what they have hitherto been best at – the Peters and Waterman proposition of 'sticking to the knitting' – but also the creation of more appropriate and supportive groupings in both the divesting and acquiring companies. The retreat from some of the excesses of growth by administrative coordination, as opposed to market performance, is a welcome development when there is such a clear national need for a wider spread of entrepreneurial management, whether in manufacturing or other sectors. While the 'leaner, fitter' image of so much of manufacturing is in particular a welcome outcome, the more longer-term requirement is a movement into new products and new processes for delivering established products that could be supplied from the UK using current and prospective technology.

The process in the context of the UK market in corporate control has, however, to be highly secretive until implemented, and this poses questions for boards of directors, in particular in terms of the exercise of their powers in relation to the interests of shareholders, employees and all others who may be regarded as 'unrepresented stakeholders'. Thus those who represent employees are understandably concerned at the extent of directors' freedom to act in divestment situations, at the dilemma of the obligation now imposed by company legislation on directors to have regard to the interests of their employees, and at the late stage at which those interests may appear to be considered.

From the wider strategic standpoint of some form of industrial policy, whether overall or sectoral, there remains the following question: where, if anywhere, is there a concern as to what capabilities are retained in the UK, and with what consequences, if exclusive reliance on market forces threatens their disappearance?

References

Argenti, J. (1976) *Corporate Collapse: The Causes and Symptoms*, McGraw-Hill.

Eliasson, G. (1976) *Business Economic Planning*, Wiley.

Harrigan, K.R. (1980) *Strategies for Declining Businesses*, Lexington Books.

Learned, E.P., Aguilar, F.J. and Valtz, R.C.K. (1963) *European Case Studies in Management*, Irwin.

Marshall, A. (1890) *Principles of Economics*, Macmillan, 8th edition (1920), p. 315.

Peters, T.J. and Waterman, R.H. (1982) *In Search of Excellence*, Harper and Row.

Slatter, S. (1984) *Corporate Recovery*, Gower, Chs 5, 9, 14.

Steindl, J. (1945) *Small and Big Business*, Basil Blackwell, Ch. 1.

Thomas, R.E. (1983) *Business Policy*, 2nd edition, Philip Allan, Ch. 11.

Tricker, R.I. (1984) *Corporate Governance*, Gower.

Whittington, G. (1972) 'Changes in the top 100 manufacturing companies in the UK 1948–68, *Journal of Industrial Economics*, Vol. XXI, No. 1, p. 17.

3

Demergers: The Case of Bowater

Mike Wright

Introduction

Other chapters in this book examine divestments (or sell-offs) in terms of the sale of a subsidiary or division of a company so that it becomes either a separate independent entity or part of another parent organisation. In both of these cases ownership is seen to be transferred to a completely new set of individuals or institutions. This chapter considers the rather different case of demergers (or spin-offs) where a separate entity is created, comprising part of the original whole, with the original owners retaining a substantial ownership stake. As yet in Britain demergers of this nature are comparatively rare, although they are more common in the United States, as will be seen below.

This chapter begins with a brief resumé of the conceptual issues which lead a firm to carry out a demerger. Following the conceptual discussion, a brief section on practical, legal and taxation issues surrounding demergers is presented. These factors are highly important since they may constrain the ability of management to change their organisational structure even when the necessary and sufficient conditions for it to occur are met. The case of the demerger of the North

American interests of the Bowater Corporation from the rest of the organisation illustrates the development of a corporate strategy which eventually leads to a parting of the ways.

It is worth stressing at the outset that demergers may fall into two main categories from an organisational point of view. Firstly, the demerged part may be 'small' in relation to the parent company. A parent may engage in a number of such demergers as part of a policy of dynamic adjustment to environmental changes in much the same way that a firm may engage in multiple divestiture of subsidiaries to new parents (see Chapter 2). The parent does, however, retain an equity interest from which its shareholders may achieve increasing returns as the demerged entity grows. This kind of demerger or spin-off has been a feature of the American economy for a number of years and often involves the setting up of new companies which can exploit potentially profitable new technological developments but which are either too small to fit into the parent organisation or are such that, if the parent entered into the market, it would dominate and possibly incur the effects of antitrust legislation (for further discussion see, for example, Cooper 1971; Sabine 1973; and Garvin 1983).

The second kind of demerger is that which is 'large' in relation to the parent and is the focus of attention here. The literature in this area defines large as comprising at least ten per cent of the parent's size (e.g. Hite and Owers 1983; Schipper and Smith 1983). In effect, the whole organisation is split into two (or conceivably more) parts of roughly equal size so that its nature changes fundamentally. It might thus be expected that this type of demerger would occur less frequently than smaller demergers and would be the culmination of a long period of strategic change and development at the end of which time there would be a clear perception that further growth could only realistically be achieved in the form of two or more separate entities. The company's shareholders may then be able to gain the benefits of further growth and, most importantly, have the ability individually to balance the amount of shares they hold in each entity according to their risk-return preferences.

Background Issues

Detailed discussion of the conceptual issues involved in the adaptation of an organisation through the transfer of ownership of a part of itself has already been covered in the first two chapters of this book. In order to set the theoretical context within which the case of Bowater took place, it is necessary to adapt the general discussion of Chapter 1 to the specific case of demergers.

It was seen in Chapter 1 that the various types of divestment could be viewed as stages in the development of an organisation's corporate strategy. Not all organisations are likely to pass through all stages but, on the other hand, the major type of demerger (to which attention is focused here) is unlikely to take place as the first strategic option. As may be observed from Figure 3.1, demerger is better understood to be the culmination of a fairly long period of development.

Taking the stages shown in Figure 3.1 in turn, it may be assumed that a company develops over many years on the basis of its original product lines. However, perhaps because the market for the products begins to decline or because the founder or original management retire, the company begins to experience a loss of direction. At this point, a need for strategy reformulation arises. Indeed, if the company has been developing for many years doing what it always has done, formal strategy development may be taking place for the first time.

As part of the strategy formulation process the need is to assess the environment, clarify corporate objectives, decide where the company wants to be and formulate a plan of how to get there. The action to achieve this plan may involve any or all of the following: internal (organic) growth; acquisition of missing parts; and divestment of parts which do not fit. Feedback of progress against the plan may at some stage require a reassessment of direction. This need may particularly arise when an environment is changing rapidly, making the initial plans and actions no longer entirely appropriate. Alternatively, reassessment may be required in order to correct past mistakes where, for example, certain acquisitions have been made which turn out to be less profitable than expected.

Following the reassessment phase, further realignment in the organisation may take place. With continued development of activities and possible further reassessments, the point may be reached where the appropriate organisational structure requires the setting up of quasi-autonomous divisions. In this way, divisional management may be given the freedom of action necessary to deal

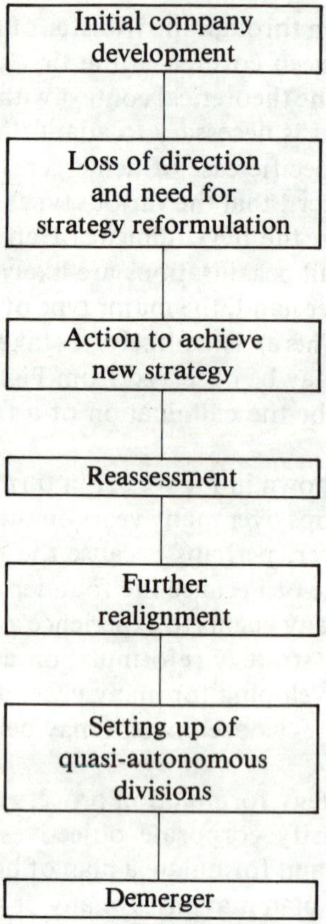

Figure 3.1 Company Development and the Route to Demerger

with particular market conditions. With appropriate central office monitoring, the organisation as a whole may best be able to achieve its objectives with such a management structure. However, as we have seen in Chapter 1, continued growth can produce increasing divergence of the activities carried out by each division, such that what is considered best for the firm as a whole may not be best for each individual division. For example, as will be seen with the case of Bowater, the capital investment funding requirements of one division may take funds from other parts of the organisation and so prevent them from taking advantage of profitable opportunities. Providing that divisions have a coherent management structure and can be viable independent entities, the demerger may offer an appropriate solution to the conflict between divisions. Each of the demerged parts of the organisation may then obtain independent access to the capital market.

As demerger involves the splitting of an enterprise but, initially at least, the retention of ownership by the same body of shareholders, there may be gains to be had from the owners' point of view. Shareholders may gain both from any increased efficiency that separation brings and from the ability to adjust the portfolio of their holdings in the two (or more) now distinct parts. Hence, for example, shareholder *A* might prefer to hold a greater proportion of his shares in demerged part *X* because it offers the prospect of a reasonable, reliable rate of return. Shareholder *B*, on the other hand, might opt for a greater proportion of his shares to be in demerged part *Y*, since it offers the possibility of a very high return, though subject to greater uncertainty. The empirical tests of shareholder gains in the circumstances of demerger/spin-off have already been reviewed in Chapter 1.

The Mechanics of Demerging

Even where the development of corporate strategy has been such as to point to demerger as the next logical step, formidable practical barriers to the pursuit of such a route may exist. Of overriding importance in determining whether or not a demerger is feasible is the nature of the corporate tax regime. In the UK, company law has provided for the separation of a large company into two or more parts for some time under the provisions of the Companies Act, 1948, s. 206. Until the passing of the Finance Act, 1965, a company wishing to undertake this kind of action could do so by distributing a dividend *in specie* derived either from capital reserves or a court-approved reduction in share capital. The only tax penalty would be stamp duty which would arise if the shares being distributed were transferred rather than allotted directly to the holding company's shareholders (Instone 1980). As part of the attempts to encourage mergers as a route to increasing economies of scale in UK industry, the Finance Act 1965 introduced taxation penalties on all dividends including those used to effect a demerger. Such action introduced a bias in the tax laws which, whilst encouraging mergers, made it impracticable from a taxation point of view for companies to demerge. With the increasing recognition in the late 1970s that many mergers had not produced the hoped-for benefits (e.g. Meeks 1977) and that it might make commercial sense to divide a company, priorities were introduced in Schedule 18 of the Finance Act, 1980, which aimed to restore neutrality in tax laws between mergers and demergers.

Schedule 18 provides for the exemption from taxation of distributions to shareholders which are used to effect the demerger of an existing subsidiary or trade as long as the parent company holds at least 75 per cent interest in the subsidiary.

It is also necessary that the demerger satisfies the following conditions: the company must be resident in the UK; the scheme must not be part of a liquidation; the demerging company must be trading and the demerger must benefit the trading activities of the parent and the subsidiary; the newly demerged entity must be left free to operate under its newly independent management; and the demerger must receive clearance from the Inland Revenue that it is not part of a scheme for the avoidance of tax. The distribution must be effected either by means of a reduction in share capital or share premium account which is confirmed by the court *or* by a dividend *in specie* (Routes (1) and (2) respectively in Figure 3.2).

The demerger by Bowater which separated the company's North American interests from its UK and rest of the world activities illustrates how the above procedure may work in practice. The scheme was effected in two stages – the reduction of the company's share capital followed by the distribution of ordinary shares (common stock) in the North American interest to the company's shareholders, as this extract from the demerger prospectus explains:

> The Scheme provides for a reduction of £90,389,440 in the Corporation's issued ordinary share capital from 180,778,880 Ordinary Shares of £1 each to 180,778,880 Ordinary Shares of 50p each. In addition, the Corporation's share premium account, amounting to £116,826,642, will be cancelled. Following the reduction of capital, the ordinary share capital will be consolidated into 90,389,440 New Ordinary Shares of £1 each and the authorised share capital will be increased to £130,000,000. Thus, Ordinary shareholders will retain 50 New Ordinary Shares for every 100

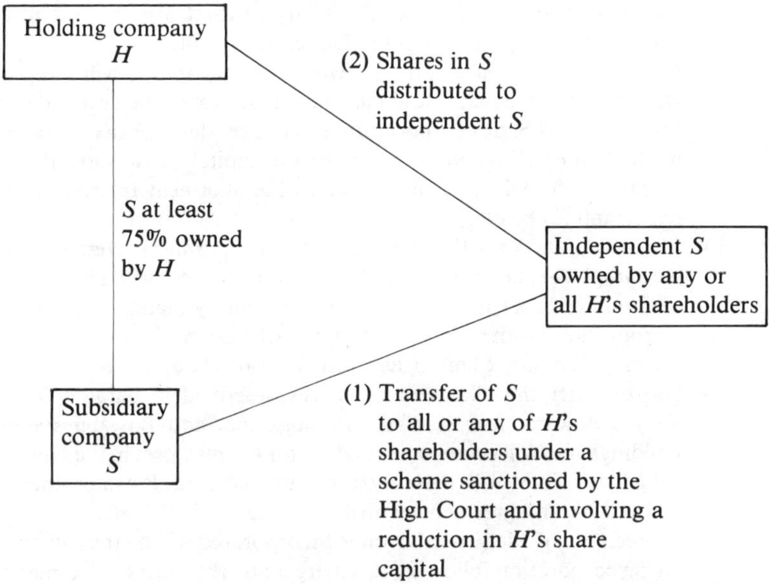

Source: Adapted from Lawton (1984).

Figure 3.2 Diagram of Demerger

Existing Ordinary Shares and so in proportion for any greater or lesser number of Existing Ordinary Shares.

The reduction of capital and cancellation of share premium account will create an additional reserve available for distribution by the Corporation by way of dividend. This additional reserve and part of its existing reserves will be used by the Corporation to distribute its 75.01 per cent holding of Common Stock in Bowater Incorporated to Ordinary shareholders pro rata in accordance with their holdings of Existing Ordinary Shares on the Record Date.

This distribution will be effected by the following technical steps which will not of themselves require any action by shareholders of the Corporation:

(a) As a preliminary step, the Corporation will shortly transfer to Bowater Intermediate Holdings Inc. its remaining holding in Bowater Incorporated. Bowater Intermediate Holdings Inc. is a wholly owned United States subsidiary of the Corporation and is resident for tax purposes in the United Kingdom.

(b) On the Effective Date of the Scheme, the Corporation will transfer Bowater Intermediate Holdings Inc. to Bowater Paper Holdings Inc., a United States corporation which is resident for tax purposes in the United Kingdom. No part of the capital of Bowater Paper Holdings Inc. will be issued prior to the allotment referred to in paragraph (c) below.

(c) In consideration for the transfer by the Corporation referred to in paragraph (b) above, Bowater Paper Holdings Inc. will allot shares of Common Stock in itself direct to the Ordinary shareholders of the Corporation on the basis of one share of Common Stock for each Existing Ordinary Share held on the Record Date.

(d) Shortly after the allotment of shares described in paragraph (c) above, Bowater Intermediate Holdings Inc. and Bowater Paper Holdings Inc. will cease to be resident for tax purposes in the United Kingdom. They will thereupon be merged into Bowater Incorporated by an agreement of merger under United States law (the 'Agreement of Merger'). Bowater Incorporated will be the sole surviving corporation following this merger and the shares of Common Stock in Bowater Paper Holdings Inc. will automatically be replaced by shares of Common Stock in Bowater Incorporated in the proportion of 12.1388 shares of Common Stock in Bowater Incorporated for every 100 shares of Common Stock in Bowater Paper Holdings Inc.

The reduction of capital, the cancellation of the share premium account, and steps (b) and (c) above will be effected under the Scheme. Step (d) will be effected under the Agreement of Merger. Once the Agreement of Merger is filed with the Secretary of State for the State of Delaware, USA, which is expected to take place on Monday 23rd July 1984, the Demerger will be completed.

As a result of the above steps, the Corporation's remaining holding in Bowater Incorporated will be held by Ordinary shareholders of the Corporation. For every 100 Existing Ordinary Shares in the Corporation, Ordinary shareholders will be entitled to 12.1388 shares of Common Stock in Bowater Incorporated and so in proportion for any greater or lesser number of Existing Ordinary Shares [and 50 New Ordinary Shares of £1 each in Bowater Industries]. (Bowater Corporation plc 1984)

The issues leading up to this particular arrangement at Bowater are discussed in the following section.

Lawton (1984) reports that up to December 1983, 570 applications had been made to the Inland Revenue for exemption from taxation of dividends made to effect a demerger. Of these, 80 had been refused clearance and a further 47 were considered to be outside the scope of the legislation. The assessment by company and tax law commentators (e.g. Lawton 1984; Instone 1980) seems to be that the legislation has not so far had the desired effect of helping to break up ill-fitting conglomerates but rather has been more useful for effecting splits in private companies. Part of the reason for this lies in the often restrictive manner in which the legislation has been framed. (For example, taxation relief may only be obtained where a trade is demerged from a trade, so that mixed groups wishing to demerge trading activities leaving investment businesses behind are not exempt; corporation tax liabilities may arise on the gains derived from the deemed disposal of a subsidiary.) Another significant part of the problem lies in the dilemma faced by the Inland Revenue in applying the rules – a balance has to be struck between encouraging companies to make use of the legislation and restricting the scheme to minimise its use by companies seeking tax avoidance. In general, the schemes appear to be of such a complexity that less detailed solutions have tended to be preferred, involving management buy-outs or capital reconstructions (Lawton 1984).

The procedure for demerging (spinning off) in the USA has been accorded favourable taxation treatment for considerably longer than is the case in the UK. Similar criteria are imposed to those just discussed for the spin-off to be tax-exempt. In particular, Section 355 of the US Tax Code requires that the distributing company owns at least 80 per cent of the subsidiary's shares and that on spin-off the parent distributes all its shares in the transfer. The transaction must not be a mechanism principally designed as a means to distribute earnings and the distributing and controlled companies must have been actively engaged in business for at least five years prior to spin-off. In addition, the transaction must not be motivated by tax avoidance considerations nor must there be any prearranged plan for shareholders to sell shares in the subsidiary subsequent to the spin-off (Fitshenry 1977). As well as tax considerations, stock-exchange regulations in the USA have since 1969 required that shares in 'spin-off' companies be registered, resulting in all the disclosure of information that registration implies. Prior to this date there was no requirement for registration of such shares which had resulted in a number of instances of fraudulent practice, particularly in over-the-counter (OTC) trading (Schipper and Smith 1983).

The Case of Bowater

The demerger at Bowater took place in 1984 and involved the separation of the Company's North American interests from the rest of the corporation. As such, it became one of the relatively few companies to avail itself of the change in the UK legislation described in the previous section.

In order that the issues which led up to the demerger can be fully understood, the discussion in this section proceeds by reviewing the stages of development of the Company. For ease of exposition, four main stages may be identified. The first takes the Company through its early development via vertical integration to its first narrow attempts at diversification. The second stage concerns the initial attempts to broaden diversification away from reliance on paper and paper products. Stage three involves the reassessment of strategy and the reorganisation of activities following the serious problems experienced with broadening diversification. The final stage takes the Company on from the early signs of the growing separation of the North American activities from the rest of the Company to the demerger. This discussion of the stages in the route to demerger is then followed by a summary of the problems that the Company overcame in getting to the final stage and a discussion of the difficulties that may need to be dealt with in the future.

The Growth and Development of the Bowater Corporation

Development, Vertical Integration and Narrow Diversification (1881–1972)

The Company began in London in 1881 as a paper merchant called W.V. Bowater and Sons. Following substantial growth in the demand for newsprint in the early part of this century, the Company moved into newsprint production on its own account with the construction of a mill in Kent in 1924. A second mill was constructed in Cheshire shortly afterwards, followed by the acquisition of other newsprint mills in the mid-1930s. By this time Bowater was the major producer of newsprint in the UK, ahead of Reed International and Inveresk (which went into receivership in 1984).

The establishment of a sales office in North America in 1912 was the precursor to the extension of the Company's manufacturing interests on that continent. Interests spread first of all to satisfy a perceived strategic need to secure greater control over raw material supplies, and took the form of the acquisition of an integrated pulp and newsprint mill at Corner Brook and extensive timber rights in Newfoundland in 1938. A similar move had taken place in Sweden a year earlier. Throughout the postwar years, the Company continued to exploit its North American interests which enjoyed favourable conditions both in terms of substantial reserves of raw materials and a large mass market for newsprint. The introduction of newsprint production in the USA in 1952, of further acquisitions of newsprint capacity in Canada in 1956 and the build-up of substantial timberland reserves throughout this period meant that by the early 1970s Bowater was the third largest newsprint producer in North America and the largest in the USA.

Although unfavoured by locational factors, the UK paper and pulp industry in general was able to survive reasonably well until the 1960s through the protection afforded by tariff barriers set up before the Second World War. Pulp was not subject to duty, unlike imported paper and board, but the inability to integrate backwards meant that UK companies were exposed to monopsonistic pricing practices by Scandinavian pulp suppliers, which were exacerbated by the devaluation of the pound sterling in 1967.

Despite the existence of tariff barriers and monopsonistic pricing, imports rose from 24 per cent to 31 per cent of UK consumption in the decade from 1954 to 1964 (British Paper and Board Industry Federation 1984). However, the phasing out of tariff barriers following the establishment of EFTA boosted the rising trend of imports, particularly between 1967 and 1973, which was not eased on UK entry into the EEC as duty-free quota arrangements were introduced for the remaining EFTA members. Concomitant with these tariff changes, structural changes occurred in the worldwide paper production industry which meant that countries hitherto only producing pulp now began to produce paper and were doing so in large production units which were able to reap the benefits of economies of scale. By 1970 import penetration had risen to 35 per cent and was destined to rise to 61 per cent by 1983.

Despite the build-up over a number of years of strong indications of a weakening UK paper market, Bowater's attempts at strategic adaptation to the new environment were limited and heavily influenced by the legacy of traditional interests and expertise. Early attempts at diversification were made in the 1950s and effectively involved forward integration into the conversion of timber and paper into items with higher added value, such as packaging and quality printing papers. In 1956 there was, however, the highly imaginative partnership of Scott Paper tissue expertise and Bowater market knowledge which established tissue partnerships in the UK, Europe and Australia. The diversification was conceived on a forest products base, where there appeared to be expertise within the organisation. Diversifications were thought to be more prone to failure where they were outside closely related areas. However, it has been argued that diversification was not as great as it might have been in this period because of a highly centralised management structure, which was resistant to change and which was heavily influenced by E.V. Bowater, Chairman and major driving force for thirty-five years of the Company's development from 1927. The management style also frustrated internal entrepreneurship on the part of those less senior managers who were able to perceive diversification opportunities but who were not able to pursue them. (*Sunday Times* 1974; Bowater's Report and Accounts 1980).

Following the death, whilst still Chairman, of E.V. Bowater in 1962, some broadening of diversification took place, with the introduction of building products in 1969 and furniture manufacture early in 1972. However, the ability of these new developments to support the weak domestic UK paper side of the Company was limited and was a contributory factor in the attempts to merge with Reed International, aimed at rationalising UK newsprint capacity to meet foreign competition. The failure of the merger attempt meant that by mid-1972 a great amount of uncertainty surrounded the future strategy of the Company. In terms of markets occupied, it was clear that dependency on paper products in the UK had to be reduced, but how this was to be achieved had not been worked out. The situation was exacerbated by the legacy of a management structure which was resistant to change, particularly if that involved a move away from paper, and an inability to generate sufficient funds to finance the scale of investment that would be required to move into different areas. The Company was thus in the position of being a potential takeover target with an asset base some fifteen per cent greater than its share price.

Broadening of Diversification (1972–75)

In October 1972 Bowater merged with Ralli Securities for an agreed bid of £82.5 million. Although the smaller Ralli technically became part of the much larger Bowater, the merger can in some ways be seen as a reverse takeover as the Chairman of Ralli became Deputy Chairman of Bowater below a non-executive chairman. This merger, which provided Bowater with diversification in the form of the international trading, banking and financial services interests of Ralli, has to be viewed against the background of the high level of merger activity in the UK at this time. (A total of 1,200 acquisitions were officially recorded in the UK in 1972 and again in 1973, the highest figure of the decade, and over a third greater than the next highest year, 1971.) Much of the merger activity was of the type whereby quoted stock-market companies bought other companies which were badly managed and undervalued. Slater-Walker Securities is probably the example *par excellence* of this type of enterprise, selling the surplus assets of one enterprise to buy another, and so on. At the time, this type of activity was generally considered to be a highly successful means of injecting new entrepreneurial management into companies which were not realising their full potential and, indeed, it was a former Slater-Walker Associate who became Deputy Chairman of Ralli. It is interesting to note the failure of a takeover bid for Bowater from Trafalgar House which was made shortly after the Ralli–Bowater deal was announced. Part of the reason for this failure was attributed to the contrasting way in which Trafalgar House had grown, which was also by acquisition but by way of diversification into all aspects of accommodation and leisure. At this time such strategies were much less well-received than the Slater-Walker type of deal, as the injection of new dynamic management was considered to be absent.

As a result of the merger with Ralli, a divisionalised structure was introduced with a high degree of decentralisation. The activities

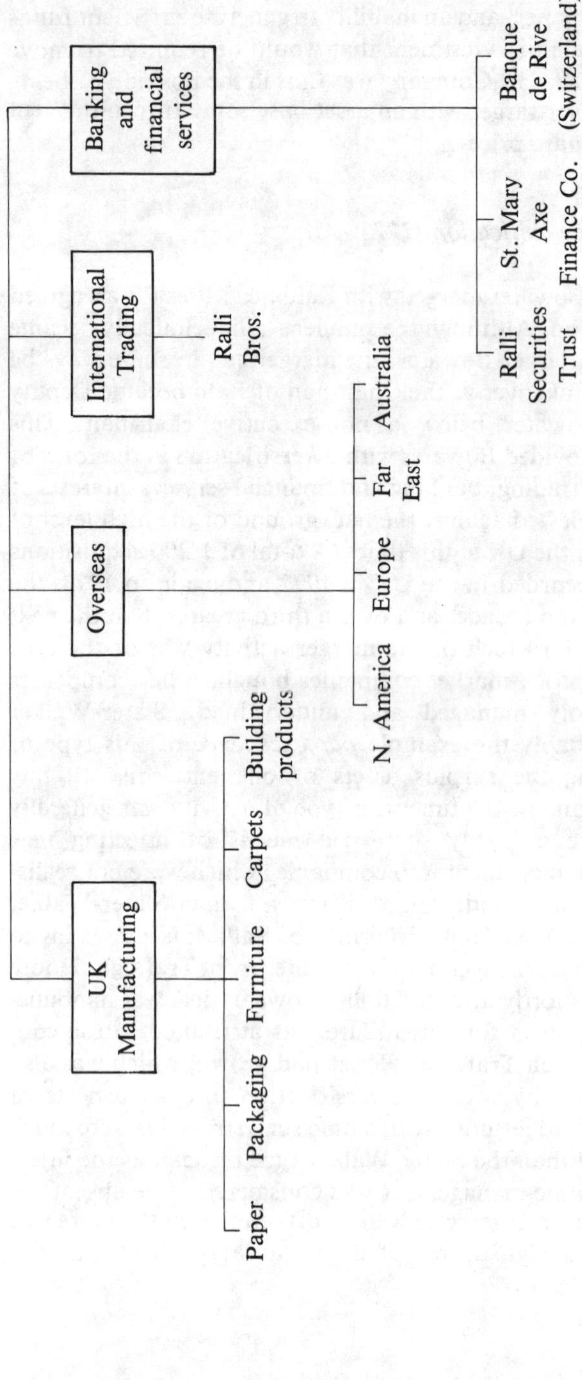

Source: Bowater Corporation (1973) *Annual Report and Accounts*.

Figure 3.3 Bowater Corporation: Divisional Structure in 1973

involved are shown in Figure 3.3 and it is reported in the Company's 1973 Accounts that the appropriate strategy in the then current environment was the wide diversification which was being pursued on two axes: domestic–international and industrial–commercial. Initially, there was widespread scepticism in newspaper reports that the new arrangement would not work, but after the first eighteen months the positive effects of diversification, decentralisation and new management were being greeted enthusiastically (*Sunday Times* 1974) and, indeed, substantial improvements in profits and sales were recorded in 1973 (see Table 3.1). However, by late 1974 the problems that many press commentators had predicted in 1972 did emerge. These problems were not so much due to the effects of a cyclical downturn in the paper market as some had feared, as to the result of the initial collapse of the secondary banking sector which included the financial interests of Ralli acquired by Bowater International. However, the North American paper interests of this time *were* considered by the Company to be earning an unsatisfactory rate of return. Commodity trading was also a problem area, so that the service activities of Bowaters moved from a return on sales of 23.3 per cent in 1973 to a return on sales of minus 4.1 per cent in 1974 (see Table 3.1). The Company was therefore faced with the serious problem that the corporate strategy it had embarked upon in 1972 was no longer appropriate to the new environment. There was still a need for diversification away from paper and for a decentralisation of management, but the form which these actions should take was not clear.

Reassessment of Strategy and Reorganisation of Activities (1975–80)

The seriousness of the problems in the service activities division meant that the organisation as a whole could not afford to absorb the losses being incurred. As a result, an attempt was made to remove the fuzziness in both the Company's activities and objectives, which resulted in a new corporate strategy being announced in late 1975. The broad strategy was for the Company to be engaged in manufacturing industries based upon the conversion of forest products, in international trading and in transportation, together with other activities which both managerially and geographically fitted

Table 3.1 Bowater Corporation: Performance by Product Area

Product area	1972			1973			1974			1975			1976			1977		
	π/T	$T\%$	$\pi\%$	π/T	$T\%$	$\pi\%$	π/T	$T\%$	$\pi\%$	π/T	$T\%$	$\pi\%$	π/T	$T\%$	$\pi\%$	π/T	$T\%$	$\pi\%$
Paper and pulp	3.9	27.4	22.3	9.4	20.0	38.0	20.2	22.1	84.5	16.9	25.4	81.7	15.2	24.2	67.3	17.1	22.3	59.6
Packaging	5.6	9.6	11.3	8.1	7.1	11.6	8.3	7.4	11.6	6.0	7.8	9.0	8.7	6.7	10.6	10.8	7.7	12.8
Tissue	10.1	7.5	16.0	10.9	5.5	12.2	8.9	6.1	10.2	6.2	8.9	10.5	8.3	7.9	11.9	10.0	7.6	11.9
Building products	8.1	9.7	16.7	7.6	9.8	15.0	(2.1)	5.5	(2.2)	(4.3)	6.6	(5.3)	(5.4)	5.6	(5.6)	0.2	5.9	0.2
Service activities	3.5	45.8	33.7	2.0	57.7	23.2	(0.4)	58.9	(4.1)	0.4	51.3	4.1	1.6	55.6	15.8	1.8	56.5	15.5
Discontinued businesses	—	—	—	—	—	—	—	—	—	—	—	—	—	—	—	—	—	—
Total:																		
Return on sales		4.7			4.9			5.3			5.2			5.5			6.4	
Sales (£m)		595.0			998.8			1,194.3			1,107.3			1,548.0			1,723.0	
Profits (£m)		28.2			49.2			63.1			58.0			84.9			110.5	

Product area	1978			1979			1980			1981			1982			1983		
	π/T	$T\%$	$\pi\%$	π/T	$T\%$	$\pi\%$	π/T	$T\%$	$\pi\%$	π/T	$T\%$	$\pi\%$	π/T	$T\%$	$\pi\%$	π/T	$T\%$	$\pi\%$
Paper and pulp	16.0	26.3	58.9	15.9	26.3	64.1	18.3	25.1	74.4	17.9	34.4	76.3	11.1	36.3	57.6	11.5	35.7	61.0
Packaging	8.6	8.9	10.6	8.2	9.3	11.6	6.2	11.2	11.2	4.0	11.5	5.7	3.7	14.1	7.4	3.6	15.7	8.5
Tissue	11.7	9.1	15.0	10.8	9.1	6.2	10.1	10.8	17.8	9.9	13.3	16.4	8.5	14.2	17.2	9.4	14.8	21.3
Building products	5.1	8.6	6.1	4.4	9.2	14.9	2.3	6.0	2.2	0.0	7.5	0.0	(0.4)	9.1	(0.4)	3.4	9.6	4.9
Service activities	1.4	47.1	9.3	0.5	46.1	3.2	2.2	10.5	3.8	2.7	15.9	5.2	4.0	17.9	10.0	4.2	17.7	11.2
Discontinued businesses	—	—	—	—	—	—	(1.6)	36.4	(9.4)	(1.7)	17.4	(3.6)	6.6	8.4	(3.6)	(7.1)	6.5	(6.9)
Total:																		
Return on sales		7.1			6.6			6.2			8.1			7.0			6.7	
Sales (£m)		1,564.0			1,723.0			1,760.0			1,728.0			1,566.0			1,623.0	
Profits (£m)		111.8			112.9			108.6			139.4			110.0			109.1	

into this pattern. The primary managerial structure was to be based on geography, with a concentration of activities in five main areas – United Kingdom industrial, international commodity trading, North America, Europe and the Far East, Australia and New Zealand. In addition, a joint venture into tissue manufacturing with Scott-Paper was being developed throughout this period, following its initiation in 1956.

This revised divisional structure comprised a chief executive for each division who reported directly to the managing director of the corporation. It was the intention that this new structure would give more autonomy to management teams throughout the world whilst at the same time securing improved coordination through closer communication links with the parent board. The development of this strategy was to be achieved, according to the 1975 report and accounts, through three main strands of action: the disposal of certain peripheral businesses which either were unlikely to earn a fair return on investment or did not fit the long-term plan; the acquisition of proven businesses where those related to the main activities; and organic growth in existing businesses. The implementation of this strategy and the realignment of the Company's activities that it required may be traced through the annual report and accounts up to 1979. The prime targets for disposal were the financial interests acquired and developed over the previous three years following the merger with Ralli, so that the Company exited completely from financial services apart from their insurance-broking interests which were trading successfully. Disposals also occurred across the whole range of activities in this period, including in the UK reductions in newsprint production, closures and disposals of window, carpet and furniture manufacturing activities, and in Europe and elsewhere removal of non-viable carton and textile activities. Acquisition activity was mainly focused on extending the Company's interests in high added-value paper-related products. For example, the Standard Cheque Book acquisition in 1976 extended paper conversion activities, whilst the acquisition of Cross Paperware in the same year complemented existing interests in disposable tableware. The building products division was also strengthened through the acquisition of Crossley Building Products in 1978 and in Europe plastics activities were strengthened through acquisitions made in West Germany.

Organic growth was achieved in a number of ways. Firstly, further heavy investment was made in the North America paper area. Secondly, the packaging, tissue and building products divisions principally based in the UK all displayed significant growth over the period. Thirdly, through a major programme of reorganisation and restructuring, a European-wide freight-forwarding network was created. In addition, international trading was also being developed in the USA, as were coated paper interests in the UK. The effects of these changes may be observed in Tables 3.1 and 3.2. The packaging, tissue and building products divisions are seen to have grown steadily over the period to account for over nine per cent of turnover each, and a third of trading profits in total. Service activities are seen to have declined over the period. This trend is mainly due to the fall in performance of the financial and commodity trading activities, but the overall figure masks the improvements being made in the freighting and forwarding sector. The paper and pulp division's performance was mixed over the period, with the UK operations declining sharply whilst the profitability of the North American subsidiary increased from a 5.6 per cent return on sales in 1972 to a 17.7 per cent return by 1979, as shown in Table 3.2. The developments that had taken place, particularly during the four years since 1975, were such that the 1979 accounts could point out

Table 3.2 Bowater Corporation: Geographical Performance Compared, 1972–1983

Year	*Return on sales (%)*			*N. America's share of activity (%)*	
	UK	*N. America*	*Total*	*Sales*	*Profits*
1972	3.0	5.6	4.7	26.6	31.1
1973	4.1	7.0	4.9	25.0	35.4
1974	2.7	13.2	5.3	26.3	65.6
1975	1.0	15.4	5.2	31.1	91.6
1976	3.8	11.4	5.5	34.3	71.0
1977	5.5	11.5	6.4	34.0	60.7
1978	5.6	17.0	7.1	23.4	55.5
1979	3.8	17.7	6.6	21.2	57.5
1980	1.4	20.3	6.2	22.7	74.7
1981	1.9	20.2	8.1	30.1	75.5
1982	1.6	15.1	7.0	35.4	76.0
1983	5.8	9.3	6.7	36.2	50.0

that the USA was the main operating base and the cornerstone of the Company.

In a change of emphasis, the UK activities were seen as providing strategic footholds, particularly in low capital-intensive areas. Moreover, the less capital-intensive parts of the business were increasingly being viewed as providers of investment funds for the paper manufacturing divisions.

The Road to Demerger (1980–84)

There were clear signs in the preceding period that the various activities of the Company were developing a clearer identity and some indications of a divergence between the North American subsidiary and the rest of the Company. This movement was given significant impetus in 1980 by two major events. Firstly, the last major link with the Ralli merger of the mid-1970s was severed with the disposal of the Company's commodity trading interests. Secondly, after a long period of poor performance and various attempts to keep it open, the Ellesmere Port newsprint mill was closed. The closure of this mill, followed in 1982 by the removal of the last machine solely dedicated to newsprint production, effectively marked the end of the UK Company's interest in high-volume low-added value paper production and virtually severed the trading connections with the North American subsidiary. The significance of both these events on the financial results of Bowater is shown in Table 3.1 where it is seen that in 1980 businesses accounting for more than one-third of turnover were discontinued.

Further realignment continued throughout this period, with the general aim of moving out of manufacturing into service provision for the European and UK parts of the Company. The withdrawal from furniture manufacture and the sale of a concrete works to the management are two notable examples of this shift towards merchanting in the building products division. In the US, diversification was being developed as an attempt to reduce overdependence on the cyclical US paper market.

However, the realignment of activities *per se* is only one aspect of the preconditions for a demerger to take place. An accompanying prerequisite, as we have seen earlier, is the development of independent and coherent management organisations in each division. For the UK and European parts of the Company, changes have involved the movement to product-based rather than geographically-based divisions and the introduction of smaller, more manageable, business units which were considered to be of a size consistent with the scale of operations. Having learned the lessons from the problems of the 1970s, Bowater decided to concentrate on the growth potential of its existing activity base, through organic developments and acquisitions targeted to fit into the existing pattern of activities.

Building further upon the decentralisation first introduced after the Ralli merger, in-house entrepreneurship was to be encouraged by making each division and business unit as autonomous as possible and by reducing substantially the number of head-office staff. In the United States decentralisation was also strengthened through the creation of profit centres. Hence, by the early 1980s the reorganisation of the Company as a whole into a coherent body of activities with a decentralised management structure was virtually complete. However, the problem of differing financial needs between the North American interests and the rest of the Company, first alluded to in the 1976 accounts, still remained.

This difference was exacerbated by an increasing recognition by Bowater of the different attitudes of the North American and UK financial communities. In America, forest-product companies have high capital intensity and investment needs which tend to dictate regular calls for new funds from shareholders, who appreciate the nature of the industry. In the UK the tendency is to prefer companies with an increasing profit trend and high positive cash flows, which allow for higher dividend payments and the avoidance of rights issues. The preference in the US is for lower dividends and an appreciating net worth. As a result of this difference, it became clear to Bowater that the two parts if demerged would be worth more than the whole. The important difference in the views of US and UK stock markets was emphasised by the return of difficulties in the US paper market in 1982 which, with increased competition and a further emphasis on the need for higher investment, highlighted the need for further finance and independence of US management action and opened the way to demerger some two years before it actually took place. The demerger was announced on 28th March 1984, with the necessary transactions being completed by August 1984. At the time of the demerger the structure of the Company could be represented as shown in Figure 3.4.

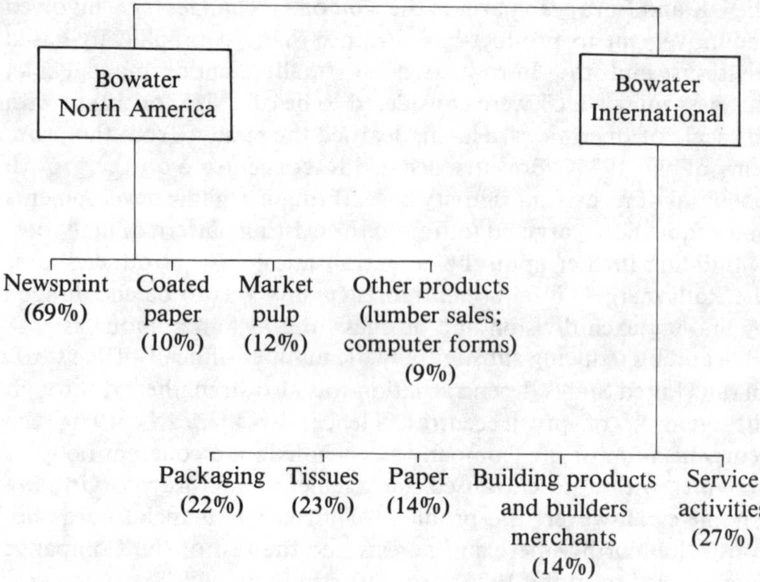

Note: Figures in brackets are percentage of sales for each of the two parts of the Company.

Figure 3.4 Bowater Corporation: Divisional Structure in 1983

Issues and Problems

In summarising the main issues involved in this case study and in considering the possible problems which remain, it is useful to divide this section into three parts: prior to the demerger, the demerger itself, and after the demerger.

Prior to the Demerger

Tracing the development of the Company, it was clear that diversification away from a narrow focus on paper and decentralisation of management style was necessary. The amount of time involved for strategy to develop and adapt to the changed circumstances and the need to change direction to rectify earlier mistakes serves to emphasise the need for flexibility in dynamic environmental conditions (Aaker 1984). Such an approach indicates two possible sources of limits to diversification activity. It may be a dangerous policy to attempt to buy into a new area far removed from the expertise of management, as the Ralli merger turned out to be. Alternatively, the diverse parts of the Company may grow so far apart that it is not possible to monitor them effectively. In respect of the former case, Bowater's appear to have been correct in changing to a policy of a gradual development of new activities which were within the competence of management to absorb. In the latter case, demerger may be the best choice of policy so long as an independent management organisation is already in place. The question of finance may be crucial in both respects. To develop new areas may require the generation of funds in other parts of the business to cushion the transition period. The failure of the Inveresk Paper Group owed a great deal to the lack of funds generated elsewhere in the business during a period of transition (Slatter 1984). When both parts of the business require substantial investment funds, it becomes increasingly difficult for these to be generated internally, and access to separate capital markets which allow each set of activities to be funded on their own merits may be the most satisfactory option.

The Demerger Itself

The mechanics of demerger have been detailed earlier, but in considering how to resolve the problem of the differences between the North American and other interests of the Company, the Board considered four main options of which demerging was one. The other three were, first, to sell-off the North American interests entirely; second, to switch the Company's base from the UK to the USA; or, finally, to float a minority of shares on the United States capital market.

Although the details of why these options were rejected have not been publicised, it seems reasonable to advance the following reasons. Selling off the North American interests entirely raised the question of where the funds so generated were to be reinvested. It is doubtful whether they could have been absorbed by the rest of the Company. If they had been invested elsewhere, it was possible that a lower return would have been forthcoming than that which could be earned from North America. In addition, any returns from investing in new ventures were likely to be subject to greater risk and uncertainty than the areas the Company knew well. The dangers in this respect had also been made all too apparent following the Ralli merger. Switching the base of the Company to the USA may have brought the advantage of greater accessibility to what was regarded as a more favourable capital market but it may well have reversed the problems that the Company was facing before the demerger. The lack of independence for the North American arm would be replaced by the same restrictions for the UK and the rest of the world interests. Moreover, although the US capital market would be better able to identify the needs of the North American activities, it may have had problems in assessing those of the rest of the Company. The flotation of a minority of shares on the US stock exchange would have provided new equity capital for the North American interests. This part of the Company had been periodically raising United States *debt-funding* for a number of years. However, the flotation of a minority of shares in the United States has implications for the dilution of control by other shareholders and still leaves the difficulties surrounding the identity of the Company unresolved. The demerger thus appears to avoid the problems inherent in the other options. However, it may itself expose shareholders to other risks which may develop after the separation of the two parts.

After the Demerger

In the short term the effects on shareholder returns seemed to be significantly positive, as the studies reviewed elsewhere suggest should be the case (see Chapter 1). The announcement of the demerger caused share prices to rise on the UK stock exchange. The demerger prospectus also estimated that the gross dividend on one hundred ordinary shares before the demerger of approximately £11.07 would rise to £12.29 following their change into a package comprising fifty ordinary Bowater industry shares and 12.1388 shares of Bowater Inc. Common stock. At the time of writing it is rather early to be precise about what the longer-term prospects are likely to be. However, performance of the two companies is likely to be related to the key questions of the availability of finance, the behaviour of product markets, the ability and behaviour of management, and the strategy pursued. It is possible at this stage to make a number of preliminary comments on these issues.

For both parts of the old Company, the gearing ratios have been reduced following the demerger, meaning that less cash generated from operations leaves the Company in loan repayments. For Bowater Inc., advantages should also be gained as dividend and taxation payments are able to fall into line with the generally lower levels found in the USA. If one of the declared major reasons for the demerger is correct, then external fund-raising benefits should arise from the companies' respective home capital markets being able to assess their identity more clearly. However, it has been suggested that in the short term the UK capital market may see it as a hotchpotch comprising the rump left over after the main North American business has been removed (Fisher and Hall 1984). Although in reality this may not be the case, it may take some time for the general view to be changed. To this end the UK Company is progressively phasing out the use of its business-logo trademark and assigning it to Bowater Inc.

The investment funds position of Bowater Inc. is still likely to be strongly influenced by the cyclical nature of the US paper industry. The attempts at diversification in the US have included a chain of home improvement stores (now divested) and the manufacture of computer stationery, but these have not been as successful as expected, leaving Bowater Inc. vulnerable through being more dependent on a single product than any of its main competitors. Bowater Inc., however, is the most efficient producer in the US industry and it has substantially increased its timberland resources to a level it considers to be more than adequate, taking advantage of favourable market conditions to source a certain amount of timber externally.

The increase in managerial freedom and the hoped-for greater access to finance following the demerger are intended to provide the means by which the American arm can minimise this problem, possibly through further diversification and development of timber reserves. Managerial freedom has been aided in Bowater Industries by the reduction in the amount of funds generated being used to help US investment programmes. As a result, the extension of the freight-forwarding side from a European to a worldwide network is being pursued vigorously, including entry into the US through the acquisition of the Imperial Air Freight Service Company of New Jersey.

The above points have touched upon a number of avenues of corporate strategy which need to be pursued if the two companies are to cope with an environment which is still changing rapidly. However, there is a further corporate strategy issue which needs to be faced – this is the question of vulnerability to takeover. The threat of takeover had been raised prior to the demerger as the Company was undervalued in the market. By raising the return to shareholders, the demerger can be viewed as a means of reducing such a threat. Alternatively, the increased flexibility to exercise shareholder risk-return preferences that the demerger has brought and which Hakansson (1982) and Hite and Owers (1983) have pointed to, could make it possible that they will be able to retain their interest in one of the companies whilst accepting, say, a share-exchange acquisition scheme for the other company which further raises their overall rate of return. It will be most interesting to monitor how matters develop on this front.

Conclusions

This chapter has built upon the theoretical reasons why the divisionalised form of organisation might reach its limits (discussed in Chapter 1) and create the conditions for a demerger to occur by examining in detail the case of Bowater. The empirical evidence concerning the effects of demerger on shareholders' rates of return, reviewed in the opening chapter of this volume, indicated that increases should be expected and are likely to be the greater the larger is the demerged part relative to the company as a whole. The Bowater case provides a classic test for this proposition. The liberalisation of UK company legislation and taxation rules is seen to have had only limited success in promoting demergers, whilst the US regime appears to have been rather more successful. The extensive and often complex case of Bowater has clearly demonstrated how the conceptual issues surrounding strategic change, particularly through demergers, are relevant in practice. The separation of one company into two fairly evenly-sized entities requires that the corporate strategies, the management structures and the product markets of the two parts be clearly and separately identified. In tipping the balance towards demerger rather than continuation as a loose federation of otherwise unrelated activities, the severity of the constraint on funds available for investment may well be crucial. But after the demerger has taken place, a number of problems will need to be resolved on a continuing basis. What is clear when talking about strategy before and after the demerger is that the level of vulnerability to takeover, and the management and shareholders' attitudes to it, need to be weighed very carefully indeed.

References

Aaker, D.A. (1984) 'How to select a business strategy', *California Management Review*, Vol. XXVI, No. 3, Spring.

Bell, J. (1975) 'Bowater plans big financial sell-off', *Sunday Times*, 14 December.

Bowater Corporation plc (1984) *Proposals for the Demerger of Bowater Inc.*, Bowater, London.

Bowater Inc. (1984) *Prospectus for Offer of Common Stock*, The First Boston Corporation, 17 May.

British Paper and Board Industry Federation (1984) 'Facts', *BPBI*, London.

Cooper, A.C. (1971) 'Spin-offs and technical entrepreneurship', *IEEE Transactions on Engineering Management*, EM 18.

Economist (1984) 'Seeing the wood for the trees', 31 March.

Financial Times (1984a) 'Bowater placing clears way for US demerger', 12 March.

Financial Times (1984b) 'UK Group's big stake in Dixieland', 16 March.

Financial Times (1984c) 'Bowater splits its paper', 28 March.

Financial Times (1984d) 'Bowater at £68m: plans demerger', 28 March.

Financial Times (1984e) 'When demerging makes sense', 28 March.

Financial Times (1984f) 'Bowater in major US air freight expansion', 10 July.

Fisher, A. (1982) 'Britain's Paper and Board Industry: the long battle to survive', *Financial Times*, 29 October.

Fisher, A. and Hall, W. (1984) 'Breaking a paper-thin alliance', *Financial Times*, 20 July.

Fitshenry, P.E. (1977) 'Using a spin-off to break up a corporation tax-free', *Practical Accountant*, Sept/Oct.

Garvin, D.A. (1983) 'Spin-offs and the new firm formation process', *California Management Review*, January.

Hakansson, N.H. (1982) 'Changes in the financial market: welfare and price effects and the basic theorems of value conservation', *Journal of Finance*, Vol. XXXVIII, No. 3, September.

Hite, G.L. and Owers, J.E. (1983) 'Security price reactions around corporate spin-off announcements', *Journal of Financial Economics*, Vol. XII, December.

Instone, R. (1980) 'Demergers', *New Law Journal*, December.

Investors Chronicle (1984) 'Bowater is split into two parts', 30 March.

Lawton, P. (1984) 'Demergers: an assessment', *The Company Lawyer*, Vol. V, No. 1.

Makinson, J. and Fisher, A. (1984) 'Bowater's amicable separation', *Financial Times*, 28 March.

Marley, C. (1972) 'Bowater could be a Rubicon', *The Times*, 2 November.

Meeks, G. (1977) *Disappointing Marriage: A Study of the Gains from Merger*, University of Cambridge, Dept. of Applied Economics, Occasional Paper.

Reader, W.G. (1981) *Bowater – A History*, Cambridge University Press.

Sabine, S. (1973) 'At Nuclepore, they don't work for GE anymore', *Fortune*, December.

Scherer, F.M. (1984) 'Mergers, sell-offs and managerial behaviour', *Paper Presented to European Association for Research in Industrial Economics Conference*, Fontainebleau, August.

Schipper, K. and Smith, A (1983) 'Effects of recontracting on shareholder wealth: the case of voluntary spin-offs', *Journal of Financial Economics*, Vol. XII, December.

Slatter, S. (1984) *Corporate Recovery*, Penguin Books.

Sunday Times (1974) 'How Bowater swam out of the treacle', 7 April.

Times (1972a) 'Questioning the Bowater–Ralli Rationale', 20 October.

Times (1972b) 'Bowater–Ralli after Trafalgar's intervention', 20 November.

4

Strategic Trading: Rationalisation in US Brewing

Gary Davis

Introduction

This chapter examines the case of strategic trading as a means by which companies may rapidly adjust to a changing commercial environment. The nature of strategic trading as a concept is outlined and the issues to be considered are assessed. The use of a strategic trade as a means of rationalisation in the US brewing industry is analysed against the background of the changing market place. The Pabst/Stroh trade of breweries is followed chronologically, and the swap itself is examined in the light of each company's strategic needs. In the final section the usefulness and future prospects of strategic trading are addressed.

Conceptual Issues

Strategic trading is the exchange of business units by two firms. There are other assets of strategic importance, such as mineral rights, patents, licences, key employees, cash, and major stakes in other firms, but 'strategic trading' applies only to going concerns that could operate independently if they were separated from their parent firm. Strategic trading is a form of barter, but it is a special kind of barter where the exchange is expected to have important long-term consequences for both firms.

Although barter is the original form of commercial exchange and its techniques are outwardly simple, the underlying decision process can be quite complex because the relative values of two unlike assets must be 'judged' by two or more people on any number of criteria. If each owner values the other's asset more than his own, then an exchange would be profitable for both firms.

Since the 1960s, mergers and acquisitions have become commonplace. More recently, divestments have occurred with increasing frequency and have been widely publicised. Business conditions sometimes change so fast that the amount of time available for making decisions and then implementing them is too short for fully satisfactory action to be taken except by the most agile and well-prepared firms. Thus, even though it may seem advisable for a firm to exit from one business and enter another, by the time the steps have been taken to identify, initiate and carry out these two transactions the opportunity may have passed. Techniques are needed that can speed up the process.

To divest a business, a firm has to find a buyer. The buyer to whom the business will be most attractive may well be one that is in that business already, or whose management is looking for ways to enter it. This puts the potential buyer in much the same position as the divesting firm, but with strengths or interests in different areas. A similar situation exists when two firms are competing in the same businesses and in the same markets but wish (a) to increase their concentration in separate businesses, (b) to serve separate markets rather than compete directly, or (c) to balance their levels of concentration across several markets.

Several factors have been cited as deterrents to divestment (Harrigan 1981). One factor that can be significant is the cost of acquiring and divesting firms. Transaction costs for selling and buying businesses, including legal expenses, financial charges and taxes, are high and can be a deterrent to acquisition or divestment. These costs might be less if the selling and buying were combined in one transaction, namely a strategic trade. In some countries, for example, when certain assets, like motor vehicles or real estate, are exchanged, taxes are assessed only on the difference in their values, rather than on the difference between current value and the original cost (less depreciation taken for tax purposes).

One way to speed up the process is the use of strategic trading. If firm *A* wished to expand in industry (or market) *Y*, and divest a business in industry (or market) *X*, while firm *B* wished to expand in industry (or market) *X* and divest a business in industry (or market) *Y*, the conditions may be right for a strategic trade. This situation is illustrated in the diagram in Figure 4.1.

	Industry *X*	Industry *Y*
Firm *A*	Firm *A* wishes to exit from industry or market *X*	Firm *A* wishes to expand in industry or market *Y*
Firm *B*	Firm *B* wishes to expand in industry or market *X*	Firm *B* wishes to exit from industry or market *Y*

Figure 4.1 A Possible Opportunity for a Strategic Trade

'Value' and the Decision Process

Most decisions are complex. Putting a value on an asset of strategic importance is a particularly complex decision. There are many ways to estimate the value of an asset, even when strictly economic criteria are used, depending on the purpose of the valuation. For example, the replacement value of an asset for insurance purposes is likely to differ substantially from its value expressed in terms of its expected contribution to the future earnings of the business. When psychological influences enter the evaluation process, it becomes even more complicated, especially when 'hidden agendas' are present. Those doing the evaluation may not even be fully aware of the criteria they are using (Stahl and Zimmerer 1984; Goldberg 1983, p. 12; Nisbett and Wilson 1977).

The value of a business can be thought of as being made up of three components. The first is the 'present value' component. Some introductory finance textbooks show that using the discounted cash-flow method of analysis, the timing of cash flows and the choice of discount rate used by a firm to calculate the present value of future cash flows together determine the ranking of alternative investments (Brigham, Kahl and Rentz 1982). When this principle is applied to business units owned by two firms with different costs of capital, it is clear that under certain conditions it would be profitable for both firms to trade business units (Davis 1984c).

In addition to the present value component, there may be instances where the managers of a firm believe that they can increase future cash flows from the acquired business unit by taking corrective action or by integrating the acquired business with its existing holdings. This is sometimes called 'synergy' (Shay 1981), although the improvements may merely result from better control or other alterations to the way business is transacted by the business unit. The potential for improvements such as this would tend to make a business unit more valuable to the acquirer than to the divestor. There may be instances where two firms see such opportunities in each other's portfolios, and this would tend to favour a strategic trade.

Finally, there are the various 'subjective' motivating influences that operate in each firm. These may range from cultural factors to forecasts of future opportunities. This depends on psychological and social conditions, but it is no less significant than the other two components.

Each of these three components of value – present value, improvements due to synergy and the subjective component – can vary over a wide range. When the three are combined, the potential exists for significant differences in values of specific business units from the viewpoints of different parent firms. When this happens, and if the rank order of values of two business units differs, the opportunity exists for both firms to increase in value if their managers execute a strategic trade.

It is perhaps worth noting that too narrow a view of the value of a business unit can lead to unnecessarily restrictive assessments of motivation or prediction of action. For example, Hearth and Zaima (1984) comment that if the value of an asset to a firm is above market value, then the firm will not divest the asset. This may seem like common sense on the surface, but if one considers that there may be two firms *A* and *B*, with assets *X* and *Y* 'undervalued' by the market, which value the other's asset above both 'market value' and the value of their own asset, then both firms would gain by trading asset *X* for asset *Y*. This is illustrated in Figure 4.2.

◄– – – – – – Lower value		Higher value – – – – – ►
Market value of asset *X* – – – –	Value of asset *X* to firm *A* – – – – – – – –	Value of asset *Y* to firm *A*
		◄– Increase in value of each firm –►
Market value of asset *Y* – – – –	Value of asset *Y* to firm *B* – – – – – – – –	Value of asset *X* to firm *B*

Figure 4.2 How a Strategic Trade can be Feasible when Selling is Not Feasible

By executing the stragetic trade of assets *X* and *Y*, the firms *A* and *B* would both increase in value by the amounts represented by the gaps on the right-hand side of the figure. In effect, strategic trading broadens the concept of 'price' to include non-monetary transactions, and increases what Harowitz and Halliday (1984) call the 'range of mutual consent', thereby increasing the number of divestment and acquisition opportunities for firms with more than one subsidiary.

Indentifying strategic trading opportunities is more complex than ordinary divestment and acquisition decisions because of the requirement that there should be greater coordination of the activities of the two firms involved. There is also the difficult task of identifying firms that may be willing to participate in a trade. For example, the most likely candidates may be firms for whom the businesses of interest form only a minor part of their current portfolio. It may be necessary to obtain the assistance of middlemen like bankers, accountants, lawyers, management consultants and business brokers. The planning divisions of the firms themselves will have to adapt their strategic management process to this search activity. Effective identification requires the gathering of information about the present and potential business activities of many firms, as well as studying the behaviour of managers faced with divestment and acquisition decisions, including ways to convince firms to divest subsidiaries which they had no previous intention of selling (Davis 1984a, 1984b).

Strategic Trade: The Case of Pabst/Stroh

Many of the issues in strategic trading can be seen by examining a case study of a strategic trade that took place in 1983. It involved the exchange of two breweries in the United States, in which no cash changed hands. The trade took place between the Pabst Brewing Company and the Stroh Brewery Company, both among the ten largest brewing firms in the country. Both firms were under a wide variety of severe pressures, mainly from government and competitors in a turbulent market. The strategic trade was the most satisfactory outcome for a large number of stakeholders, certainly more than if the most obvious alternatives had been chosen.

It is necessary to place the trade in context by giving a brief overview of the brewing industry in the United States.

The United States Brewing Industry

General Background

In 1900 there were more than 1,000 brewery firms in the United States, most serving very small local markets. When the sale of alcoholic beverages was prohibited by an amendment to the United States Constitution in 1919, legal production of beer stopped. Some firms converted their plants to manufacture other products, such as ice cream and carbonated soft drinks. When 'prohibition' was repealed in 1933, about 750 breweries reopened, but trends towards national distribution and home consumption resulted in a continuous decline in the number of firms, as the stronger ones expanded and the weaker firms were taken over or closed. The decline accelerated after the Second World War, and by 1950 there were less than 400 firms, some with plants in several locations. The number had dropped to 200 by 1960, to 100 by 1973 and to 50 by 1976. In 1980 there were only 41 firms left in the industry.

Most brewery firms still operating in the United States in the 1980s were owned or controlled and bore the names of the families that founded them more than a century earlier. Most were still essentially one-product businesses, although a few had begun to diversify. The proportion of the market held by the eight largest firms rose from 30 per cent in 1947 to 91.6 per cent in 1981. The share of the top ten rose from 70.4 per cent in 1971 to 95.5 per cent in 1981 (see Table 4.1). This was disturbing to the Antitrust Division of the United States Department of Justice. These changes took place against a background in which the total market was increasing. Between 1971 and 1981 the total market increased from 127m barrels to 180m barrels.

Antitrust measures (see Chapter 7) provide a continuous thread running through the story of the United States brewing industry since 1945 – far beyond that reported here. The United States government had some success in slowing concentration in the industry, but only managed to hold back the tide temporarily. This raises questions about the effectiveness of the antitrust system, and whether the eventual outcome was much different than it would have been if no government action had been taken (except perhaps for the names of the firms). Such an issue is beyond the scope of this chapter. However, it is clear that antitrust action was a strong deterrent to acquisition activity. Of particular relevance here has been the adoption in recent years by the Antitrust Division of the Justice Department of the concept of 'regional' antitrust attitudes: if a firm was seen as having too great a share of the market in a part of the country, rather than in the country as a whole, it was still considered grounds for ordering divestment or disallowing an acquisition.

Marketing

The definition of 'beer', according to the United States Department of Justice Antitrust Division, is:

Table 4.1 The Ten Largest United States Brewing Firms, 1971 and 1981

1971	*Volume (m. barrels)*	*Market share (%)*
Anheuser-Busch Inc.	24.3	19.1
Jos Schlitz Brewing Company	16.7	13.1
Pabst Brewing Company	11.8	9.3
Adolph Coors Company	8.5	6.7
F. & M. Schaeffer Corporation	5.6	4.4
Miller Brewing Company	5.2	4.1
Falstaff Brewing Corporation	5.2	4.1
Carling Brewing Company	4.4	3.5
Theo Hamm Brewing Company	4.1	3.2
Stroh Brewery Company	3.7	2.9
Total for top ten companies	89.5	70.4
Total market	127.1	100.0
1981	*Volume (m. barrels)*	*Market share (%)*
Anheuser-Busch Inc.	54.5	30.3
Miller Brewing Company	40.3	22.4
Jos. Schlitz Brewing Company	14.3	7.9
G. Heileman Brewing Company	14.0	7.8
Pabst Brewing Company	13.5	7.5
Adolph Coors Company	13.3	7.4
Stroh Brewery Company	9.2	5.1
Olympia Brewing Company	5.7	3.2
Genesee Brewing Company	3.6	2.0
C. Schmidt & Sons Inc.	3.5	1.9
Total for top ten companies	171.9	95.5
Total market	180.0	100.0

Sources: NYTI, 1972:209; NYT, 24 Jan 1982, NTY 2 Jun 1982, Higgins 1979:373.
Note: Volumes are in millions of barrels; market shares are as a percentage of the market.

. . . any fermented malt beverage containing one-half of one per cent or more of alcohol by volume, brewed or produced from malt, wholly or in part, or from any substitute for malt. Beer includes lager beer, dark beer, bock beer, malt liquor and ale. (US Justice Department 1982)

The US industry has generally adopted a number of terms to describe the different price, quality and image categories of beer-product offerings, including the following:

(a) Popular prices (low-price/low-margin brands)
(b) Premium (higher-priced brands with an 'up-market' image)
(c) Super-premium (higher priced, to compete with imports)
(d) Light beer (with fewer calories, less 'filling')
(e) Imports (generally from Europe or Canada)
(f) 'Domestic imports' (US-made European brands)
(g) 'Price' beers (private brands)

The United States beer market in the 1980s is characterised by a very large proportion of sales of beer packaged in small containers, principally for consumption at home or outdoors. Beer consumption per capita (population 18 years and over) in the United States rose rapidly until 1947, when it reached 27 gallons (consumption was calculated in United States 'wine gallons', defined as 231 cubic inches, or 3.785 litres, i.e. 0.833 imperial gallons). This growth was followed by a period of decline which reached about 24 gallons between 1955 and 1960 before it started to rise again. By 1980, per capita annual consumption had reached nearly 35 gallons, an increase of 45 per cent in 20 years. There was also a shift in consumer preferences to the more expensive brands of beer. Per capita consumption of distilled spirits increased by 55 per cent over the same period. The rate of increase in per capita wine consumption was even more noticeable: while still far less than beer, per capita consumption of wine had doubled from 1.40 gallons in 1960 to 2.82 in 1980. The population in the 18 and older group increased from 115 million in 1960 to 159 million in 1980, or by 39 per cent. Total beer consumption had doubled in the two decades, spirits volume had more than doubled, and wine sales had nearly tripled.

In the early 1980s, however, the annual per capita rate of consumption of beer appeared to be levelling off at about 36 gallons, and the growth of the population 18 and over, and particularly the 18–34 age group, was also slowing. Combined, these indicated a slowing in the growth rate of the beer market. This was expected to lead to even more intense competition among the few remaining brewers.

Market Segments

Wide regional and demographic differences existed in the marketing and consumption of beer in the United States. One influential factor was the variation in population densities: many states were sparsely populated while there was heavy population concentration in the big cities. Until the mid-1970s, two-thirds of United States beer consumption was in the eastern states (*Business Week* 1976a). Beer drinkers could be classified according to a variety of factors which correlated with their preferences for specific products. This led to products being designed to appeal to such groups. There was a distinct difference between the markets in the northern, colder areas where growth was slow or markets were shrinking, and the warmer 'sun belt' where consumption was increasing. There was strong competition in all markets as firms fought to preserve market shares in the northern areas while establishing themselves in the 'sun belt'. Even the rankings of individual firms varied widely from place to place. In 1976, for example, Coors had 40 per cent of the market in the twelve western states in which it operated (*Business Week* 1976b). Recent market shares for the six leaders in the Minnesota market are given in Table 4.2. The large market shares of some firms in some areas made antitrust approval of acquisitions less likely because of the 'regional antitrust' concept referred to earlier.

Product images were created to suit each major market segment. The rapid growth of Miller in the 1970s was attributed to its ability to identify rapidly growing market segments early, particularly in the case of Miller Lite, which was aimed at beer drinkers who wanted to feel 'less filled' (rather than those who were weight conscious, who tended to avoid all kinds of beer). Most other brewers scrambled to copy Miller's marketing and production techniques. Anheuser-Busch had a similar, if less spectacular, success with their super-premium Michelob, which was positioned to compete directly with Miller's 'domestic import', Lowenbrau.

In the United States market it was possible for a brewery to change the image of a product in order to 'reposition' it to make it

Table 4.2 The Top Six Brewers in Minnesota in 1981 and 1982[a]

		Market share (%)	
Rank	*Firm*	*1981*	*1982*
1	Heileman	39.4	38.6
2	Miller	18.7	19.7
3	Pabst[b]	15.0	14.1
4	Stroh[c]	11.3	11.2
5	Anheuser–Busch	8.2	9.9
6	Olympia[d]	3.7	2.8
Total of the top 6		96.3	96.3

Notes: (a) No other firm had more than 1 per cent of the market in 1981 and 1982.
(b) Excluding Olympia.
(c) Stroh was selling Schlitz only in Minnesota.
(d) Including Hamms.

more appealing to a growing market segment, sometimes with little or no change in the 'formulation' (the ingredients and manufacturing process) of the beer. This was done by several firms, including Anheuser-Busch and Stroh.

Packaging was important because it was part of the product's image and because profit is sensitive to production costs. Competition was strong in several dimensions: the type of container (cans or bottles), the materials (steel, aluminium or glass), the size (12 oz regular or 7 oz 'pony'), the type of opening (flip-top cans, easy-opening bottles), and the degree of permanence (reusable or non-returnable bottles). This competition became an interesting battle on the sidelines during the increasingly competitive 'beer wars' from the 1950s onwards. A few of the larger brewers, as heavy users, produced some of their own containers.

Economies of scale in advertising in the United States are significant because the large commercial television networks are able to offer very low costs per viewer to national advertisers. Small-scale producers are unable to afford these advertisements and could not satisfy the demand they would generate.

Brand loyalty was not strong in the United States beer market in the early 1980s. Demand was sensitive to 'images' created mainly through advertising. Consumers also reacted strongly to events covered by the news media. They were willing to switch away from a brand and not return to it, even if they lost interest in its replacement. A change in the formulation of Schlitz beer in the 1970s was not acceptable to many Schlitz customers, and was a major factor in the collapse of Schlitz's business. The Coors brand of beer experienced a surge in sales when it became a fashionable drink, benefiting from free publicity such as the revelation that on separate occasions Mr Henry Kissinger and President Gerald Ford had taken several cases of Coors from the western United States to Washington DC on government aircraft (*New York Times* 1975).

Production

Major factors affecting costs of production were labour, packaging, distribution and inventory. Beer-production technology had changed to the extent that large, automated, plants could be built eliminating much of the labour needed in older breweries. Elzinga (in Glueck and Jauch 1984, p. 624) estimated that 1.25m barrels capacity was the minimum efficient brewery size. Anheuser-Busch's total output in 1965 was 10.2m barrels, but by 1980 it had single plants that could produce that much. Packaging played a major role in the creation of the image of each individual product, but container costs were high – often more than the beer inside. Transportation costs were rising. This tended to work against the use of very large breweries, but in the early 1980s the savings from building large plants had outpaced increases in transportation costs. Distribution at the local level was done by independent wholesalers who were able to maintain close contact with retailers. In the early 1980s at least one major brewer (Miller) was considering dealing directly with retailers. Inventory costs depended partly on the length of the lagering (ageing) stage in the production cycle. This was short for Miller and long for Anheuser-Busch. Shortening the lagering time would have the effect of increasing plant capacity, but it could affect the flavour of the beer.

Strategy and Market Change

In the 1970s the larger firms embarked on huge modernisation and expansion programmes. A rule of thumb in 1980 was that it cost $40–50 per barrel of annual production capacity to build a new plant. This rule was applied to some extent when firms bought existing breweries, but in those cases adjustments had to be made for the labour intensity of the older plants. These older breweries would have a shorter useful life because of these inefficiencies, as evidenced by the large number of closures of old breweries, notably in the New York City area.

However, some breweries closed because of weak marketing and an inability to compete, not because of inefficient production. Schlitz sold its newest, most efficient brewery near Syracuse, New York, to Anheuser-Busch in 1980 because of declining demand. Pabst's Peoria Heights, Illinois, plant was described as profitable, but it was shut down in 1982.

The competitive situation in the 1970s which provided the background to the strategic trade was characterised by crises of profitability and survival that affected even the largest brewers. As can be seen from Table 4.1, the rankings changed dramatically over the decade 1971–81. These changes were the result of major strategic initiatives by firms in the industry which had marked effects on individual fortunes.

Anheuser-Busch has been the market leader since 1957 when it took over from Schlitz. Schlitz remained its prime competitor until 1975 and much of its strategy was designed to meet this threat. Policy concentrated on quality. After 1975, Schlitz was replaced by Miller as the major threat. Schlitz had seen its market share decline as customer resistance to its product intensified. Anheuser-Busch embarked upon a programme of diversification but maintained 90 per cent of its business in beer in 1980.

The rise of Miller was by far the most significant event in the industry and had a major effect on all firms' strategies. Its rise followed its acquisition at the beginning of the decade by Philip

Morris, a tobacco company. Utilising the marketing flair which had characterised its new parent's success with low-tar cigarettes, Miller identified and exploited a market segment for 'light' beers. To do this, it sacrificed short-term earnings to build market shares, notably through the repositioning of Miller High Life and Miller Lite.

Coors managed to increase market share over the period 1971–81. The company has benefited from the strong brand image, despite spending less than half the industry average on advertising. Its overall strategy has generally been described as conservative but it has usually held its own despite all the turmoil around it.

Four large firms disappeared over the decade, three through acquisition by competitors (Theo Hamm, Carling and Schaeffer). Carling, part of the Canadian firm Carling-O'Keefe, itself acquired by Rothmans, suffered from inadequate local management and saw its market share slip progressively from 6 per cent in 1969 to 3 per cent in 1975. Despite acquiring the National Brewing Company in an attempt to buy market share and a stronger management, it was subsequently acquired itself by Heileman in 1979.

Schaeffer suffered as a result of financial over-commitment following the family sell-out, which resulted in reductions in advertising and a consequent inability to compete at a time when others in the industry were becoming more aggressive. In terms of brand image, Schaeffer was particularly vulnerable because of its long-established reputation as a heavy, working man's beer. It was subsequently purchased in 1980 by Stroh (see below).

Falstaff had held sixth place for a number of years but was suffering from increasing costs. It was taken over by a firm with both real estate and brewing interests, possibly attracted by the city centre locations of many of its breweries, but still could not turn the tide. The new owners made a strategic shift into production of 'own brands' for supermarket chains and, whilst losing market shares, they have made the company profitable once more.

There were four new entrants to the rankings, but the most significant impact was at Heileman and Olympia, both of whom were aggressive acquirers and took over competitors not dissimilar in size to themselves in their attempts to move from being regional to national brewers. Heileman moved from 39th position in 1960 to 4th in 1981. After a number of early acquisitions in which they bought up the victims of intensifying competition, they acquired the declining Carling National Breweries in 1979 and added two further small breweries in 1980 and 1981.

Olympia had been one of the most important regional brewers and sought to become a national force through acquisition. It purchased the Hamms brewery in St. Paul, Minnesota, for $22m, and in a $75m deal in 1976 added the Lone Star Brewery Company of San Antonio, Texas, becoming the 6th largest brewer in the market. The rate of acquisition and ambitious expansion plans took their toll on the company which went into decline in the late 1970s; by 1981 it had slipped to 8th place in the national league table.

The remaining two companies still in the top ten in 1981, as in 1971, were Pabst and Stroh. Their strategies are considered in more detail as the events leading up to the strategic trade are examined.

The Case Study: Company Strategies

Stroh

The Stroh Brewery Company had decided in the late 1970s that it had to change the company from a relatively small regional brewer selling a single brand in the Middle West region, to a national producer of a full line of beer products on a scale comparable to Anheuser-Busch and Miller. The alternative, as the company's president, Mr Peter W. Stroh said in an interview in 1983, was stagnation and eventual failure, as the country's beer drinkers switched to nationally-advertised premium brands (*New York Times* 1983).

The company's acquisition activities were later described as 'a survival effort' amidst consolidation in the industry (*New York Times* 1982b). Analysts agreed that in order to survive in the long-term, a national market presence was required. This was mainly because of the aggressive marketing efforts of the major national companies in the context of market concentration.

By 1980 Stroh's products were beginning to gain national recognition. Although it was known in its home market as a working man's beer, by 1980 Stroh's sales had grown rapidly among college students, especially in the Middle West states. This was reminiscent of a temporary surge in sales of Coors beer when it became 'fashionable' a few years earlier, but it did indicate the possibility of wider acceptance. In May 1980, Stroh made a commitment to buy more than 75 per cent of the large regional brewer based in New York, the F. and M. Schaeffer Corporation. When the agreement was announced, the two companies had claimed that its purpose was 'to increase cooperation' by sharing production and distribution facilities. The deal gave Stroh two valuable assets: a foothold in the lucrative North-East market and access to Schaeffer's huge modern brewery in Allentown, Pennsylvania. Perceptive observers saw the deal as a thinly-disguised takeover by Stroh. At that time, Stroh was the country's eighth largest brewer and Schaeffer was tenth; combined, they would be seventh in sales volume in 1980.

It was no surprise when Stroh completed the acquisition of Schaeffer in May 1981, and Stroh made its initial effort a $30 million addition to Schaeffer's brewery to equip it to produce Stroh's beer. The plan was to introduce the Stroh brand to the East Coast from the new facility over a two-year period. The Stroh brand was to be marketed as a premium beer, while Schaeffer's brands would continue in the popular price bracket. It was felt that the distinctive taste and appeal of Stroh's beer would sustain a premium price in the East. The new facility would reduce the demand on Stroh's Detroit plant, which could then start producing for new markets in the West.

Stroh surprised many observers when, in April 1982, it took over the Jos Schlitz Brewing Company, a firm with annual beer shipments half as big again as Stroh's. Schlitz had five big breweries, located in Los Angeles, California, Tampa, Florida, Memphis, Tennessee, Winston-Salem, North Carolina, and Longview, Texas, while Stroh's plants were located in Detroit, Michigan and Allentown, Pennsylvania.

The Schlitz takeover moved Stroh from seventh to third place in 1982 sales volume with 22.9m barrels sold compared with 59.1m for Anheuser-Busch and 39.3m for Miller.

Pabst

Pabst had been late in altering its strategy when the brewing industry changed in the 1970s. As a result, it missed opportunities it may have had to consolidate its position as number three in the industry. Turnover of top executives was rapid in the decade prior to 1982. The company's lack of marketing aggressiveness despite a strong balance sheet made it a vulnerable takeover target.

In November 1980, a group of businessmen led by Mr Irwin Jacobs had acquired over 8 per cent of Pabst, signalling a takeover bid. Mr Jacobs, who specialised in managing turnrounds, considered Pabst a solid firm that just needed an infusion of leadership. Mr Jacobs' strongest criticism was that Pabst had not pursued the acquisition of Schlitz when they had an opportunity to acquire it and had lost out to Heileman.

In February 1982, C. Schmidt & Sons, a regional brewer in Philadelphia, Pennsylvania, bid for Pabst shares, but the offer was rejected. Schmidt stopped bidding in April, although it continued to express interest until the summer. Also in February, Pabst announced plans to take over the small but profitable Pittsburgh Brewing Company. A 'definitive agreement' was reached in March, but because of uncertainties about the future of the Pittsburgh plant and in view of the possible acquisition of Pabst by Mr Jacobs, the Pittsburgh Company withdrew from the deal in June (*New York Times* 1982d).

Heileman entered the bidding for Pabst in May 1982. The Antitrust Division opposed the takeover because of the concentration of market share which the combined firms would have in the Middle West states. The Jacobs group then increased its offer and announced that if it was successful it would immediately sell Pabst's Newark, New Jersey and Perry, Georgia plants, which constituted about half of Pabst's production capacity, to Heileman.

The next step occurred in June when Pabst 'startled the financial community' by announcing a plan to acquire 49 per cent of the Olympia Brewing Company, a move which might have been designed to make Pabst a more difficult firm for Heileman to take over by putting more antitrust roadblocks in the way. Olympia quickly announced that it had accepted in principle a Pabst offer to take it over completely, and a definitive merger agreement was signed. By 9 July, 90 per cent of Olympia's shares had been tendered to Pabst, and it moved quickly to acquire those remaining. The deal was not without its complexity and had involved a two-way tender offer where Olympia had been counterbidders for Pabst to offer an alternative to the Jacobs deal.

A subsidiary of Olympia called OBC Acquisition Inc. was specially created to make an offer to buy approximately 49 per cent of Pabst. The bid was to compete with the Jacobs offer and to bring Olympia and Pabst closer to a full merger. A simultaneous statement by the Pabst board recommended rejection of Jacobs' offer for Pabst shares because it was inadequate and not in the best interests of the company or its stockholders.

The New York Times of 16 July reported that the Olympia offer was being financed by Pabst. Under the plan, Pabst shareholders would be able to exchange up to half of their holdings for cash, and the remainder for convertible, preferred shares in OBC, which would then hold shares of both Olympia and Pabst. Pabst recommended to its shareholders that they accept the OBC offer.

This two-way tender offer was described as one of the wildest merger strategies ever seen. When the Jacobs group's offer was withdrawn, it was quickly followed by a withdrawal of the OBC offer. The 'status quo' was more or less restored and although Jacobs still held a stake, a full takeover had been averted.

On 5 November, 1982, Heileman and Pabst announced a merger agreement based on the assumption that the Pabst/Olympia merger would be completed. Heileman would then take over three Pabst/Olympia plants and spin off the remainder as a 'new' Pabst. The deal excluded Jacobs and, on 16 November, he filed a suit against Pabst, Olympia and Heileman in a final attempt to block the transaction that was to take place without him as a participant. The issue was finally resolved on 26 November when Heileman made an agreement with Jacobs which gave his group a multimillion dollar profit on their Pabst shares and removed Jacobs from the battle (*New York Times* 1982i).

When the dust had settled, Heileman had acquired breweries in Perry, Georgia and Portland, Oregon (from the 'old' Pabst), and San Antonio, Texas (a former Olympia brewery). The remaining four breweries were spun off by Heileman to be managed by existing Pabst management, to avoid antitrust action against Heileman. This 'new' Pabst consisted of breweries in Milwaukee, Wisconsin and Newark, New Jersey (from the 'old' Pabst), Tumwater, Washington (a former Olympia plant) and St Paul, Minnesota (the former Hamm's brewery Pabst had acquired in the merger with Olympia).

1983: The Build Up to the Strategic Trade

Some observers were not optimistic about Stroh's future given the combination of the massive debt load it had taken on, the burden of trying to revive Schlitz's declining brands, and competing against Anheuser-Busch, Miller, Heileman and Coors. Stroh had pledged the assets of the company for a $336 million short-term loan to buy Schlitz, and had hoped to raise cash by liquidating some of Schlitz's assets.

When the acquisition of Schlitz by Stroh was announced in April 1982, the Antitrust Division immediately went to court demanding that Stroh divest either the Schlitz brewery in Winston-Salem, North Carolina or the one in Memphis, Tennessee, within one year. Stroh had already said it was prepared to divest one of these breweries, but had asked to be allowed two years to find a buyer. When the matter was decided in court, Stroh was given one year from the date of the final judgement, 10 November 1982 (US Justice Department 1982b).

As a result of its acquisition activity, Stroh had six large new breweries in addition to its home brewery in Detroit, but it had none in a large section of the country north of California and west of Michigan, comprising nearly half the area of the United States.

All four of Pabst's breweries were near the northern border of the United States (excluding Alaska). One was on the Pacific coast, and one on the Atlantic, and the company had two breweries in the Middle West region. Pabst had no production facilities in the sun belt, although it had an arrangement under which Heileman would produce Pabst beer in its Georgia plant but on a declining basis for five years. Pabst was not a *truly* 'national' firm.

Stroh had been trying to sell one of its two southern breweries since April 1982 but there were few possible buyers. (Anheuser-Busch and Miller were ruled out on antitrust grounds. Coors said it would build its own plants from the ground up, not buy and remodel someone else's. Heileman had just acquired Pabst's plant in nearby Georgia. No-one seemed interested.) In January 1983, however, Pabst announced that it was prepared to consider purchase of the Memphis plant, which would give Pabst production facilities in the attractive South-East market (*Advertising Age* 1983). At the same time, Pabst disclosed that it might have to close the St Paul 'Hamm's' plant because it was operating far below capacity, was unprofitable and was close to their Milwaukee brewery, which had enough unused capacity to serve the whole Mid-West region by itself. Pabst and Stroh executives met to discuss the sale of one of Stroh's breweries, but it became clear that Pabst could not afford either the Memphis or the Winston-Salem plant, though it told Stroh that it was interested in and *could* afford to buy the Tampa brewery. It was at one of their meetings that an executive suggested that Stroh might have a use for the St Paul brewery, and that a trade might be feasible if the Justice Department would allow Stroh's Tampa brewery to be substituted for the two named in the court decision. Justice Department approval was granted, and detailed negotiations proceeded.

The Trade

The trade was announced publicly in the first week of May 1983 and approved by the court in September of the same year. The exchange included all the assets and employees of both plants, and no cash changed hands.

It is possible to identify for both parties a number of reasons why each favoured the strategic trade. As far as Stroh was concerned, production facilities in St Paul would relieve production pressures on its Detroit plant, thus allowing it to produce more of the Stroh brand in Detroit. The St Paul plant, which had twice the capacity of the Tampa brewery, could serve the 'West North Central' market, saving transportation costs from Detroit, thus giving it good locational coverage of all major market areas. In addition, they would acquire access to a valuable network of distributors along with the St Paul plant. The antitrust implications were acceptable as the trade satisfied the requirement of the Justice Department to divest a plant in the South-East region, while it allowed Stroh to keep the large, efficient, modern and expandable plants in Winston-Salem and Memphis, and to make more permanent plans for them. The capacity utilisation of both plants would be increased.

On the financial side, no cash was needed to acquire the St Paul plant, and no cash was received for the Tampa plant. Thus, the deal could be structured as a tax-free exchange of assets.

Pabst favoured the exchange because it obtained modern 'permanent' facilities in the South-East market, filling a big gap in the geographical distribution of its plants. It could aggressively push existing products in the South-East, and would save transportation costs in serving the sun-belt market. It already feared it might have to close the St Paul plant because of local overcapacity. A recent closure of a plant in Illinois had demonstrated how expensive closure could be as it had cost Pabst nearly $9 million in severance payments alone. The Tampa brewery which it would get in exchange, although it had only half the production capacity of the St Paul plant, was modern and efficient and had room for expansion. Indeed, the smaller size was actually an advantage in the short term because Pabst was forced to honour an agreement to buy beer from Heileman's Georgia brewery for five years. The deal gave extra flexibility to Pabst who now had three breweries with locations suitable for producing beer for export, an option it was considering. The brewery also included a can-manufacturing plant capable of making 600 million cans per year, which Pabst felt could save it money.

The financial advantages at Stroh were mirrored at Pabst. No cash was involved (Pabst did not have much cash) and the deal was structured as a tax-free exchange of assets. The Justice Department was content to see the trade take place because it would increase competition in the Great Lakes region and reduce concentration in the South-East. There were also potential benefits to other parties which the trade would bring. Not least, it would remove a 'cloud of uncertainty' affecting the workers and communities involved in several breweries, and through increased competition it was likely to lead to lower prices and greater variety for consumers.

The movement of Pabst production from St Paul to Milwaukee would mean more jobs in Milwaukee, while movement of Stroh production from Tampa would mean more jobs in Winston-Salem and Memphis.

The Workers' Interests

The consequences of the strategic trade were felt by both the employees of the affected plants and the residents of the communities in which they were located. A committed workforce should not be underestimated as part of a company's assets. The workers at the breweries in Winston-Salem, Memphis and St Paul's were enthusiastic about the trade after the uncertainties of its former acquisitions, but this was not matched in Tampa where the workers expressed their concern to the Antitrust Division. The workforce at St Paul's had become used to change after several changes of ownership since 1960.

In all, there were 1,675 workers at the Winston-Salem, Memphis and St Paul's plants and 290 in Tampa. The 500 at St Paul, where the average age was 53, had been very uncertain about their future and the trade was met with undisguised enthusiasm. It was seen as a means of securing a future for brewing in the city. On completion of the trade, the unions accepted new work contracts which removed many restrictive practices and increased productivity. The renegotiation was described as a means of streamlining operations while keeping union jurisdiction intact.

The reaction over uncertainty at Winston-Salem and Memphis was more dramatic. It was embittered by a lack of communication from Stroh when it took over Schlitz. The change in the court approval from the antitrust authorities, agreeing to replace breweries in the original order, reassured the workers in Winston-Salem and Memphis but led to fears in Tampa. Pabst sought to reassure the Tampa workforce that there were to be no redundancies and that expansion was planned for Tampa, but in the short term some 100 hourly workers were temporarily laid off.

The Aftermath

Competition in the beer market intensified in 1983 and 1984, and *Business Week* reported that it was becoming a battleground. The traditional target group – young men – was decreasing and turning increasingly to other beverages.

In 1984, overcapacity in the industry was estimated at 40 million barrels, leading to widespread price cutting to keep plants operating. Miller was hardest hit, losing market share in both 1983 and 1984 and suffering a 25 per cent fall in operating profit. Coors aggressively launched new products and entered new markets, having lost market share in its traditional ones. Industry-wide advertising budgets were increased substantially, by an estimated 60 per cent from 1980 to 1984, to $700 million. With such intense competition in the industry, it seemed inevitable that more firms would fail, or more mergers would take place.

Pabst after the Trade

At the time of the strategic trade, informed opinion was that Pabst had gained more from the deal than Stroh, but the benefits to Pabst appeared to have come too late. The company admitted that unless it could acquire, through merger or acquisition, instant volume, then it would be in trouble. The lack of confidence spread right to the Pabst president himself.

By the end of 1984 it seemed as if it was indeed 'over' for Pabst, as its sales volume and market share continued to decline. It was subject to competing merger approaches from S & P (who owned the old Falstaff brewery) and Heileman. Pabst eventually accepted an offer from Heileman and in order to get antitrust approval, Heileman agreed to sell Pabst's Tumwater, Washington, plant and the Olympia, Hamm's and Olde English '800' brands to S & P. It was later reported that Pabst had agreed that if Heileman's takeover bid failed, Pabst would sell it certain brands, along with Stroh (*Wall Street Journal* 1984d). This was seen as a move to make competing bids difficult. Stroh and C. Schmidt reacted quickly and succeeded in getting a preliminary injunction halting further action by Heileman until they could make a counter-offer for Pabst (*Wall Street Journal* 1984e). Although the specific outcome was not clear, it seemed certain that Pabst was about to disappear as an independent entity.

If the Heileman takeover went through, it would make Heileman the third largest brewer in the United States, slightly ahead of Stroh. It would also give Heileman capacity of 33 million barrels, far in excess of its after-merger projected sales of about 24 million barrels. This was expected to lead to plant closures, probably of former Pabst breweries; but which plants were threatened was not specified (*Wall Street Journal* 1984c).

Stroh after the Trade

Stroh held third place in 1983 with a volume of 24.3 million barrels, an increase of 6.2 per cent over 1982. The company planned expansion and expected to be selling the Stroh and Stroh Light brands in all parts of the country within about a year and a half. A super-premium brand, Signature, was also to be gradually marketed nationally. Despite the sales gains, and an aggressive new marketing strategy designed to change consumer perceptions about its products, there was no uniform confidence in the company's long-term prospects (*New York Times* 1983).

Stroh continued its aggressive marketing in 1984 by increasing its advertising budget and bringing out a popular new series of television commercials, and as a result it was able to maintain about the same sales volume as in 1983. This was better than the performance of Miller and Pabst, but not as good as Anheuser-Busch, Heileman and Coors. Stroh gave every sign of continuing to be an aggressive competitor.

The Effectiveness of the Strategic Trade

When the strategic trade took place, analysts saw it as favouring Pabst. That is, they saw the increase in value to Pabst as exceeding the increase in value to Stroh. However, the underlying weakness of Pabst meant that the survival of the firm as an independent unit was still threatened. The increase in its value as a result of the strategic trade does not appear to have been sufficient to overcome that more fundamental weakness, even when combined with other measures such as cost-cutting – including the wage rollbacks accepted by the company's unions.

Perhaps events would have turned out differently had the market for beer not been shrinking. Pabst was poised to compete, but it had been severely weakened by the 'beer wars'.

In Stroh's case, the strategic trade appears to have been vital in freeing the Memphis and Winston-Salem plants for long-term use. In the face of relentless competition, resources had to be available for whatever purpose Stroh could use them. With Miller and Pabst facing marketing difficulties, the firms which were ready to capitalise on their weaknesses were the ones likely to benefit most.

Anheuser-Busch, Stroh, Heileman and Coors were in that position, and without the freedom provided by the strategic trade, Stroh might have been severely hamstrung.

The Future of Strategic Trading

This case illustrates the usefulness of strategic trading as an instrument to facilitate rapid adjustment by more than one firm to major strategic factors in the business environment. It shows that a strategic trade can be executed where a straight sale would not have been financially possible. It also indicates that both participants in the strategic trade can benefit (even though in the present case Pabst was unable to take full advantage of its gains). While the situations in which strategic trades are feasible may be relatively few and may take extra effort to organise, the benefits can be significant. Strategic trading should not be ignored as a strategic alternative.

References and Further Reading

Advertising Age (1983) 'Smaller Pabst Brewing considers its options', by Robert Reed, 17 January, pp. 4, 52.

Brigham, Eugene F., Kahl, Alfred L. and Rentz, William F. (1982) *Canadian Financial Management*, Rinehart and Winston.

Business Week (1973) 'A struggle to stay first in brewing', 24 March, pp. 42–9.

Business Week (1975a) 'Brewing up a rescue at Falstaff', 30 June, p. 31.

Business Week (1975b) 'How Miller won a market slot for Lite beer', 13 October, pp. 116–18.

Business Week (1976a) 'Olympia Brewing aims to go national', 20 September, pp. 32–3.

Business Week (1976b) 'Miller's fast growth upsets the Beer Industry', 8 November, pp. 58–67.

Business Week (1980) 'Anheuser's plan to flatten Miller's head', 21 April, p. 171.

Business Week (1981) 'Asset redeployment: everything is for sale now', 24 August, pp. 68–74.

Business Week (1982) 'Stroh's gamble in swallowing Schlitz', 26 April, p. 31.

Business Week (1984) 'Bairnco: an empire that spins off companies to grow', 30 April, pp. 68–9.

Business Week (1984a) 'A shrinking market has beermakers brawling', 20 August, pp. 59–63.

Business Week (1984b) 'At Philip Morris, soda and beer are still falling flat', by Judith H. Dobrzynski and Ellyn S. Spragins, 17 December, pp. 61–2.

Davis, M. Gary (1984a) 'How strategic trading can help firms adapt quickly to changing conditions', *Financial Times Mergers and Acquisitions*, January to March, pp. 45–8.

Davis, M. Gary (1984b) 'The industrial structures of diversified firms', *Conference on New Challenges for Management Research* (Leuven, Belgium), European Institute for Advanced Studies in Management, Brussels, Belgium.

Davis, M. Gary (1984c) 'The relative values of business units', *Proceedings of the Conference of the Atlantic Schools of Business*, Halifax, N.S., Canada: Mount St Vincent University.

Dun's Review (1981) 'Divestitures: a new business rage', March.

Economist (1984) 'Beer as a soft drink', 2 June, p. 71.

Ernst and Whinney, Management Consultants (1984) *Corporate Divestitures: A Results-Oriented Approach.*

Financial Times (1983) 'The struggle to keep up with the leaders', by Paul Betts, 4 October.

Forbes (1984) 'Is the game over?', by Barry Stavro, 16 January, p. 95.

Fortune (1979) 'August Busch brews up a new spirit in St Louis', by Thomas O'Hanlon, 15 January, pp. 92–103.

Fortune (1983a) 'Selling the subs: the latest thing in finance', 8 August, p. 6.

Fortune (1983b) 'Jimmy Goldsmith's US bonanza', by Gwen Kinkead, 17 October, pp. 125–44.

Glueck, William F., and Jauch, Lawrence R. (1984) *Business Policy and Strategic Management*, 4th edn., McGraw-Hill.

Goldberg, Walter H. (1983) *Mergers*, Gower.

Harowitz, Howard and Halliday, Doug. (1984) 'The new alchemy: divestment for profit', *The Journal of Business Strategy*, Vol. 5, No. 2, Autumn.

Harrigan, Kathryn Rudie (1981) 'Deterrents to divestiture', *Academy of Management Journal*, Vol. 24, No. 2.

Hearth, Douglas and Zaima, Janis K. (1984) 'Voluntary corporate divestitures and value', *Financial Management*, Spring.

Higgins, James M. (1979) *Organizational Policy and Strategic Management*, The Dryden Press.

Milwaukee Journal (1983) 'Pabst, Stroh to swap plants in St Paul, Tampa', 5 May.

Milwaukee Sentinel (1983) 'Pabst–Stroh plant swap could lead to jobs here', by Kent Krauss, 6 May.

National Review of Corporate Acquisitions, see Ernst and Whinney above.

New York Times (1975) 'Coors: beer of beers or "kool-aid"?', by James P. Sterba, 4 February.

New York Times (1980) 'Schaeffer pins hope on Stroh', 17 May.

New York Times (1981a) 'Stroh's brewery bid for Schaeffer completed', 21 May.

New York Times (1981b) 'Pabst post sought by entrepreneur', 14 July.

New York Times (1982a) 'The Blue-Ribbon battle for Pabst', by Ray Kenney, 24 January.

New York Times (1982b) 'Stroh's "Survival" bid', 22 April.

New York Times (1982c) 'Pabst sets bid for 49% of Olympia', by Kirk Johnson, 2 June.

New York Times (1982d) 'Pittsburgh brewer ends Pabst talks', 24 June.

New York Times (1982e) 'Olympia brewing unit in Pabst bid', by Kirk Johnson, 6 July.

New York Times (1982f) 'Pabst asks shareholders to accept offer by Olympia', by Thomas J. Luecki, 7 July.

New York Times (1982g) 'Olympia extends Pabst deadline', 16 July.

New York Times (1982h) 'Olympia reports on Pabst tenders', 21 July.

New York Times (1982i) 'Olympia brewing ends its offer for 49% of Pabst', by Kirk Johnson, 27 July.

New York Times (1982j) 'The perils of cutting quality', 22 August.

New York Times (1982k) 'Heileman wins the battle for Pabst', by Sandra Salmans, 24 December.

New York Times (1983) 'Stroh's big-league gamble', by John Holusha, 27 August.

New York Times Index (1972) Vol. 60: The New York Times Company, 1973, p. 209.

Nisbett, Richard E. and Wilson, Timothy DeCamp (1977) 'Telling more than we can know: verbal reports on mental processes', *Psychological Review*, Vol. 44, No. 3, May.

Pabst (1983) Annual Report of the Pabst Brewing Company.

St. Paul Pioneer Press and Dispatch (1983a) 'E. Side brewery closing studied', by Steve Massey and Dave Beal, 16 January.

St. Paul Pioneer Press and Dispatch (1983b) 'Stroh swaps for brewery on East Side', by Lee Egerstrom, 5 May.

St. Paul Pioneer Press and Dispatch (1983c) 'Locker room beer runs low as employees celebrate', by Ozzie St George, 6 May.

St. Paul Pioneer Press and Dispatch (1983d) 'Stroh "bullish" on Minnesota as "bear" market heads south', by Lee Egerstrom, 7 May.

St. Paul Pioneer Press and Dispatch (1983e) 'Marketing', by Lee Egerstrom, 9 May.

St. Paul Pioneer Press and Dispatch (1983f) 'Stroh, unions ratify 3-year wage contract', by Steve Massey, 14 October.

Shay, Scott A. (1981) 'Setting the "right" premium in an efficient market', *Mergers and Acquisitions*, Spring, pp. 23–8.

Stahl, Michael J. and Zimmerer, Thomas W. (1984) 'Modelling strategic acquisition policies: a simulation of executives by acquisition decisions', *Academy of Management Journal*, Vol. 27, No. 2.

Tampa Tribune (1983a) 'Stroh, Pabst plan to swap Tampa, Minnesota plants', by Bernice Stengle, 6 May.

Tampa Tribune (1983b) 'Brewery swap delayed until 1 October', by Bernice Stengle, 2 July.

Tampa Tribune (1983c) 'Schlitz plant becomes Pabst next Monday', by Mike Vizvary, 27 September.

Tampa Tribune (1983d) 'Pabst to lay off 100 workers', 14 October.

Tampa Tribune (1983e) 'New brew on tap at former Schlitz brewery in Tampa', by Bernice Stengle, 16 October.

Thomas, R.E. (1981) *The Government of Business*, 2nd edn., Philip Allan.

Times (1982) 'BP Chemicals and ICI in asset-swapping deal', by Derek Harris, 18 June.

US Bureau of the Census (1974) *Statistical Abstract of the United States: 1974*, 95th edn., Washington D.C.

US Bureau of the Census (1983) *Statistical Abstract of the United States 1984*, 104th edn., Washington D.C.

US Justice Department (1982a) USA v The Stroh Brewery Company, *Complaint for Injunctive Relief*, 16 April.

US Justice Department (1982b) USA *v* Stroh, *Stipulation*, 10 November.

US Justice Department (1983) USA *v* Stroh, letter from Employees of the Stroh Brewery Co. (sic) to Mr Anthony V. Nanni, attachment to *Plaintiff's Certificate of Compliance with Order Directing Publication of Notice*, 15 September.

US News and World Report (1983) 'The merger drive goes into reverse', by Clemens P. Work, 2 May, pp. 55–6.

Wall Street Journal (1983a) 'Paul Kalmanovitz acquires Falstaff and pursues Pabst', by Victor F. Zonana, 7 April.

Wall Street Journal (1983b) 'Pabst battles back', by Tim Metz, 15 June; reprinted in Thompson, Arthur A., Strickland III, A.J. and Fulmer, William E. (1984) *Readings in Strategic Management*, Business Publications.

Wall Street Journal (1984a) 'Paul Kalmanovitz continues his quest for Pabst Brewing', 12 November.

Wall Street Journal (1984b) 'J. Walter Thompson wins competition for coveted Miller High Life Account', by Bill Abrams, 14 November.

Wall Street Journal (1984c) 'Pabst accepts sweetened offer of G. Heileman', by Marj Charlier, 7 December.

Wall Street Journal (1984d) 'Heileman, Pabst amend options to buy certain Pabst assets', 21 December.

Wall Street Journal (1984e) 'Court halts Heileman's purchase of Pabst shares', 27 December.

Winston-Salem *Journal and Sentinel* (1982a) 'Stroh reassures Schlitz workers', by Michael Wade, 14 May.

Winston-Salem *Journal and Sentinel* (1982b) 'Teamsters here join walkout against Schlitz', by Pete Mantius, 17 June.

Acknowledgements

I would like to thank particularly the following people (listed in alphabetical order) who helped me obtain information needed to write this chapter:

Ms Darlene Banks (US Department of Justice)
Mr John Byrd (Winston-Salem *Journal* and *Sentinel* Newspapers)
Ms Mitzi Dahnke (Pabst Brewing Company)
Mr A. James Dooley (Pabst Brewing Company)
Ms Lori A. Harbour (The Stroh Brewery Company)
Mr William Kerr (Ward Chipman Library, University of New Brunswick)
Mr Steve Massey (*St Paul Pioneer Press and Dispatch*)
Ms Bernice Stengle (*The Tampa Tribune*)

I would also like to thank Professor R.E. Thomas for his many insights into the subject of mergers and acquisitions and business policy.

5

Foreign Divestment and International Rationalisation: The Sale of Chrysler (UK) to Peugeot

Mark Casson

Introduction

Foreign divestment may be defined as a situation in which a corporation with headquarters in a foreign country relinquishes control of the production activities of a local subsidiary.

Early studies of foreign divestment include an analysis by Franko (1971) of factors influencing the survival of international joint ventures, a study by Kitching (1973) of successes and failures amongst US acquisitions in Europe, and an analysis of US divestments by Torneden (1975). Business International (1976), Sachdev (1976) and Chopra *et al*. (1978) present further case study evidence, and survey the strategic issues from the standpoint of the divesting company.

A wave of foreign divestments in Europe, beginning in 1973, emphasised the need to consider more carefully the social and economic impact of divestment on the host country. Van Den Bulcke (1979) examined the case of Belgium and found that during the two years 1975–76 foreign affiliates were responsible for 32 per cent of job losses arising from plant closures and collective dismissals in manufacturing industry – a proportion very similar to their share in total manufacturing employment. However, foreign affiliates were more inclined than their Belgian counterparts to close down smaller plants and to retain large ones, which suggests that they were involved in a more coherent form of rationalisation than were indigenous firms. In a more recent study, however, Van Den Bulcke and Halsberghe (1983) noted that this difference between foreign and indigenous firms has since disappeared. This is confirmed in a study of employment losses in Irish manufacturing industry by McAleese and Counahan (1979), who found no significant differences at all between foreign subsidiaries and indigenous firms. Figures published by the Industry Department for Scotland indicate that this applies in Scotland too.

A number of recent case studies have focused upon the political economy of foreign divestment. Grunberg (1981) has examined Leyland's divestment of the Italian motor manufacturer Innocenti and Litton Industries' closure of its British Imperial Typewriter subsidiary, whilst Hood and Young (1982) and Young, Hood and Hamill (1985) have examined foreign divestments in Scotland by Singer, Hoover, NCR, Honeywell, Goodyear, Timex, Hyster and IBM. Both Grunberg and Hood and Young also discuss Chrysler, although their emphasis is different from the present study. Grunberg focuses upon the negotiations between Chrysler and the British Government in 1975 while Hood and Young focus upon Peugeot's closure of a major Scottish factory in 1981. More specific studies of the impact of foreign divestment on a local economy are provided by Gaffikin and Nickson (1984) for the West Midlands and Lloyd and Strutt (1983) for the North West.

The object of this chapter is to use the Chrysler–Peugeot divestment of 1978 to illustrate certain general points which can be established independently from other sources of evidence. These general points concern the nature of the economic forces which induce foreign divestment, and the particular way in which these forces have recently manifested themselves in a drive towards the rationalisation of production in the motor industry. This chapter does not present a case study of the machinery of the corporate decision-making process (see Boddewyn 1983b), but rather a case study of the way that economic circumstances dictated a particular rational response by the managements of the two companies to adverse trading conditions in their industry. In describing the response as rational, it is assumed that both managements had well-defined objectives and attempted to choose the appropriate means to fulfil them. It is recognised, however, that managements were responding to the situation as it was perceived at the time, and not as it might now be perceived with the benefit of hindsight. It should be clear, therefore, that this case study is informed by the insights of economic theory rather than by insights gained from the study of organisational behaviour.

The following section outlines the general theory of foreign divestment. The third section provides general background information on the motor industry, whilst the fourth introduces the specific issue of the rationalisation of production, which provides the key to understanding the Chrysler–Peugeot divestment. The highlights of the Chrysler–Peugeot story are described in the fifth and sixth sections, whilst details of attempts to rationalise production are presented in section seven. The future prospects for the divested operations are assessed in section eight. The policy issues raised by the divestment are discussed in section nine, and finally the conclusions are summarised.

The Motives for Foreign Divestment

The motives for foreign *divestment* can be examined by adapting the theory of foreign *investment* to deal with what is essentially the reverse case (Boddewyn 1983a, 1984).

It is useful to distinguish two main forms of foreign divestment. The first is associated with the closure of an overseas subsidiary, whilst the second involves transfer of ownership of the subsidiary to someone else. Different factors are likely to be important in the two cases. In the first case it is probable that the location of production is wrong, in the light of the current market environment in the industry. It is possible, of course, that the location may be suitable for use by a different industry, or for the production of a different product within the same industry. It is, however, normally very expensive to convert a facility from one use to another. Since highly specific fixed assets based in the wrong location are of little value to other firms, closure of the plant is the natural policy.

In the second case it is more likely that it is the ownership structure of production that is wrong. The location must be reasonably satisfactory if someone is willing to take over the production facility.

The takeover occurs because the acquiring company can offer the divesting firm more than the plant is worth under existing arrangements. This offer may still provide the acquiring company with savings over the cost of purchasing a similar plant elsewhere or of building a new plant from scratch somewhere else. Divestment occurs in this case, it may be said, because the acquiring company has an advantage in owning the assets concerned. The possible nature of this advantage is considered in some detail below.

The distinction between the locational structure of an industry and its ownership structure is an important one (Dunning 1977). It should not, however, be turned into a complete analytical dichotomy. Ownership and location structure interact in several ways. To begin with, a parent firm and its subsidiary normally trade more regularly with each other than they do with independent firms outside their group. Transport costs incurred in connection with the movement of goods and services normally vary directly with the distance travelled. The need to economise on transport costs thus encourages parent and subsidiary to locate as close as possible to one another. Likewise, communication between parent and subsidiary is normally more intensive than between a pair of unaffiliated establishments. Communication costs, like transport costs, vary with distance, though in this case it is 'psychic distance' rather than 'geographical distance' that is important. Psychic distance is shorter the greater are the cultural and linguistic affinities between the two locations. Economy in communication costs encourages parent and subsidiary to locate in places that share a common language and culture.

Fiscal relations between countries also forge a link between ownership and location structure by creating advantages to transfer pricing (see, for example, Rugman and Eden 1985). Transfer pricing occurs when the price set in a transaction between two affiliated companies differs from the price which would prevail in a similar transaction between two unaffiliated companies in the same locations. A parent company, for example, which under-invoices a foreign subsidiary for a supply of components can benefit in three possible ways. If profit taxation rates are lower abroad than they are at home, then a low internal accounting price notionally redistributes profit to the subsidiary and so reduces the global tax liability of the group. Secondly, if imports of components are subjected to *ad valorem* tariffs, then tariff liability will be reduced by under-declaring the value of the subsidiary's imports from the parent company. Finally, if exchange controls in the home country prevent the export of capital to more profitable locations abroad, then the controls can be bypassed by concealing the export of capital in a subsidised transaction between parent and subsidiary. When conditions are the reverse of these discussed here, the group can profit through either the *over*-invoicing of the subsidiary or the *under*-invoicing of the parent by the subsidiary.

In general, the profitability of transfer pricing is greater, the greater are the fiscal differences and the impediments to trade and capital movements between the countries concerned. When political differences impede trade between countries that have much to gain from it, it is likely that multinational ownership of production will predominate. The advantages of conducting trade *within* firms rather than *between* firms mean that ownership structure and location structure become inextricably intertwined.

When analysing the closure of a foreign subsidiary, it is useful to distinguish three main ways in which the subsidiary may fit into the overall structure of the group. Firstly, the subsidiary may be concerned with producing one of the group's products for sale in a local market. In this case the operations of the subsidiary allow local production to be substituted for imports supplied from the parent firm. Such 'import-substituting' investments allow the group as a whole to economise on transport costs and tariff payments that would otherwise be incurred on products exported by the parent to the subsidiary's market. Against these savings must be set any additional costs arising from loss of economies of scale due to the dispersal of production over different plants (Vernon 1966, 1974, 1979). The changes most likely to precipitate the closure of a subsidiary of this kind are outlined below:

(a) The size of the market being supplied by the subsidiary may shrink due to lower domestic incomes, a switch in tastes towards new and better products offered by rival firms, or an increase in the cost of distributing the product, which reduces the market area that the subsidiary can profitably supply. Economies of scale mean that lower sales incur unit-cost penalties, and so the subsidiary may be closed and production switched to the parent firm.
(b) A fall in transport costs, a reduction in tariffs, or the removal of non-tariff barriers on imports from the parent firm may also encourage production to be switched to the parent firm.

The second way in which the subsidiary may fit into the activities of the group is through offshore processing. It receives raw materials and semi-processed products from an affiliate in one country, processes them further, and then exports them, either back to their country of origin or to an affiliate in a third country. The profitability of offshore processing depends crucially upon low labour costs and low international transport costs. The closure of an offshore processing facility is most likely to be caused by either:

(a) a rise in domestic labour costs relative to labour costs elsewhere, due to a rise in money wages, a strengthening of the domestic exchange rate, or lagging domestic productivity growth; or
(b) a rise in international transport costs or increased impediments to international trade.

Finally, the subsidiary may be involved in primary production of agricultural or mineral products processed elsewhere within the group. Closure of a subsidiary of this kind is most likely to be due to either

(a) increasing costs of utilising land or mines which are close to the point of exhaustion; or
(b) the discovery of alternative sites which are either cheaper to operate or located closer to the rest of the group's operations and closer to the major centres of final demand.

There are, of course, other types of subsidiary, such as the sales and distribution subsidiary, the finance subsidiary and the group management services subsidiary. Subsidiaries of this kind are extremely important, but they cannot be discussed here because of limitations of space. Until recently, however, these other types of subsidiary did not figure prominently in discussions of foreign divestment.

A similar classification of subsidiaries is useful when considering divestment from one company to another. It has already been noted that in this case it is ownership structure rather than location structure that is crucial.

A group that successfully produces and markets a product abroad in competition with indigenous producers presumably enjoys some advantage relative to its indigenous competitors which enables it to survive in spite of its additional costs of operating away from home. This advantage may stem from a superior product design, superior production technology, an internationally-known brand name, and so on (Hymer 1976; Kindleberger 1960; Caves 1971). Advantages of this kind are, however, subject to obsolescence, and a point may be reached where another company acquires superiority over the foreign investor. Under these circumstances the investor may sell out to its rival, who can make better use of its production facilities. This exemplifies divestment stimulated by the passing of competitive advantage from the divesting to the acquiring firm.

Another possibility is that the parent firm may decide to license its know-how and skills, instead of exploiting them itself through a network of production subsidiaries. The company may then sell off its production operations to its local licensees. This is most likely to occur when a company realises that while it can successfully innovate new products and processes, it has difficulty in managing the overseas production that utilises them. Alternatively, such behaviour may represent a strategic response by the company to host government regulation and restriction of foreign investment. The hostility of the governments of many developing countries towards foreign direct investment in the 1970s led many companies to divest by substituting alternative contractual arrangements for outright ownership of foreign subsidiaries. These alternative contractual arrangements included not only licensing but franchising, subcontracting, and joint ventures with local firms (Casson 1979; UNCTC 1983).

A foreign subsidiary involved in offshore processing has an advantage over purely indigenous competitors in that its processing activities are integrated into the activities of a wider group. The subsidiary participates in economies of vertical integration which confer secure supplies of material inputs, a secure market for output, better planning of capacity expansion in related activities, avoidance of monopolistic price distortions in arm's length trade, easier organisation of quality control, better opportunities for transfer pricing, and so on (Casson 1984). Divestment occurs when the benefits of vertical integration are so small, or the administrative costs of achieving them are so great, that it is better either for the subsidiary to 'go it alone', or for it to be integrated into the operations of some other group instead. A common occurrence is for the product range produced by the group to change as a result of competitive pressures, so that there is no longer much demand within the group for the subsidiary's processing activity. At the same time, a rival firm may have expanded its product range and be seeking a processing facility to be integrated with its existing operations. This realignment of product ranges induces the first group to divest its subsidiary to the second group.

A company involved in agricultural and raw-material production may divest for reasons similar to those affecting offshore processing – namely, that these activities no longer fit in well with the other activities undertaken within the group. During the 1960s and 1970s, forced divestments were quite common within developing countries as host governments claimed land and mineral rights as the property of the state.

Production, Management and Marketing in the Motor Industry

The motor car is built up by the assembly of many diverse components: the internal combustion engine, mechanically engineered transmission and suspension, pressed steel bodies, synthetic rubber tyres, electrical and electronic components, plastic trim, and so on. Each component is produced to fine tolerances to allow spare parts to be interchanged. Mass production was introduced into the motor industry by Henry Ford, who adapted techniques from the Chicago meat-packing trade to generate the moving-track assembly line now widely used for mass production in manufacturing industry. Ford also used the techniques of scientific management pioneered by F.W. Taylor – in particular, time and motion study – to determine the optimal speed of the track.

The problem of organising a continuous supply of components was one of a number of factors that encouraged the President of General Motors, Alfred P. Sloan, Jr., to apply multidivisional organisation to his company. Although the multidivisional concept originated with E.I. du Pont Nemours, a large US chemical conglomerate, which at the time had a stake in General Motors, its application in General Motors proved extremely influential (see, for example, Chandler 1962; Rae 1965; and the numerous references given therein).

Quite recently, the Japanese have formed 'quality circles' amongst their key employees to improve component reliability, and have developed the 'just in time' production concept to reduce component inventories by promoting punctuality amongst their suppliers. Many motor manufacturers are now introducing robots to undertake welding, wheel assembly, paint spraying, etc; the pioneers include Volkswagen at Wolfsburg in West Germany, and Nissan in Japan.

The variety of components used in the motor industry means that many different types of manufacturing process are found. Body panels, for example, are pressed from sheet steel using high-volume dies which can produce 5–10 million stampings before replacement. Maxcy (1981, p. 201) estimates that the presses into which the dies are inserted can produce up to 2 million pressings a year, which means that minimum-cost production of body panels requires a rate of output of 2 million units per annum sustained over $2\frac{1}{2}$–5 years. (For further information on cost structures in the motor industry, see Rhys (1977).)

It has been estimated that the minimum efficient scale (mes) in the casting of engine blocks is 100,000 units per annum, in the machining and assembly of the power train (engine and transmission) 500,000 units per annum, and in final assembly 200,000 units per annum.

The importance of economies of scale means that the profitability of motor production depends crucially upon the intensity of demand for the product. At given prices, the higher the volume of sales, the greater is the margin of profit on each unit sold. In the early motor industry some of the most sophisticated vehicles were produced in France, but they were usually custom-made and sold only to a limited number of wealthy people.

Henry Ford was one of the first to create a mass market for motor vehicles amongst middle- and low-income families. Demand was particularly strong in rural areas, such as the mid-western states of the US. In interwar and early postwar Europe there were two main segments of the motor market: the mass production sector dominated by Citroën, Volkswagen, Fiat and Ford (UK), and the luxury sector dominated by smaller British and Italian firms.

Within the last 25 years a third segment of the motor vehicle market has emerged. Narrowing after-tax income differentials, higher oil prices, the trend towards hypermarket shopping and the increasing availability of motorways has created a large demand for medium-size 5-door vehicles which offer low running costs but provide some differentiation in styling.

The multicomponent character of the motor vehicle can be exploited to meet some of the needs of this market. Superficial differentiation of the product can be achieved by substituting one type of component for another in the final assembly process. By developing a standardised range of components, the same basic vehicle can be offered with different sizes of engine, with manual or automatic transmission, with different levels of trim, and with or without power-steering, turbochargers, electronic displays, and so on.

The introduction of robots on the assembly line has eliminated many of the delays which were caused by retooling production using manual labour. Thus when robots are used, the capacity of the assembly line effectively determines not the efficient output of a single model but the efficient output of the entire range. This has tended to reduce the importance of economies of scale in assembly (see Altshuler *et al.* 1984). On the other hand, the high capital cost of robots means that the cost penalties of operating the assembly line at below its rated capacity are much greater than before.

The fact that so many differentiations of the motor vehicle are possible means that the choice of model tends to reflect the lifestyle of the owner. This allows skilful marketing to exploit the consumer's social aspirations by suggesting that a particular model will allow him to achieve his desired lifestyle. The versatility of the motor vehicle also calls for marketing skill in explaining to the customer the precise range of functions that any particular model can perform.

One of the crucial issues in marketing is how far the manufacturer should market the model rather than the range. This is related to a wider issue of the advantages of selling a 'full line' under a single brand name, or 'badge'. The badge is a symbol of the quality of product: Ford, for example, is widely associated with mechanical reliability, Volkswagen with durability, Volvo with safety, Citroën with technical sophistication, and so on. Customers for motor vehicles progress through a life cycle during which the pattern of their movements and the size of their family change. By marketing the badge rather than the model, the manufacturer can attract customers for life, who will trade up and down the model range, confident that each of the models shares with the others the quality that they value most. When promoting the badge, it is important that the range includes a model at the bottom end with which the young customer can begin. It is less important to have a model in the extreme luxury category, since few customers are likely ever to earn sufficient income to afford one, except perhaps at the very end of their life cycle.

Novelty is a major aspect in attracting customers, and the annual sales of most models peak fairly early during their life. But the large number of different components involved means it is difficult to introduce an all-new vehicle, and many new models are, in fact, restyled versions of older models with updated specifications, effected by modifying a few components. R and D is thus an ongoing process in which information from salesmen and from service engineers about deficiencies in the performance of existing components is continuously fed back to prompt further improvements. Likewise, marketing is an ongoing process in which much of the emphasis is placed on explaining to consumers the advantages of the latest specification changes, or drawing their attention to new styling.

The Pressure for Rationalisation

The cost structure of the motor industry indicates that component production should be concentrated upon a small number of very large plants in order to fully exploit economies of scale. To justify large-scale production it may be necessary for the same component to be used in several different models in the range. If the sales of the range are fairly modest, the producer may buy in the components from a specialist who supplies a number of different firms in the same industry. The specialist producer enjoys economies of scale which he may be able to pass on to his customers in lower prices. The disadvantage of this arrangement is that economies of vertical integration are lost.

It may be advantageous to produce different components in different locations because of the variety of different components involved. Sophisticated components can be produced where skilled labour is abundant, larger and heavier components where raw materials and energy are cheap, and so on. Production of components such as engines and transmissions, which afford substantial economies of scale, should be concentrated on the fewest plants. Components that are difficult or costly to transport should be produced close to the assembly line. The assembly line itself needs to be located somewhere near the 'centre of gravity' of the major sources of component supply and the major centres of consumer demand.

In interwar Europe, economic nationalism encouraged high protective tariffs to stimulate domestic motor production for military and strategic reasons. It was not until the postwar period, with the formation of the European Community and the improvement of infrastructure through motorways and container-handling systems etc, that production could be specialised internationally to fully exploit economies of scale (Foreman-Peck 1985).

In Britain, the industrial heritage of protectionism was a large number of relatively small plants, most of which survived the war intact. Most of them needed to be enlarged and modernised, or closed down altogether in favour of new plants on greenfield sites. Only Ford's highly integrated Dagenham plant approximated to an efficient scale.

Reconstruction along these lines was, however, inhibited by regional policy which encouraged investment in declining peripheral regions remote from the major metropolitan markets of Europe. A system of industrial development certificates was introduced to restrict investment outside designated development areas. Companies that wished to rationalise by building new factories were often obliged to locate them in areas far away from the rest of their operations (Young and Lowe 1974). Moreover, companies that had high-cost plants already located in the regions were under political pressure not to close them down. The designation of development areas became a party political issue, particularly when the areas seeking designation contained marginal parliamentary constituencies. In the early 1970s, for example, when the Scottish National Party was challenging many traditional Labour seats, a substantial budget was available for attracting companies to Scotland and discouraging those already there from closing down.

Employment protection policy also discouraged rationalisation. Government was reluctant to see high-cost production units closed down. It preferred to avoid bankruptcies and liquidations by arranging the takeover of unprofitable firms. After a takeover or merger, the new management would often find itself preoccupied with the short-run problems of the 'lame ducks' it had acquired. The short-run losses incurred by the weaker operating divisions of the company also absorbed funds which could otherwise have been used to finance restructuring and long-term growth.

The Redundancy Payments Act of 1966 reflects another aspect of employment protection which discouraged rationalisation. It encouraged employers with high-cost plants to run them down through natural wastage rather than to shut them down and make all their employees redundant. The pace of rationalisation was almost certainly slowed down as a result.

The delay in rationalising production led to growing problems in the British motor industry. These were exacerbated by the OPEC oil price rises beginning in 1973, which escalated British wage costs, because the incomes policy in force at the time linked wage rates to the cost of living. In Japan, however, productivity improvements continued apace and import penetration by their low-price high-quality vehicles reached such a point that several countries, including Britain, negotiated voluntary export restraints.

Background Narrative to Peugeot's Acquisition of Chrysler (UK)

The highlights of the Chrysler/Peugeot story are well known (see, in particular, Young and Hood 1977; Bhaskar 1979; Maxcy 1981; Grunberg 1981, Chapter 5; Wilks 1984). Chrysler is one of the fifty largest private manufacturing corporations in the US in terms of sales, and the third largest US motor manufacturer, behind General Motors and Ford. By 1960 its two main rivals both had long-established European operations, but Chrysler did not. From about this time, Chrysler headquarters in Detroit pursued a deliberate policy of diversifying into the European motor industry. Approaches were made to a number of established European firms and this eventually led to acquisitions in Britain, France and Spain. As a late entrant into the European market, however, Chrysler was unable to negotiate acquisition on favourable terms. It finished up acquiring those companies which its major indigenous competitors had, in many cases, already decided not to acquire.

In 1964 Chrysler took a 30 per cent stake in Rootes Motors, a British family-controlled firm whose Hillman, Humber and Singer saloons enjoyed a reputation for quality in the medium–large size sector of the market. At the time this minority interest was acquired,

Rootes had just entered the small car market with the launch of the Hillman Imp, a rear-engined car which was a close competitor of the Mini. The Imp was manufactured at a new factory at Linwood, near Paisley on Clydeside, some 250 miles north of the main centre of Rootes operations around Coventry.

Sales of the Imp were disappointing, and industrial relations at Linwood were poor. In its first full year of operation, Linwood operated at under half capacity. By 1967 Rootes was losing £10.7 million on a turnover of £171 million (Hood and Young 1982, p. 64). At this time Chrysler increased its stake to 66 per cent of the voting shares. This acquisition of control required the consent of the British Government because of an undertaking given by Chrysler in 1964.

A new family saloon, the Hillman Avenger, was launched from the Ryton factory in Coventry, but the launch of two other models – the Chrysler 180 and the Chrysler Alpine – was switched to Chrysler's French subsidiary, apparently because of labour problems in Britain.

At the end of October 1975 the Chairman of the Chrysler Corporation, John J. Riccardo, indicated at a press conference in Detroit that in view of the corporation's adverse financial position, it was considering withdrawing from Britain. Riccardo's statement appears to have taken the British Government by surprise. After intensive negotiations, the Government agreed to support Chrysler to the tune of a maximum of £162.5m. between 1976 and 1979, while in return the company committed up to £64m., agreed to the launch of new models, and signed a Planning Agreement with the Government (United Kingdom, House of Commons 1976).

Notwithstanding the consultative arrangements called for by the Planning Agreement, it was announced abruptly on 10th August, 1978, that Chrysler's European operations would be acquired by the French motor manufacturer PSA Peugeot–Citroën. Chrysler would receive US$230m. and a 15 per cent stake in the French company. It also obtained a seat on the supervisory board of PSA. The Planning Agreement continued in force, and the financial arrangements with the British Government were taken over by the French company with certain minor modifications.

Altogether, PSA Peugeot–Citroën acquired control of 11 Chrysler European subsidiaries at this time, including a 99.62 per cent stake in Chrysler France and a 46.51 per cent stake in Chrysler

Espana. It also acquired six import subsidiaries and two property subsidiaries in a separate deal shortly afterwards. The Chrysler Europe operation was renamed Talbot at the end of 1978 and in 1980 the management structure of the Peugeot and Talbot operations was unified. Also in 1980 the name of the Peugeot group was changed to Peugeot SA.

Chrysler's stake in Peugeot was valued on the Chrysler balance sheet at $323.9m., as compared to a value on the Paris stock exchange on the date of agreement of $202m. However, Chrysler reported that an independent valuation from a leading European investment banking firm valued the stake at above the balance-sheet figure.

The European divestment was one of several undertaken by Chrysler about this time. Also in 1978 Volkswagen acquired a 67 per cent equity stake in Chrysler's Brazilian operation, and Chrysler reduced to 49 per cent its own stake in Chrysler Argentina. In 1979 General Motors agreed to purchase Chrysler's interests in its Columbian subsidiary and to purchase the fixed assets of its Venezuelan subsidiary. By 1980, Mexico was host to the only major Chrysler operation outside North America. The overseas operations divested by Chrysler between 1978 and 1980 had lost the company approximately $40m. in earnings between 1974 and 1977. Losses had been particularly heavy in France during 1977 because of a combination of cost inflation, falling market share, and government price controls.

Since the divestment, both the Chrysler parent company and the Peugeot group have been in financial difficulties. Both have been committed to heavy investment expenditures to launch new models. Having lost the confidence of their bankers, and of the private capital market in general, both have been obliged to obtain government underwriting for new loans. Chrysler was guaranteed up to $1.5 billion via a Loan Guarantee Act in 1979, but it has had to make its US models comply with increasingly exacting pollution and safety standards, and adapt them to provide greater fuel efficiency at the same time. Peugeot has been financially stretched by losses incurred by the Citroen operation which it acquired in 1976. Another major acquisition coming only two years later has compounded the financial difficulties. As a result of these two acquisitions, Peugeot has suddenly risen to become one of the six largest motor manufacturers in Europe, and its management has had to face the problems of imposing an overall corporate strategy on a diverse group of enterprises, each with their own independent traditions. Chrysler management, on the other hand, has been liberated from concern over its European operations and has been able to concentrate on re-establishing its position within the US domestic market.

The Logic of the Divestment

The causes of Chrysler's poor performance in Europe are not hard to find. To begin with, Chrysler did not have the same kind of international reputation, marketing skills and technical know-how as did its two main US rivals. In the 1960s Chrysler's profitability in the US rested upon an exciting range of large high-performance vehicles with a sporting image (Iacocca and Novak 1985). The models were, however, far too large to appeal to the European consumer. The relatively staid vehicles produced by Rootes could not easily be promoted using Chrysler's marketing techniques.

The quality of Chrysler's US management appears to have begun to deteriorate in the late 1960s and early 1970s. New models were less successful than the old ones that they replaced. Chrysler's share of the US car market fell from 16.1 per cent in 1970 to a mere 8.6 per cent in 1980. The US management does not appear to have had the kind of general expertise within the motor industry that could usefully be transferred to Europe. Indeed, it was one of the company's European-designed vehicles that helped the company to make substantial progress in the sub-compact segment of the US market at a time when it was rapidly losing ground in its traditional stronghold, the standard segment of the market. The popularity of the Plymouth Horizon and Dodge Omni allowed the company to increase its share of the sub-compact market from 4.8 per cent to 17.4 per cent between 1975 and 1978, at a time when its share of the standard market fell from 9.6 per cent to 2.7 per cent.

Chrysler US had few skills in the management of vertical integration. Compared to its two rivals, it relied heavily upon independent suppliers for components. In 1978 the company was using over 30,000 independent suppliers and purchased from them substantially all its requirements for batteries, bearings, bumpers, carburettors, passenger compartment interior trim, radiators, glass, steel, tyres and wheels.

Financially, the company was highly geared, and relied extensively on short-term bank loans. This insecure financial structure meant that it faced a higher cost of capital than its rivals. It also exacerbated many of the company's problems when its trading difficulties became public knowledge during 1978.

In no sense, therefore, did Chrysler US have skills that were particularly relevant to its European subsidiaries. The company also faced particular difficulties in Britain because of problems that it had inherited from Rootes.

In Britain, Chrysler was affected more seriously by the oil price rise than were its major rivals because its engines were relatively old, and therefore less fuel-efficient, and because Chrysler was weak in the small-car segment of the market to which consumers were switching. These defects in the Chrysler range were in turn the consequence of problems that had begun some ten years earlier.

Chrysler inherited from Rootes the problem that its most modern production facility, Linwood, was bedevilled by poor industrial relations, by component supply problems caused by its remoteness from the heart of the UK engineering industry in the West Midlands, and by its commitment to producing a vehicle – the Hillman Imp – for which there was very little demand. It was extremely difficult for Chrysler to boost sales of the Imp by cutting prices because its main competitor, the Mini, was itself underpriced due to shortcomings in the British Motor Corporation's cost-accounting methods and its marketing strategy.

Political pressure and financial inducements had taken Rootes to Linwood in the first place, and the maintenance of employment at Linwood formed an integral part of the 1975 rescue plan. It was hoped that the Linwood plant would generate its own local supply industries, but this never materialised, possibly because the Government underestimated the volume of demand needed to take advantage of economies of scale in the supply industries.

The failure of the Imp meant that the company could not generate sufficient internal funds to finance the development of new models. It has already been noted that R and D is an ongoing process. A buoyant demand for current models generates finance for further improvements to the range, helping to boost sales even further. If sales of existing models are low, however, then this virtuous circle becomes a vicious one. When R and D has to be cut back, models get older and their sales decline further; eventually a company faces extinction if there are no new models in the pipeline.

Chrysler management appears to have recognised fairly early that rationalisation was required, but the shortage of funds meant that only a very limited programme could be pursued. They followed what must have seemed the obvious strategy of concentrating the production of the few new models they could afford on their French subsidiary, whose productivity was much higher, and turning UK production into an assembly operation using mainly French components. From the British Government's point of view, of course, this strategy seemed more like adverse discrimination than rationalisation.

It is instructive to compare Chrysler's European operations with those of Ford, because Ford pursued the kind of policy that Chrysler needed to emulate. Ford had, however, been much longer established in Europe, and so had more time in which to develop a coherent model range and to rationalise its production. Ford had relied heavily on greenfield investments to build up its European operations, and so when the 'Ford Europe' division was formed to impose integration, it avoided the problem of dealing with subsidiaries that had previously enjoyed a separate identity (although it did have to buy out certain minority interests). It had also by this time built up an effective dealer network offering a high standard of servicing with a uniform scale of charges. Ford's small cars which, until the development of the Cortina/Taunus, were the basis of its model range, were all highly successful. In particular, the new Escort, introduced in 1980, was designed as a 'European' car. The succcss of these models has generated the finance necessary to support the development of the next. Ford has concentrated the production of key components on special factories, creating a considerable volume of intra-firm trade in components. As a result of these measures, the company regularly claims to be the most profitable of the six major motor manufacturers in Europe.

It was clear by 1978 that Chrysler's financial position was so parlous that it had an urgent need to cease its loss-making European operations and to convert fixed assets into hard cash as quickly as possible. What is not so clear, at first sight, is why Peugeot was so willing to take over Chrysler's European operations.

Peugeot is essentially a family firm that began operating a steel foundry in 1810, commenced producing bicycles in 1885, automobiles in 1889, and in 1965–66 underwent structural reorganisation as part of a programme to become a major European motor producer. In 1976 the company took over the ailing Citroen company, which would otherwise have had to be nationalised (although Peugeot itself received government funds to help it 'turn around' its new subsidiary).

It appears that Peugeot planned to consolidate its position in the European market by becoming one of the very biggest producers. Peugeot management believed that only a small number of very large producers could survive in Europe in the long run, and it hoped that by becoming larger it could increase its own chance of survival. Peugeot management also believed that it possessed substantial managerial expertise that could be transferred to Chrysler's European operations. The performance of the Citroën company had improved remarkably within two years, and it appears that Peugeot management considered itself responsible for the recovery of the company. With the benefit of hindsight, however, Citroën was mainly sharing in a temporary general revival of European motor sales, and very little of its success was due specifically to Peugeot management.

There was clearly a potential to integrate Chrysler and Peugeot production in France, and in particular to exploit economies of scale in component production by designing new cars which used similar parts. There was also the possibility of integrating the marketing of Chrysler and Peugeot models. Peugeot's acquisition also made sense from the point of view which asserts that US multinationals find it more difficult than European firms to adjust to a social and political climate which favours the gradual run down of an unsuccessful manufacturing facility to precipitate outright closure. There is some evidence that US managements in general find that a run down of production through natural wastage in the workforce etc. is too expensive both in terms of finance and management time, and so prefer divestment to accepting responsibility for closure. They divest to indigenous companies which have greater expertise in raising funds from host governments. These funds are offered in order to 'save jobs' and avert redundancies. European governments are more willing to support indigenous firms for such purposes than they are to support foreign firms. This is particularly important in the case of France, with its tradition of government antipathy towards US multinationals. The Citroën case had already demonstrated Peugeot's skill in negotiating substantial loans from the French Government.

On balance, therefore, it seems that Peugeot's acquisition of Chrysler had more to recommend it than did Chrysler's original investment in Europe. Although Peugeot overestimated its management skills, the underlying economic logic was probably sound. The value of Chrysler's European operation was probably higher to Peugeot than it was to Chrysler, though whether it was worth all that Peugeot paid for it remains a moot point.

The fact that Peugeot acquired the whole of Chrysler's European operation, rather than just the French part, may indicate the company's willingness to build upon the very limited intra-European integration that Chrysler had achieved. Alternatively, it may simply reflect Peugeot's desire to strengthen its dealer network in the UK, and Chrysler's need to find someone to take over its Planning Agreement with the UK Government.

The Progress of Rationalisation, 1975–82

The business strategies pursued by Chrysler and Peugeot in the few years immediately prior to and immediately following the divestment are examined below under six headings.

Marketing

Demand for Chrysler vehicles in the UK contracted sharply between 1975 and 1982. Table 5.1 shows that the company's share of the market for cars and light vans fell from 8.0 per cent in 1975 to 3.6 per cent in 1982. The ratio of the 1982 market share to the 1975 share is even lower than for BL, for which the corresponding figures are 30.7 per cent and 17.8 per cent. Over the same period Ford increased its market share from 21.5 per cent to 30.5 per cent, and Vauxhall (a General Motors' affiliate) from 8.2 per cent to 11.7 per cent. A number of foreign manufacturers performed extremely well over this period, especially BMW, Volvo and Volkswagen, whilst the Japanese producers consolidated their position. The proportion of the UK market supplied by vehicles produced abroad increased from 33.1 per cent to 57.7 per cent. These figures include intra-firm imports of finished vehicles by multinational producers such as Ford, General Motors and, of course, Chrysler–Peugeot.

Given the shortage of new models to promote, marketing strategy has tended to concentrate upon mainly cosmetic changes. For example, 'limited editions' of a number of established models have been produced, offering additional accessories and trim.

Table 5.1 Leading Manufacturers' Shares of the UK Market for Cars and Light Vans, 1975–82 (%)

Company	*Source of production*	*1975*	*1982*
Ford	Various	21.5	30.5
BL	Britain	30.7	17.8
Vauxhall	Various	8.2	11.7
Datsun	Japan	5.3	6.0
VW Audi NSU	W. Germany	4.0	5.9
Renault	France	4.7	4.1
Talbot	Various	8.0	3.6
Volvo/Daf	Sweden (mainly)	1.9	3.3
Fiat	Italy.	3.2	2.8
Toyota	Japan	1.7	1.8
Citroën	France	1.8	1.5
BMW	W. Germany	0.6	1.5
Fiat licensees total		0.8	1.5
Lada	USSR	(0.6)	(1.1)
Polski-Fiat	Poland	(0.2)	(0.2)
Zastava	Yugoslavia	(0.0)	(0.2)
Peugeot	France	1.2	1.3
Honda	Japan	0.8	1.0
Mazda	Japan	0.9	1.0
Mercedes-Benz	W. Germany	0.5	0.8
Alfa-Romeo	Italy	0.7	0.6
Saab	Sweden	0.6	0.6
Skoda	Czechoslovakia	0.8	0.6
Colt	Japan	0.3	0.6
Daihatsu	Japan	0.0	0.3
Lancia	Italy	0.0	0.3
Hyundai	Republic of Korea	0.0	0.2
Suzuki	Japan	0.0	0.2
Subaru	Japan	0.0	0.2
Others	Various	1.5	0.3
Total		100.0	100.0
Total imports		33.1	57.7

Source: Society of Motor Manufacturers and Traders, *The Motor Industry of Great Britain*, Various issues.

In 1976–77 the Chrysler brand name replaced the Hillman name on the Avenger and the Hunter. This may have reflected an attempt to promote the Chrysler identity worldwide, or simply to reverse the bad impression created in the UK by the earlier attempt to pull out. In retrospect, however, the change seems to have done little to reassure consumers who were worried about the future availability of spares, and about the prospective resale value of their vehicles. In any case, the Hillman name had acquired a reputation for quality which, although it became somewhat tarnished in the 1960s, was probably still more valuable than the Chrysler name. Finally, it had the unfortunate consequence that, because of the subsequent Peugeot takeover, the names were changed twice within three years.

The Talbot name, revived by Peugeot, is easily pronounced both in French and English. The company considered that it enjoyed a sporting image. However, the historical significance of the name in the early development of the motor car does not seem to have been fully appreciated in Britain. The introduction of the name in fact caused some confusion because the Chrysler Sunbeam (a rear-wheel drive family hatchback) became the Talbot Sunbeam, which could be mistaken for the Sunbeam Talbot produced some twenty years earlier by Rootes. With the benefit of hindsight, it might have been better to have retained the Hillman name throughout in the UK. It is interesting to note that the company has since revived the old Rootes names Rapier and Minx for badging Alpine/Solara models produced at Ryton.

Following the acquisition, leading Chrysler dealers became Peugeot–Talbot dealers, of whom there are approximately 500 in the UK. There has been no effort to integrate Peugeot and Citroën dealerships, presumably because Citroën products are highly distinctive, attract loyal customers, and require special maintenance skills because of their ingenious and unusual engineering.

Peugeot–Talbot models do not, however, form an integrated range. In the spectrum from small to large vehicles, the Talbot Samba occupies a similar niche to the new Peugeot 205 (and the old Peugeot 104), while the Talbot Solara and Alpine models occupy a similar niche to the Peugeot 305. The Talbot Horizon, however, has a distinctive place as a short, spacious, and relatively high performance front-wheel drive hatchback, filling the gap between the 205 and the 305. (The Talbot Sunbeam, a small car emanating from the 1975 Rescue Plan, ceased production in 1981.)

The Samba and the Solara/Alpine models appear to be sold at a discount relative to their Peugeot counterparts. The current premium for a Peugeot model over its Talbot counterpart is approximately 6 per cent, and this probably reflects the relatively modern engine and transmission, the more sophisticated suspension, and general reputation for higher standards of manufacturing quality control. The Horizon has sold extremely well relative to other vehicles in the Talbot range, and at quite high prices – the 1.5 GL 5 speed Horizon was listed in the UK in July 1984 at £5,715, compared to £5,660 for the Peugeot 305 GR.

The top end of the Peugeot–Talbot range is weak. The aging Peugeot 604 is being phased out, and its potential successor, the Talbot Tagora, has been a disaster ever since its launch in 1981; only the Peugeot 505 has adequate sales. This weakness at the top of the range is somewhat ironic in view of the relative strength of the Rootes group in this niche under its Singer and Humber names.

Scale of Production

The poor sales performance means that there has been little opportunity to exploit economies of scale in production. Table 5.2 reports the outputs of the major models of Chrysler UK, Chrysler France, Peugeot and Citroën in 1975 and 1982. In 1975 Chrysler had just commenced production of the Alpine, which was highly acclaimed by the motoring press and sold well for the first two years. By 1982, however, production of the Alpine had fallen to 6,500 units. The other major model, the Hunter, was kept in production only because of an export order for kits, supplied from Ryton to a state-owned assembly plant in Iran; it had been withdrawn from the UK market in 1979. The Iranian contract was considered important for Britain's reputation as an exporter to the Middle East, and the need to avoid its cancellation was a major factor in the Chrysler rescue of 1975.

The scale economies enjoyed by Chrysler France are greater than those of Chrysler UK because of the relatively high volume of Samba and Horizon production. The figures for Peugeot are even better: the 104, 305 and 505 all achieved outputs of over 100,000 units in 1982. Citroën produces the best-selling Visa, although the proliferation of the less successful Citroën models has caused problems for the Peugeot group.

Table 5.2 Production of Chrysler–Peugeot Vehicles in Britain and France, 1975–82

	Production of cars and light vans ('000 per annum)	
Model	*1975*	*1982*
Chrysler UK/Talbot UK		
Imp	8.0	—
Avenger	86.0	—
Hunter	} 136.0 (Hunter, Alpine, Sceptre, Rapier)	27.1
Alpine		6.5
Sceptre		—
Rapier		—
Solara	—	8.4
Sunbeam	—	14.2
Total	230.0	56.2
Chrysler France/Talbot France		
Simca 1000	71.3	—
Simca 1100	193.2	0.0
Simca 1301	36.1	—
Simca 1501	11.3	—
1307/8	46.7	—
180/2 litre	24.6	—
Samba	—	102.7
Horizon	—	71.3
Alpine	—	10.3
Solara	—	32.1
Tagora	—	3.3
Others	—	14.7
Total	383.2	234.5
Peugeot		
104	114.5	117.9
204	88.2	—
304	93.3	—
305	—	186.5
404	15.8	—
504	239.4	80.7
505	—	145.7
604	10.3	5.7
Total	561.4	536.5

Table 5.2 Production of Chrysler–Peugeot Vehicles in Britain and France, 1975–82 (continued)

Model	*Production of cars and light vans ('000 per annum)* 1975	1982
Citroën		
2CV6	106.3	83.1
Dyane-Mehari	107.7	26.0
LNA 11	—	26.6
Ami	47.2	—
Visa	—	206.9
GS	187.8	—
GSA	—	108.8
BX	—	13.5
CX	96.8	57.4
D–DS	0.8	—
SM	0.1	—
Total	546.8	522.3

Source: L'argus de l'automobile, Various issues.

It is when these production figures are compared with those of Chrysler's rivals that the true magnitude of the problem is revealed. Table 5.3 shows that in 1982 168,000 Escorts were produced by Ford in the UK, and 281,200 in West Germany; 352,000 Renault 5s, 284,700 Renault 18s and a staggering 494,800 Volkswagen Golfs were produced in the same year. The scale economies available to these producers far outweigh anything that can be achieved with Chrysler or Talbot models.

Location of Production

Between 1975 and 1982 the number of different models produced by Talbot in Europe fell from eleven to eight. Much of this reduction occurred in 1976 when the Hillman Imp, Humber Sceptre and Sunbeam Rapier were all withdrawn; the Talbot Sunbeam, introduced in 1977, was withdrawn in 1981.

Table 5.3 Production by Chrysler–Talbot's Major European Competitors

	Production of cars and light vans ('000 per annum)	
Company and Model	*1975*	*1982*
Ford UK		
Fiesta	—	42.0
Escort	152.5	168.0
Cortina	140.4	54.5
Sierra	—	26.5
Consul, Capri, Granada	36.8	15.7
Total	329.6	306.6
Ford (West German)		
Escort	215.8	281.2
Others	197.4	237.3
Total	413.2	518.4
Renault		
R5	299.0	352.0
R12	250.4	—
R18	—	284.7
Others	479.7	854.1
Total	1,029.1	1,490.9
Volkswagen		
Golf	419.6	494.8
Others	630.7	625.7
Total	1,050.3	1,120.5

Source: L'argus de l'automobile, Various issues.

Three of the six new models introduced since 1975 were until recently produced only in France or Spain; they are the Samba, Horizon and Tagora. Since 1980 the Horizon has been produced in the UK as well. Two of the new models were then produced in both France and Britain – the Alpine and the Solara – and only one, the

Talbot Sunbeam, was produced in Britain alone. Many of the components for the Alpine and Solara came from France, so that the British side of the joint manufacturing operations was little more than assembly.

The policy of concentrating production in France appears to have been followed by both Chrysler and Peugeot. It is reflected in a large volume of intra-firm exports from France to Britain. In 1982, 44 per cent of Talbot registrations in Britain were sourced from France (see Table 5.4). In the same year, less than 0.1 per cent of Talbot registrations in France were sourced from Britain. If intra-firm trade in components is considered as well, the use of French production to source British operations becomes even more marked.

Table 5.4 shows that in the period 1980–82 both Ford and

Table 5.4 Changes in the Sourcing of the UK Market, 1980–82

	Registrations of cars and light vans (vehicles per annum)	
Country of production	*1980*	*1982*
Talbot	90,874	56,149
UK	62,876	31,560
France	25,481	24,534
Eire	1,853	47
Spain	664	6
Others	0	2
Ford	464,706	474,192
UK	247,946	244,140
West Germany	85,091	100,349
Belgium	49,135	66,911
Eire	13,537	10,472
Spain	68,878	52,187
Others	119	133
General Motors	133,078	181,737
UK	82,233	102,573
West Germany	29,147	30,062
Belgium	20,708	48,862
Others	990	276

Source: L'argus de l'automobile, Various issues.

General Motors also sourced the UK market extensively from continental Europe, although it must be remembered that their European operations were much more extensive than those of Talbot. What is particularly striking, however, is that between 1980 and 1982 the dramatic reduction in Talbot sales in the UK was almost entirely accounted for by the contraction in UK production, consequent mainly on the closure of Linwood in 1981. UK production was halved, while French imports to the UK remained practically unchanged. UK production has now become almost negligible within the Peugeot group as a whole.

Use of Common Components

Chrysler models, like those of other manufacturers, utilised engines which were interchangeable. Since the Peugeot acquisition, there has also been common use of engines between the Talbot and Peugeot models. The Peugeot 205 uses the same engines as the Talbot Samba, and the Tagora SX uses a V6 engine that is also fitted to the Peugeot 604. The Peugeot 104 coupés share a body shell with the Citroën LNA and the Talbot Samba. Other examples of standardisation include the use of Avenger and Alpine components in the Talbot Sunbeam, and the use of certain paint colours which are common to Talbot and Peugeot.

Vertical Integration

During the 1970s Chrysler UK – like its US parent – was sometimes criticised for relying too heavily upon outside suppliers of components. It was alleged that the company was obliged to pay too high a price for its components and also had difficulty guaranteeing supplies. However, the minimum efficient scale for producing many components was much higher than Chrysler's output of finished vehicles, so that in many cases it would have been impossible for the company to produce its own components on an efficient scale. Moreover, the company suffered so many disruptions of production in its own plants that it is difficult to see how internal sources of supply could be more reliable than external ones, especially when the company was able to 'shop around' among competing suppliers for a number of components. It seems likely, therefore, that reliance on external suppliers was a rational response to the company's inability to exploit economies of scale.

In Europe matters are rather different, however, now that Chrysler operations have been incorporated within the automobile division of Peugeot, because the Peugeot group is both larger and more diversified. It is involved, for example, in the cold-rolling of special steels, in the manufacture of transmissions, cycles, motor cycles, electrical and plastic components and armour-plating.

Even a large diversified company, however, may be unable to take full advantage of scale economies in components such as large engines for luxury cars. An alternative to relying on outside suppliers is for the company to undertake joint ventures with its competitors to produce these components, or to enter into a specialisation agreement whereby companies can trade or barter components for one another's use. Inter-firm collaboration affords many of the advantages of full integration without some of the costs; it is of growing importance in the world motor industry.

Inter-Firm Collaboration

Continental European motor producers have for many years been more heavily involved in collaborative arrangements than their British and US counterparts. Fiat, for example, has at one time or another held financial interests in Citroën and Unic (a commercial vehicle manufacturer) in France and NSU in West Germany, and has licensed production of its models to Spain, Yugoslavia, Poland and the USSR. In France, state-owned Renault and privately-owned Peugeot have collaborated on a number of ventures in recent years.

Peugeot is a member of the Joint Research Committee with Renault, Volkswagen, Volvo, Fiat and BL which undertakes research into combustion technology, new materials, computerised engineering and a number of other subjects. Peugeot is involved with Fiat in the development and production of a new one-litre engine for the Fiat Uno and Peugeot 205, and in the production of a new van in Italy. The Peugeot subsidiary, Cycles Peugeot, has an agreement to manufacture motor-cycle engines for Honda in Belgium and to assemble a Honda scooter in France for the Belgian market (Automotive Industry Data 1983). Peugeot and Chrysler also entered into negotiations about industrial collaboration, soon after the acquisition, that explored the possibility of producing small Peugeot cars for the sub-compact market in the US, but so far there has been little to show for this.

Peugeot and Renault are involved with Volvo in a joint venture, manufacturing engines at Douvrin in France, and also jointly produce automatic transmissions in France. In 1981 Renault purchased a stake in Karrier Motors, a commercial vehicle manufacturer whose British operation was inherited by Peugeot from Chrysler UK, and acquired full control from Peugeot in 1983. The sale of commercial vehicle operations by Peugeot to Renault has a precedent in the disposal of the Berliet commercial vehicle subsidiary of Citroën to Renault when Peugeot acquired control of Citroën. It represents the continuation of a policy, beginning with the Renault acquisition of Saviem in the 1950s, by which heavy commercial vehicle production in France has been concentrated upon Renault.

The fact that Talbot operations are now beginning to be integrated within the operations of a company which is, in turn, heavily involved in inter-firm collaboration with other motor producers is perhaps one of the most hopeful aspects of the current situation. It suggests that any future Talbot model will be able to incorporate much more modern components than any of its predecessors, and that it will be produced more cheaply because of the more effective exploitation of economies of scale. Only skilful design can, of course, guarantee success. However, some of the conditions necessary for success have now been met, even though these conditions alone are not sufficient to guarantee Talbot's future.

Future Prospects

It has been estimated that there was approximately 15 per cent excess capacity in the Western European motor industry in 1984. Some of this is aging high-cost plant, kept going in the hope that jobs can be maintained until there is an economic recovery, whilst other excess capacity is modern highly automated plant, utilised more intensively but often still with a margin of spare capacity.

The consumer market is highly competitive, particularly in countries such as Belgium which produce very few of their own models. Competition is less intense in France because of the obstruction of

Japanese imports by French customs procedures. British conditions are also special because of the high costs of the only major

Table 5.5 Income Statements and Balance Sheets for Peugeot, 1980–82 (FFm.)

	1980	*1981*	*1982*	*1983*
Assets (end of year)				
Property, plant and equipment	19,313	21,076	22,944	23,606
Other fixed assets	2,879	3,526	3,886	4,532
Accrued assets	—	—	2,050	2,648
Inventories	16,815	16,054	16,962	18,471
Other current assets	12,634	14,715	12,177	14,384
Total	55,641	55,371	58,019	63,641
Liabilities (end of year)				
Shareholders' equity	12,132	10,178	8,150	5,712
Minority interests	653	594	490	313
Provisions and long-term liabilities	1,824	1,615	2,190	2,356
Long-term loans	9,772	11,590	13,806	15,417
Current liabilities	27,260	31,394	33,381	39,843
Total	51,641	55,371	58,019	63,641
Depreciation	8,841	10,367	12,035	13,255
Accounts receivable and bills receivable (net)	7,056	8,859	7,254	9,555
Accounts payable and bills payable	6,123	9,336	11,067	13,371
Turnover	71,103	72,389	75,263	85,207
Additional revenues	320	379	506	499
Operating expenses	70,081	70,982	75,651	83,314
Operating margin	1,342	1,786	118	2,392
Other costs and revenues	3,995	4,164	4,332	5,518
Share in the results before tax of companies accounted for on the equity method	19	292	318	522
Pre-tax profit	–2,672	–2,086	–3,896	–2,604

Source: Company accounts.

indigenous producer, BL, and because the demand for right-hand drive rather than left-hand drive vehicles encourages price discrimination against British consumers. The EC Competition Directorate has recently attempted to discourage producers from using their tied retail outlets to enforce discrimination of this kind.

Many major motor producers incurred losses in Europe in 1983, which was an exceptionally difficult year. Table 5.5 shows that Peugeot has been incurring losses continuously since the acquisition of Chrysler Europe, though its performance in 1983 was significantly better than in 1982. In 1983 the company lost FF 2,604m. (approximately £250m.). Sales were up over 12 per cent on the previous year, reflecting the successful launch of new models – the Peugeot 205 and the Citroën BX – which enabled the company to increase its share of the French market at the expense of its main rival, Renault. Both French companies have, however, been losing ground in Europe to rivals such as Ford. It is also unfortunate for Peugeot that the impact of its new models has been less than it might have been if the overall market had been more buoyant.

Funding the development of these new models has imposed a considerable burden of debt on the company. Financial restructuring has marginally diluted the interests of the major shareholders (the Peugeot family and their trusts 33.9 per cent; Chrysler Corporation 14.1 per cent; and the family-controlled Michelin tyre company 9.0 per cent). Between 1980 and 1983 the company's current liabilities have risen steadily relative to its total assets, and long-term loans have increased substantially. At the end of 1983 the ratio of long-term loans to assets net of current liabilities was 65 per cent, which is very high, at least by British standards. Accounts payable and bills payable have risen from FF 6,123m. in 1980 to FF 13,371m. in 1983. A company in such a shaky financial position would normally find it difficult to increase its credit with suppliers in this way; the company's good standing with its creditors almost certainly reflects their perception that the company's obligations are underwritten by the government.

As already noted, the group's UK operation is now peripheral to its main activities, and indeed the number of production workers in the UK is currently less than 4,000. The reduction in employment has been associated with a substantial increase in productivity at the company's main plant at Ryton and with a notable lack of industrial disputes. In 1984 Ryton workers produced a phenomenal 37 cars per man without the use of robots. Coupled with the recent weakness of sterling, this has enabled UK production costs to fall relative to those in France. In 1983 the automobile division, which is dominated by French operations, had a productivity of 8.3 vehicles per employee per year, compared to 8.7 for Volkswagen and 10.9 for Fiat. These figures need to be interpreted with caution because of different degrees of vertical integration within the companies concerned. Nevertheless, they suggest that productivity in the company's French factories is unimpressive, and it is well known that some of these factories have recently been the scene of serious industrial disputes, especially the Talbot plant at Poissy near Paris. Thus if UK production costs continue to fall relative to those in France, it is not inconceivable that the company might decide to invest in a cheap and docile labour force in the UK.

The future of the company's Stoke plant, near Coventry, remains uncertain because of its heavy dependence on the continuation of the Iranian contract. It is currently planned to produce a new Peugeot car, possibly under the Talbot badge, at Ryton; it is hoped that the use of the Talbot name on a brand new car will help the company to break back into the UK fleet market, where the 'high profile' business customers still nominally prefer to buy British.

If this scenario is taken seriously, then the major obstacle to investment would be the company's financial dependence on the French government. So long as this dependence persists, political considerations are likely to prevent any substantial 'export of jobs' from France to the UK. Whether it is long-run or short-run considerations that finally prevail will probably be determined by whether or not there is an imminent recovery in the West European economy.

Policy Issues

The potential influence of the French government on Peugeot investment policy illustrates an important policy issue in both foreign investment and foreign divestment, namely the way that the interests of the company's home country are likely to prevail over those of the host country whenever crucial decisions have to be made. A multinational company is likely to look first to its home government for the exercise of political influence and military strength in defence of its property overseas, as well as for financial support in case of commercial difficulties. It is therefore in the company's long-term interests to demonstrate reciprocity by acting first and foremost as a 'good corporate citizen' of the home country, with the interests of the host country being kept firmly in second place. Reliance on the home government for financial support is evident in the case of both Chrysler and Peugeot. It is therefore not unreasonable to suggest that UK interests may have been prejudiced by a desire to safeguard jobs in the home country at the expense of those in Britain. Having said this, however, it is difficult to demonstrate that in these particular cases there has been any contraction of employment in Britain in excess of what would have been likely to have occurred under British management.

Although the British government disliked the way that Chrysler management disclosed its problems with its UK operations to its US shareholders before it informed the British government, and although it disliked Chrysler's hard-line bargaining tactics, the government got what it wanted from Chrysler during the 1975 negotiations – namely the preservation of employment at Linwood and the production of new models in the UK. A purely British solution to the UK operations had been ruled out as early as 1967, when the Labour Government failed to find acceptable alternatives to the Chrysler acquisition of Rootes. By the time of the divestment in 1978, it was widely appreciated that BL management could not cope with the acquisition of Chrysler, and that Chrysler would not fit in to the European operations of either Ford or General Motors. Given Chrysler's financial difficulties, therefore, and the government's own reluctance to provide further finance, it was forced to admit that there really was 'no alternative' to the Peugeot takeover if jobs were to be preserved.

There is no doubt that if Chrysler had pulled out from the UK without divesting to another company, then plant closures would have resulted in large job losses occurring at short notice. This did not happen, however. Although Peugeot closed the Linwood plant in 1981, employment there had been contracting steadily for a number of years and by the time of the closure the workforce appears to have accepted the outcome as inevitable. The steady run down of employment under Peugeot management is preferable, from the standpoing of social policy, to precipitate closure, and the scale of the run down has been unexceptional given the prevailing conditions of world recession.

It is possible that when a foreign company sells off a plant, there may be a capital outflow which temporarily worsens the host country's balance of payments, or weakens the exchange rate. This applies, however, only when funds are raised in the host country to buy out the foreign firm. In the case of the Chrysler divestment, the capital account of the British balance of payments was largely unaffected because the transfer of funds occurred between France and the US.

It could be argued that it was wrong of Chrysler management to convert into cash assets whose purchase had been partly subsidised by the UK government through the rescue agreement of three years earlier. This argument does not, however, make very good economics if the assets would in fact be better managed by another company. Moreover, Peugeot agreed to take over Chrysler's outstanding commitments under the rescue plan, and in so far as these obligations reduced the market value of Chrysler's UK assets, the final distribution of rewards may have been quite equitable.

So far as the wider implications of the Chrysler divestment are concerned, therefore, the UK government should perhaps count itself lucky that Chrysler managed to find another foreign buyer that was willing, at least in the short run, to continue producing in the UK.

Conclusion

Given the importance of rationalisation for the long-term future of the European motor industry, the closure of some high-cost plants in Britain was inevitable. Chrysler management recognised the need to implement a rationalised European production strategy along the lines pursued by Ford Europe, but the company never had the financial security necessary to do this. The lesson seems to be that it is unwise for host governments to oppose foreign divestments where these divestments form part of a cogent rationalisation programme designed to secure the future of a European industry. In the long run there must be a transfer of labour from aging high-cost plants to modern low-cost plants, and divestment may be an integral part of this process. A more constructive policy for government is to stimulate new investment in plants which fit into a rational European production structure, in order to create jobs which will make good the loss of employment elsewhere.

References

Altshuler, A. *et al.* (1984) *The Future of the Automobile*, Allen and Unwin.

Automotive Industry Data (1983) *Joint Venture and Collaboration Agreements*, AID.

Bhaskar, K. (1979) *The Future of the UK Motor Industry*, Kogan Page.

Boddewyn, J.J. (1983a) 'Foreign direct divestment theory: is it the reverse of FDI theory?', *Weltwirtschaftliches Archiv*, 119, pp. 345–55.

Boddewyn, J.J. (1983b) 'Foreign and domestic divestment and investment decisions: like or unlike?', *Journal of International Business Studies*, Winter 1983, pp. 23–35.

Boddewyn, J.J. (1984) 'Theories of foreign direct investment and divestment: a classificatory note', mimeo, Baruch College, City University of New York; forthcoming in *Management International Review.*

Business International (1976) *International Divestment: A Survey of Corporate Experience*, Business International.

Casson, M.C. (1979) *Alternatives to the Multinational Enterprise*, Macmillan.

Casson, M.C. (1984) 'The theory of vertical integration: a survey and synthesis, *Journal of Economic Studies*, 11 (2), pp. 3–43.

Caves, R.E. (1971) 'International corporations: the industrial economics of foreign investment', *Economica*, New Series, 38, pp. 1–27.

Chandler, A.D., Jr. (1962) *Strategy and Structure: Chapters in the History of the Industrial Enterprise*, MIT Press.

Chopra, J., Boddewyn, J.J. and Torneden, R.L. (1978) 'US foreign divestment: a 1972–1975 updating', *Columbia Journal of World Business*, Spring 1978, 14–18.

Dunning, J.H. (1977) 'Trade, location of economic activity and the multinational enterprise: a search for an eclectic approach', in B. Ohlin, P.O. Hesselborn and P.M. Wykman (eds), *The International Allocation of Economic Activity*, Macmillan.

Foreman-Peck, J. (1985) 'The motor industry', in M.C. Casson and associates, *Multinationals and World Trade: Vertical Integration and the Division of Labour in World Industries*, Allen and Unwin.

Franko, L.G. (1971) *Joint Venture Survival in Multinational Corporations*, Praeger.

Gaffikin, F. and Nickson, A. (1984) *Jobs Crisis and the Multinationals: Deindustrialisation in the West Midlands*, Russell Press.

Grunberg, L. (1981) *Failed Multinational Ventures: The Political Economy of International Divestments*, Lexington Books.

Hood, N. and Young, S. (1982) *Multinationals in Retreat: the Scottish Experience*, Edinburgh University Press.

Hymer, S.H. (1976) *The International Operations of National Firms: A Study of Direct Investment*, MIT Press (previously unpublished doctoral dissertation, 1960).

Iacocca, L. and Novak, W. (1985) *An Autobiography*, Sidgwick and Jackson.

Kindleberger, C.P. (1960) *American Business Abroad*, Yale University Press.

Kitching, J. (1973) *Acquisitions in Europe: Causes of Corporate Successes and Failures*, Business International.

Lloyd, P.E. and Strutt, J. (1983) *Recession and Restructuring in the North West Region: The Policy Implications of Recent Events*, Working Paper No. 13, North West Industry Research Unit, University of Manchester.

McAleese, D. and Counahan, M. (1979) '"Stickers" or "Snatchers"? Employment in multinational corporations during the recession', *Oxford Bulletin of Economics and Statistics*, 41, pp. 345–58.

Maxcy, G. (1981) *The Multinational Motor Industry*, Croom Helm.

Murray, R. (ed.) (1981) *Multinationals Beyond the Market: Intra-Firm Trade and the Control of Transfer Pricing*, Harvester Press.

Rae, J.B. (1965) *The American Automobile: A Brief History*, University of Chicago Press.

Rhys, D.C. (1977) 'European mass-producing car makers and minimum efficient scale: a note', *Journal of Industrial Economics*, 25, 313–19.

Rugman, A.M. and Eden, L. (eds) (1985) *Multinationals and Transfer Pricing*, Croom Helm.

Sachdev, J.C. (1976) *A Framework for the Planning of Divestment Policies for Multinational Companies*, unpublished Ph.D. thesis, University of Manchester Institute of Science and Technology.

Torneden, R.L. (1975) *Foreign Disinvestment by US Multinational Corporations: With Eight Case Studies*, Praeger.

UNCTC (1983) *Transnational Corporations and World Development: Third Report*, United Nations.

United Kingdom, House of Commons (1976) *Eighth Report from the Expenditure Committee: Public Expenditure on Chrysler UK Ltd., Volume 1: Report*, HMSO, HC 596–I (1975–76).

Van Den Bulcke, D. (1979) 'Existing data', in D. Van Den Bulcke, J.J. Boddewyn, B. Marten and P. Klemmer, *Investment and Divestment Policies of Multinational Corporations in Europe*, Saxon House for ECSIM, 1–59.

Van Den Bulcke, D. and Halsberghe, E. (1983) 'Divestment and loss of employment: a comparison between foreign and Belgian enterprises', Paper presented to European Institute of Advanced Management Studies Workshop on 'European Unemployment and Productivity', Oslo, 16–17 December, 1983.

Vernon, R. (1966) 'International investment and international trade in the product cycle', *Quarterly Journal of Economics*, 80, pp. 1901207.

Vernon, R. (1974) 'The location of industry', in J.H. Dunning (ed.), *Economic Analysis and the Multinational Enterprise*, Allen and Unwin, pp. 89–114.

Vernon, R. (1979) 'The product cycle hypothesis in a new international economic environment', *Oxford Bulletin of Economic Statistics*, 41, pp. 255–67.

Wilks, S. (1984) *Industrial Policy and the Motor Industry*, Manchester University Press.

Young, S. and Hood, N. (1977) *Chrysler UK: A Corporation in Transition*, Praeger.

Young, S., Hood, N. and Hamill, J. (1985) *Decision-Making in Foreign-Owned Multinational Subsidiaries in the United Kingdom*, International Labour Office.

Young, S. and Lowe, A.V. (1974) *Intervention in the Mixed Economy*, Croom Helm.

Acknowledgements

I am grateful to Messrs D. Dyster and Z. Hakam for their advice on statistical sources, and to my colleagues John Board and Michael Bromwich for their advice on the interpretation of company accounts. I am also indebted to Garel Rhys, Stephen Young, Neil Hood, Jean Boddewyn, Peter Buckley and Danny Van Den Bulcke for their comments on an earlier draft. Finally, I should like to thank Mike Wright and John Coyne for their advice on the structure of the paper, and for their patience in awaiting the final draft!

6

Divestment by Management Buy-Out: Variant and Variety

John Coyne

Introduction

An increasingly important means by which a divestment may be concluded is through sale of a subsidiary, division or part of an enterprise to its management. When all the corporate examination has been concluded and corporate strategies assessed in the manner outlined earlier in Chapters 1 and 2, and a decision to sell has been reached, then the search for a buyer commences. It is with the specific instance where the buyer is found from within rather than from outside that this chapter is concerned.

The first task of the chapter is to define precisely what is meant by a management buy-out, and perhaps more importantly what is not! The development of the buy-out market place in the United Kingdom can then be reviewed. Sources of buy-out will be examined in order to place the divestment route firmly in context with the totality of the experience. The specific reasons why, when all other strategic options have been examined, there is a particular case for considering a sale to management will also be analysed, and the various strategies that the parties can adopt in order to either effect a desired transfer or defend against an unwelcome advance will be outlined. The mechanics of management buy-outs, and the reality behind the concept, will then be illustrated with reference to recent buy-outs in the UK which specifically illustrate some of the major aspects of the phenomenon.

What is a Buy-Out?

A management buy-out occurs when a management team within a company or division purchases that company from its current owners, thus becoming owner–managers. The buy-out is applicable to both the private and the public sector and is one means by which privatisation may take place. It has usually been in the private sector that most of the initiative has come and it is this sector which is the focus here. The owners from which such a purchase may be effected could be absentee shareholders, a current owner–manager, very often a family firm, the receiver, either acting for the company itself or a parent in difficulty, or it could be from a parent company which is still trading. In the latter case the sale may be regarded as a specific variant on conventional divestment in so far as a clean break takes place, but the new owners are already in place in management positions within the bought-out company. It is with this latter case that we are concerned here.

There are certain features of the buy-out which need to be distinguished: first, to explain more fully the nature of management's involvement and how it may expect to make the purchase; and, second, to distinguish the buy-out from other forms of ownership transfer which may involve management but which are more aptly described and grouped under different titles.

The management team, in order to make the purchase, is usually expected to put up a proportion of the purchase price from its own resources and to offer some degree of personal security for sums invested. For example, Spicer and Pegler suggest that on a £1.5m purchase, management might be expected to find 10 per cent (Spicer and Pegler 1984). In return, it may expect a substantial equity stake in the company, more often than not the major slice and in many instances a controlling, majority stake. The rest of the funds are usually provided in the way of loans, and so the purchase is generally going to leave the company very highly geared. The rationale behind this kind of arrangement is that the company will benefit from the remarriage of ownership and control and the personal vested interest in its success which the new owner–managers will have. The institutions are generally prepared to make conventional loans and trust to the structure of incentives to safeguard their interests too. They very often hedge their bets so as to take advantage of any more favourable trading conditions by taking some equity for the time when a quotation may be sought, and by including some cumulative convertible redeemable participative preferred ordinary shares.

Management is faced with the need to generate sufficient cash, particularly in the early years, to meet the interest payments, although some arrangements do include payment holidays to enable the company to get into its stride. If the payments are met and the loans repaid, the company then becomes an extremely effective cash generator and the prospects for massive returns to the very successful are real indeed. It is this potential for high future reward that is often the motivating force behind a management wish to buy out.

In some instances, the buy-out has included all employees of the firm as providers of capital. Although the purchase is led by a small management team, the employees are invited to invest and in such cases the term 'employee buy-out' may be more appropriate. The privatisation of NFC and the sale of the Victaulic Co. Ltd by British Steel fall into this category.

In order to realise this potential, the management team clearly has to be up to the task of successfully managing its own company and there must be the potential both within the management team and the structure of the company and its products. One reason for the importance of the phenomenon and its increased attention is the way in which the realisation of potential requires the exercise of entrepreneurship by the new owners. The phenomenon is seen as epitomising the re-emergence of classical entrepreneurship into industry, emphasising alertness, independence, action and an appropriate structure of incentives and rewards (see Kirzner 1979; Hayek 1978; Binks and Coyne 1983).

The freedom to act without internal constraints, the ability to exercise judgement in the face of risk, and a renewed impetus to motivation are regularly cited by buy-out team leaders as the moving force behind their decisions (see Anslow 1984).

The management buy-out shares some characteristics with other forms of ownership transfer where divestments may seem to have been effected which include management involvement, and it is important to make the necessary distinctions between these. There are a number of terms applied to the mechanisms which share characteristics such as 'leveraged buy-outs', 'spin-offs' and 'hive downs'.

The *leveraged buy-out* is a concept and term which originated in the United States and which has enjoyed considerable popularity since the early 1970s as a means of purchasing a company. The target company is usually bought using loans and the deal is therefore highly geared as in the management buy-out. However, it need not be the internal management who purchase the company, nor need it be involved. It is often a means by which an individual or small team, with institutional backing, can take a public company into private ownership by buying out the existing shareholders (Wallner 1980). There is thus a break of ownership, a remarriage of ownership and control, and a highly geared new company, but the existing management need not be involved.

A *spin-off* also shares some of the characteristics of the buy-out, particularly the personnel aspect. However, a spin-off is where some employees of a company take an idea, or some part of the assets, and set up an independent company to exploit them. The spin-off may be with the parent company's blessing as a means of developing further an idea to which the parent would not wish to commit further internal resources but which could be traded in the future. A parent may even go so far as to initiate the break and keep a continued arm's length involvement in the newly created company. This type of arrangement has been most common in high-technology areas and new firms formed in this way have often taken ideas out of large company research and development programmes. The spin-off usually therefore only involves part of any assets, part of any personnel, and there may be a strongly implied continuing trading relationship (Garvin 1983).

A *hive down* is where a parent management purposely assembles a set of assets into a new company which it then registers as a separate company. This new company may then be offered for sale as a discrete legal entity, but there is no presupposition that the eventual purchasers will be the current management. There may be circumstances where the gathering of assets into a saleable bundle through hive down triggers off a desire to buy on behalf of management as it sees the hive-down process as a threat to its own security and current standing.

Thus, whilst all three mechanisms discussed share some

characteristics with the management buy-out, and whilst, in the case of the last two, situations may arise where a management buy-out is effected, in their basic form there are important distinctions which need to be made.

Where Do Buy-Outs Come From? The UK Market Place

The past six years have probably seen something of the order of 1,000 buy-outs successfully completed, and they are probably continuing at a rate of just over 200 per year. This figure compares quite dramatically with the figures for conventional divestment produced by British business and presented in Chapter 2 of this book. The route is therefore a major and established part of the current UK industrial scene. The growth in the number of deals per annum has been quite significant, rising fourfold between 1979 and 1983.

Keeping a precise track of actual deals completed is rather hazardous as many are concluded with the minimum of fuss and publicity and some financiers are reluctant to give details of buy-outs which they have supported. Nevertheless, the magnitude of the phenomenon as estimated above will not be far from the true picture. The deals vary enormously in terms of size, from just a few thousand pounds to over £50m. A recent survey has shown the average size to be under £1m., but the data on which that estimate is based excluded a number of very big recent deals, and the large employee buy-outs (Wright and Coyne 1985). It would not be too far from the mark to suggest that the phenomenon could be responsible for approaching £250m. of venture capital in 1985. The increased willingness of financiers to lend for buy-outs, and the growing sophistication of the financial market place with the development of the second market, the over-the-counter market and the development of Business Expansion Funds under the government Business Expansion Scheme, have all given a boost to buy-outs. As has been noted earlier, management buy-outs may be of independent companies or those which are part of a larger concern. In a recent survey it has been seen that over 75 per cent of buy-outs are of companies that were previously members of groups. The orthodox divestment from a parent still trading accounted for just over 60 per cent of all buy-outs (Wright and Coyne 1985).

The buy-out is, therefore, well-established as a means by which a parent company may effect a divestment and there are a large number of companies around which there are now thriving independent units having spent a good part of their lives under a larger corporate umbrella. Even in the case of divestment by the receiver, many profitable buy-outs survive. There are often cases of groups which are unsuccessful when viewed as a whole but which contain viable subsidiaries. For example, a number of companies continue successfully out of the Alfred Herbert collapse of which one, Melville Technologies, has been a successful buy-out. The collapse of toymakers Lesney has left behind a bought-out company specialising in small industrial die castings which is trading successfully, serving only a portion of the market which the former parent sought to serve. Opportunities for successful businesses therefore often exist in unlikely places.

Some of the 'conventional' divestments may also arise out of adversity rather than from a positive forward corporate plan. The sale may be to raise cash to reduce the possibility of receivership for the whole group. In these circumstances it is often simply the most easily saleable parts with the best, quietest prospect of generating the required cash which get sold off first.

Buy-outs are, therefore, an established part of the UK scene, comparable in number to conventional divestments, which maintain their place as a tool of corporate strategy. They are present in almost every geographical region and across almost all of the Standard Industrial Classification (Coyne, Wright and Lockley 1984). There is a concentration in minimum list headings 2 to 4, which cover the bulk of UK manufacturing industry, with approximately 75 per cent of all buy-outs in these areas, but they are represented also in transport, retailing, distribution, financial services, etc. Irrespective of type of location and industry, the buy-out can offer an option to effect a transfer of ownership for a parent wishing to divest itself of one part of its operation. The general point applies whether the company is part of a UK-owned group or a subsidiary of a foreign parent.

There is some evidence to suggest that other European economies, notably France and West Germany, are also discovering the buy-out as a means of corporate adjustment. Just as the UK took its early expertise by looking to similar circumstances in the United States, and mirroring its venture capital sophistication, so Europe is looking towards the UK to offer expertise and guidance in this field. One leading financial institution has already concluded deals in West Germany, and the establishment of funds by Paribas in France suggests that growth will come fairly quickly.

Why Divest to Management?

If we assume that a company has decided, for whatever reason, that a subsidiary or division does not fit in with its corporate plan and has, therefore, decided to sell, we need to examine why the management buy-out route may be followed. What advantages or disadvantages are there in selling to management as opposed to pursuing a conventional sale to an external purchaser?

Before a buy-out can take place there must be a simultaneous coincidence of desires on the part of both the vendor and the purchaser. The vendor's decision to sell, in which local management may or may not have been involved, must be matched by the perception of opportunity and a desire to buy on the part of the management team. If the desired sale is made public, either formally or informally (Professor Thomas has discussed the delicate issues of information dissemination in Chapter 2), one may expect that there will be more than one prospective purchaser and that the management team may be up against outside competitors.

The vendor's sole concern is to get the best deal for itself, though defining best in these circumstances will encompass many dimensions. We must assess the 'pros' and 'cons' of a sale to management particularly closely given that until fairly recently there were often greater legal, financial, and taxation difficulties associated with a buy-out than with a conventional sale. These difficulties were partly because of the lack of experience in dealing with a relatively new (1970s) phenomenon, partly because company and taxation law had not anticipated such moves and made them easy to facilitate, but overall because of the difficulties surrounding the legal rights, responsibilities and obligations of management as employees to their board, and the board to the body of shareholders. To complete the early buy-outs often took a great deal of will, patience, perseverence and ingenuity. The barriers have eased somewhat in the past three years and the provisions of the Companies Act 1981, particularly the exception allowed in Section 43 easing the path to share purchase and transfer, have made buy-out arrangements less complex. The utilisation of measures contained in successive Finance Acts, and the ingenuity of specialist advisers, have all helped to clear the path to more and more straightforward buy-outs (Hardman and Young 1983).

The specific rationale for sale to management will vary from case to case according to the material circumstances of the divestment and the vendor's perception of his own best interest. The elements which will undoubtedly figure in that assessment will be the desire to get the best price and the need to facilitate an easy sale. In so doing the vendor will have due regard to the shareholders' interests to whom the board is ultimately accountable. Complications may be introduced where the subsidiary to be sold is a well-known name in its market and/or trades using the parent's name. The vendor may also have regard to its own corporate image in so far as it may continue to be associated with the subsidiary post-buy-out, (in customers' minds at least) and will also be aware of a need to maintain corporate confidence once a sale is announced. One aspect which will concern the parent, and would be well to the fore in any decision to sell, is the extent to which the independent company post-buy-out would be a competitor in any of the existing lines of business and the knowledge of the parent, its operations and corporate plans that the management leaving in the bought-out company may take with it. In this final respect it must also be remembered that an important part of the assets of any company is the value embodied in the management team.

The parent will need to weigh up all these elements in making a decision to sell to management and will be aware that management's insider knowledge will be a vital factor in negotiations.

The management team, once alert to an opportunity, will have its bargaining position enhanced for a number of reasons. Firstly, there may be a certain asymmetry of information within the company such that the central strategists have less information on the actual performance and potential of any division than the management within that division itself. The local team will be more aware of the extent to which the full potential of current assets is being realised.

Secondly, the local management will know its own value to the subsidiary and the contribution that it has made to its current position and could make in the future. A disaffected management team would be unattractive to an outside purchaser unless the outsider already had the necessary specific expertise available to manage the post-purchase company. This might rule out outsiders whose desire to buy was for diversification.

Finally, the local management should have early warning of impending sale, and have full and free access to all information pertinent to concluding a successful deal. On this latter point there is a problem of conflicting interest once a decision to bid has been made, as the local management then has a clear incentive for its subsidiary or division to be valued as cheaply as possible in order for it to be given the best start post-buy-out. The dividing line between acting under the obligations of the contract of employment and pursuing independent self-interest is a thin and problematical one. In a number of run-ups to buy-out it has led to managers leading strangely dichotomous lives as they attempt to wear two hats and to be seen to act without prejudice.

The potential conflict between the parties will generally be resolved through a negotiating process in which a third dimension will always exist: the degree to which the deal can be financed. If the sale is insupportable in the financial community other than at a particular price, then the boundaries of negotiation are more clearly defined. As far as managements buying out are concerned, this should ensure that they do not take unacceptable risks. In the United Kingdom this bargaining process may be an entirely secret affair and external purchasers may never be aware that the opportunity exists if the vendor decides at the very outset to pursue only the buy-out route. This does not happen in the United States where such sales must be made public and where third parties are invited to bid. The objective of such an arrangement is to ensure that the sale takes place at a figure which is acceptable in the general market place, thus avoiding excessive discounts which might be contrary to the general shareholder interest.

Although this procedure may result in a 'fairer' price in the eyes of the vendors' shareholders, it does create other problems which are not without their costs, though the precise value to be attached to them is rather more nebulous and subjective. Firstly, the scheme may introduce delay; secondly, it may lead to a breakdown in confidence within the company; and, thirdly, it may lead to management losing an auction in such a way that its own value to the company is diminished. Alternative schemes may also be introduced in this process such as the asset swap/strategic trade arrangements discussed in Chapter 4. Management veto and disaffection will tend to be played down by the vendor, and issues such as price and ease of sale will tend to be to the fore.

Overall, the general conditions under which a sale to management will usually prevail are where only management is prepared to pay the required price; where a quick, quiet and internal sale is required for strategic reasons by the parent; where sale to management will better preserve the overall reputation of the parent; and where, for whatever reason, there is a personal bond such that the internal management will be preferred. In the final two cases the corollary exists. A parent would not wish to sell to a weak management which it felt would not be up to making a success of the new venture. It would not wish to see its own reputation tarnished by being seen to sell a bad deal to its former employees. In one large group this view was expressed very forcefully. Indeed, it was suggested that if the management were good enough to run a successful business in their own right, then they were the kind of people whom they would like to keep in the group; and if they were not, then could they in all conscience be responsible for setting them on the path to disaster! This group, which wished to remain anonymous, conducted management audits and moved on its promising talent elsewhere in the group before any potential candidates for sale were offered to the market.

In the final analysis, when a desire to sell and a desire to buy coincide, and where the vendor chooses to sell to management so that a buy-out is cffected, the potential success depends upon the underlying fundamentals of the new business: Is its product good enough? Does a market exist for the product or service? Does management have the necessary ability? And is the venture adequately and sensibly financed at a fair price?

The Buy-Out and Broader Corporate Strategy

There are circumstances in which the existence of the buy-out route may lead to a more wide-ranging consideration of corporate strategy. In this wider sphere the concern is not so much to consider whether or not to pursue the buy-out route once an appraisal has identified some element as being ripe for disposal, so much as to examine the way in which buy-out consciousness may fundamentally affect the whole notion of management and the division of responsibility and rewards within a company.

The existence of successful buy-outs, their growing numbers and the spectacular and public successes which some buy-out teams have enjoyed, has raised the awareness of corporate managers of the rewards which may exist in independent business were they to take their current charges out from under the corporate umbrella. The vast majority of the buy-out team members that have 'gone it alone' over the past seven years are first-time entrepreneurs. Whilst it is well-documented that most new firm founders come from other small and medium-sized firms, and have often had exposure to some form of risk-related decision taking in their previous roles (Storey 1983), the buy-out phenomenon is characterised by the release of 'organisation men'.

Most of the buy-out teams are mid-career 'company men' with over ten years' experience, on average, in their current positions (Wright and Coyne 1985). If we do some simple arithmetic with about 1,000 buy-outs and an average team size of 4.5, then we have seen the release into independent business on their own account of some 4,500 individuals. This is not an insignificant number of people and certainly sufficient to be seen, examined and become an aspiration model for those left within companies.

How does this affect corporate strategy? First of all, it indicates that there is a pool of entrepreneurially-minded individuals lurking within companies seeking the opportunity to exercise their entrepreneurial skills on their own account. Here, then, is a pool which could be usefully harnessed within companies if appropriate organisational forms could be designed. Secondly, it perhaps demonstrates the difficulties which parent groups may face in assuring themselves that the management of their subsidiaries are always acting in the parent's interests.

If an opportunity to buy can be 'created' by the management of a subsidiary, it can ensure a very good deal for itself perhaps by running the firm below potential but by preparing the ground for going independent. The ability to buy-out may therefore, to some extent, sow the seed of a threat from within which the parent company may need to defend. In the development of corporate strategy it may therefore be necessary to have tight control procedures to safeguard against secure, complete management teams in place in subsidiaries which are vital to the centre, or it may be necessary to introduce means of equity participation, profit sharing and rewards to entrepreneurial initiative.

Another aspect where the existence of the buy-out route may require the parent to be defensive is where it receives an unsolicited bid from an independent outsider which it wishes to consider but may be predisposed to reject. The bid may bring forth a counter-bid from management which may be more difficult to defend/reject than an outside bid as any lingering dissatisfaction from the management team prevented from buying out may affect future performance.

However, it is also possible to see the buy-out in a wider corporate strategy sense from the aggressive point of view, that is the means by which a company may nurture the concept of the buy-out as a means of progress. It could well be possible for a company to specialise in corporate development by buying companies, assembling teams, putting them on their feet, then selling to the management in place (probably retaining some small equity participation), and using the funds generated to buy more companies, etc. The company would take its profit from the short-term turnround, and perhaps in the long-term when the bought-out companies become listed. Alternatively, the spawning company could lend in the normal way alongside institutions. This aggressive exploitation of the buy-out would have the advantage of allowing the parent speedy adaptation and great flexibility.

Whilst there are a number of instances where a particular group has sold off a number of subsidiaries through management buy-out, there is no suggestion yet that such consciously adaptive parents exist in the form described in the last paragraph.

Thus, in the widest sense the existence of buy-outs, their popularity, and the publicity surrounding their success, poses broader corporate questions of both a defensive and an aggressive nature.

The Wider Issues

The management buy-out raises a number of issues which are of interest to and applicable across a wider spectrum of industry. These relate particularly to the restructuring of an economy through divestment, the exercise of entrepreneurship and its importance to economic development, and the relationship between ownership and control and its effect on efficiency.

The divestments which have led to buy-outs are often the result of previous acquisitive behaviour in the pursuit of anticipated economies of scale. The acquisition and merger boom of the 1960s fuelled by general government exhortations that 'big was best' created a number of ill-conceived conglomerates which have been in the process of being untangled following the failure of the larger unit to deliver the promised returns (Meeks 1977; O'Brien 1978; Chiplin and Wright 1980, 1983).

The move towards returning parts to independence has also been encouraged by the shift in emphasis to a belief that 'small may now be better', and that small and medium-sized firms should be encouraged for their flexibility, innovativeness and responsiveness to the market (Curran and Stanworth 1982; Binks and Coyne 1983). The process has undoubtedly been exaggerated by the general recession and high interest rates which have encouraged firms to take a critical look at the returns currently being earned by all their constituent parts. There is some temptation to characterise the buy-out as a phenomenon of recession, and undoubtedly in some of its dimensions – purchases from the receiver and the obtaining of discounts on the book value of assets – poor trading conditions have helped management to acquire the company. However, it would be wrong to totally consider the buy-out in terms of economic difficulty; there are positive strategic aspects which will ensure that the mechanism survives as a useful adaptive tool for companies beyond the current recession.

Recent financial developments taking place simultaneously with the recession have given buy-outs a boost, notably the development of the venture capital market and the opening of the Unlisted Securities Market. These financial developments have made it easier to raise finance to restructure by buy-out, and for the management buying out to see an early and inexpensive way of getting a listing which enables it to get a return on its personal investment (Wright and Jarrett 1982). Similar moves in Europe may lead to the buy-out being more widely used there also (Fairley 1984).

The role of the entrepreneur in industry in general has enjoyed something of a resurgence in the 1970s and into the 1980s. The attention attracted by the entrepreneur in both academic and popular deliberation is as high as it has ever been. His skills of co-ordination and administration, and the willingness and ability to take risks, are widely appreciated (Cantillon 1755; Casson 1982). In the economics literature this current appreciation comes from a rediscovery of the 'Austrian' school of economists whose modern proponents include Hayek and Kirzner (Littlechild 1977). The 'golden age' of British industry was attributed by Say to 'the wonderful practical skills of her entrepreneurs' (Say 1854). Once again the exercise of entrepreneurship and its importance in economic development is being encouraged to help pull the UK economy out of recession. The buy-out is one of the most striking examples of how this can be done, and the buy-out teams can be considered as fulfilling the 'entrepreneurial function' within the new firms (Kirzner 1980).

The management team generally contains a leading light who is the personification of the entrepreneurial individual in an almost stereotypical way. It is he who is usually instrumental in giving impetus to the venture. One of the foremost skills he generally exhibits is the ability to choose an effective team (Wright and Coyne 1985).

The desire to take on this entrepreneurial role is fuelled by the structure of incentives and personal rewards that flow from success, and is tempered by the prospects and possibility of loss. These may be described as 'pull' and 'push' factors which are relevant to all decisions to enter independent business (Binks and Coyne 1983). The importance of incentives in ensuring efficiency and the closeness of ownership and control have been major issues in organisational and economics literature for a number of years. The existence of a divorce between ownership and control in both the UK and USA has been generally recognised (Berle and Means 1932; Prais 1976). Whether this divorce has serious implications for control has been questioned in some studies in which the particular holdings of directors and the stability of boards is considered (Beed 1966; Marris 1964).

Entitlement to profit, as the residual from production and as an incentive to promote efficiency, is the central theme of some studies where the organisation is seen to be efficient only if someone has the incentive to monitor production (Alchian and Demsetz 1972). The performance of buy-outs immediately after the change of ownership would certainly support the view that the remarriage matters, and that incentives generate efficiency. The issue is seen particularly starkly in the successful management of turnrounds which have occurred in a number of cases.

On each of these issues the experiences of management buy-outs may give useful indicators which are capable of generalisation within industry as a whole. The phenomenon will certainly be examined closely to see if the early good experiences are maintained and will influence whether managers continue to present themselves as potential buyers-out!

The Mechanics of Buy-Out

There are a number of important issues surrounding the mechanics of the buy-out itself including the way negotiations are conducted, the form of ownership transfer used and the choice of financial arrangements in the agreed purchase.

The negotiations are often complicated by the fact that the management team was formerly in a subordinate relationship with the people with whom it is negotiating for the purchase of the company. In the run up to the purchase, the question of conflicting interest may also be problematic. Both difficulties are eased by the use of intermediaries in the negotiating phase, either as advisers or to conduct negotiations entirely on their client's behalf. It is usual to go to an intermediary, often an accountant or financial institution, for a preliminary assessment of the feasibility of the deal before committing time, resources and the potential for embarrassment to the idea. After this initial screen, an informal discussion with the parent could take place at which management would have to declare its hand. Life is seldom the same after this has been done. Further meetings can then fill out the detail and should cover the points listed in Table 6.1.

Only a good deal which has the right calibre management and a sound business will get financing of the type required, but there are great benefits in putting the proposal to alternative funding sources who may have quite different attitudes to certain businesses, as the Dennis and Robinson experience mentioned later shows.

Once negotiations reach an advanced stage, then the fine detail needs to be attended to, and the management commitment must be 100 per cent as the fees and expenses incurred to get a proposal to

Table 6.1 Example of Topics to be Covered in a Company Appraisal in the Case of a Buy-Out from a Parent Company

Topics

1. Company histories
   Of subsidiary to be bought out
   Of parent
2. Markets and marketing
   The overall state of the market in which the subsidiary is operating
   The subsidiary's marketing policy
   The subsidiary's customers and suppliers
   Seasonal trading characteristics
3. Performance (past and expected future)
   Summary of past five years' audited accounts
   Profit forecast for first three years after buy-out
   Cash-flow forecast for first year after buy-out
   Statement of assumptions on which forecasts based
   Production and sales statistics for previous five years
4. Assets to be acquired
   Fixed assets
   Stocks and work in progress
5. Existing financial resources
   Long-term capital structure and shareholders
   Working capital (including detailed debtor and creditor position)
   Taxation aspects
6. Manpower
   Directors and their personal histories
   Union representation
   Workforce size and characteristics (including charges)
   Key employees and management and their effectiveness
7. Organisation of the company
   Organisation chart
   How the company is managed and controlled
   The effectiveness of the current management and control of the company
   State of industrial relations

Source: Wright, M. and Coyne, J. (1985) 'Management buy-outs', Croom Helm.

this stage can be quite substantial. For example, in one recent deal where approaching £50m was raised, the management team incurred expenses and fees of almost £1m. The fine detail usually requires a careful examination of all the legal and taxation implications, for both the parent and the bought-out company of the changeover. The precise detail changes with each Finance Act, together with amendments to the Companies Act. The services of specialist company lawyers and accountants experienced in handling buy-outs can be invaluable in ensuring that the full legal requirements are complied with and that unnecessary difficulties and costs are avoided. Care has usually had to be taken to make the most advantageous arrangements with respect to pension transfers, redundancy payments and continuity of service, and the carrying forward of tax allowances (Hardman and Young 1983).

There are four main ways in which the transfer can be effected. They break down into either a transfer of shares or a transfer of assets and are summarised in Table 6.2. The share route has been eased by the Companies Act 1981, particularly the exemption to Section 42 allowed in the provisions of Section 43.

There are an increasing number of sources from which the necessary finance may be raised and these include merchant banks, commercial banks, enterprise agencies, local authorities and Business Expansion Scheme funds. Most financial institutions, pension funds and the like now list management buy-outs as preferred areas of lending which shows the extent of their current popularity. Institutions vary in their preference for loans as against equity, the stake they look for from management, and the terms on which they want repayment. The eventual structure of any deal will depend upon these preferences as well as type and size of deal, perceived risks and time horizon.

The balance of equity to loans in the package has important implications for the inescapable annual repayments commitment. A package biased towards loan funding means regular fixed payments whilst an equity bias means that dividends are paid only when profits are earned. As a general rule, management teams are extremely unhappy about the dilution of equity and tend to over-favour the loan arrangements. On the whole, most of the funding is provided in the form of loans and it is unusual for financial institutions to take straight ordinary shares. Institutions usually prefer to take cumulative convertible redeemable participative preferred ordinary shares which have catch-up clauses and rank first for extra slices of profit. They usually reflect the strength of the institutions' bargaining position in setting up the finance.

Table 6.2 Main Buy-Out Arrangements on Divestment

1. Subsidiary Company of a Parent Still Trading

   Target company pays a dividend to its parent and shares in the target company are then acquired by new company or by the managers. This scheme requires that target company has sufficient distributable reserves. Alternatively, the financier can replace a loan from the parent company to target company.

2. Purchase from a Group (or Company in Receivership)

   Subsidiary of target company is formed, with trade of target being transferred to new subsidiary ('hived down') on loan account. Financier replaces loan and new company or managers personally purchase shares in target's new subsidiary. For purchasers from receiver, hive down must take place before liquidation of target and sale of its subsidiary. For purchase from a group, new subsidiary must commence trading before sale takes place.

3. Purchase of Assets from Vendor Company

   New company is formed and used to purchase assets of target company. (*Note*: Although in principle a very simple method, it can, if purchase is at a discount, often cause serious conflicts of interest between the vendor and the purchaser in terms of liabilities and allowances for taxation. As a result, one of the previous methods may be preferred.)

4. Purchase of Target Company when Management Team already Owns Some Shares

   Either shares in target company can be distributed as dividend to buy-out team and its shares in the distributing company become worthless (a 'demerger' as provided for in the Finance Act 1980) or target company purchases for cash shares of outgoing shareholders leaving managers in control (as provided for in the Companies Act 1981).

Source: Adapted from Hardman, J.P. and Young, M.R. (1983) 'Management buy-outs', *Accountants Digest No. 133*, Spring.

One source of finance which can be used on divestment is from the parent itself. This could take several forms from a conventional commercial loan, to deferred payments of part of the purchase price, through to some equity participation of the new company. There are probably as many different balances of financial package as there are deals! The availability of finance, the terms offered, and the structure of the deal are all vital ingredients in making the divestment by buy-out possible.

Case Studies

The preceding discussion raises a number of questions concerning the use of the management buy-out as a means of divestment by parent companies. These issues are very broad and range from the corporate-strategic type, such as assessing to what extent a company fits into future plans, to the personnel-specific type, such as whether there is a personal relationship which makes the buy-out route possible. It is difficult to illustrate these points from just one case, yet an examination of case material is useful in cementing the conceptual considerations and the mechanics of buy-out. The major points are illustrated here from a number of recent buy-outs on divestment which reflect the diversity of the phenomenon.

Crisis management and the need to make a rapid shift was at the centre of the decision of Dunlop to sell its Energy Engineering Division to its management, who formed a new trading company called Lanemark. The parent, Dunlop, had tried over a number of years to diversify away from its principal tyre business, a core which was in decline partly as a direct consequence of the company's own product development success in producing longer-life tyres. The diversification came too late, and the decline of the core business was too rapid for Dunlop to really give a full opportunity for the new businesses to develop. The Energy Engineering Division is an example of this failure.

The division had been developed to provide a commercial outlet for products arising out of research and development and had been set a target turnover of £3m. per annum. A need to produce cash-generating parts of the business was seen starkly in 1982 when Dunlop's financing costs were over £56m. Failure to meet the turnover target, despite the core of a successful business, led to the decision to sell. The disposal was small scale when compared with

Dunlop's disposal of Malayan interests for £119m., Angus Fire Armour for £20m. and, of course, the disposal of the tyre facility to Sumitomo. The sum required to purchase the new Lanemark was £170,000, of which £45,000 was provided by the buy-out team in the ratio 25 per cent ordinary shares to 75 per cent cumulative redeemable preference shares, and £125,000 was provided by the financial institutions, of which £100,000 was in straight loans. The four-man team thus bought a £1m. turnover company in which the principal assets were the copyrights and patents in the new products being developed. Dunlop got rid of a division whose performance had not matched its internal targets, and received some return for the development work put in on the new products such as liquid heaters, petrochemical and chemical burners.

Having to change the name on buy-out has meant that the company has needed to establish a market presence all over again and cannot rely on any spin-off from the well-known name of a parent.

The need to start up under a new name was also a characteristic of the sale of the Kings Norton fasteners business of GKN as part of the rationalisation of its UK activities. In the highly competitive engineering, automotive supplies and steel stockholding business which has been the core of GKN's UK operation, a major consideration in divestment is always the effect that a new independent company, or addition to a competitor's portfolio, may have on existing GKN business. Thus, in any internal review each operating division or subsidiary is viewed with respect to the capacity existing in the industry and the ability of other parts of GKN to meet current and prospective demand. Within overall GKN policy there appears to have been two clearly discernible strands: first, a switch in the emphasis of operations from the UK to overseas so that overseas operations in 1985 are a more significant part of the total company than they were even five years ago; second, a regrouping within the UK around the core of the business both in terms of geographical location and product area. GKN has kept potential growth markets and high added-value businesses and consolidated them around its West Midlands base. Where over-capacity has existed in a market in which it chooses to remain, it has preferred to close plants rather than consider their sale in any form, including piecemeal sale of assets and equipment. Where the above criteria have not applied and a business is surplus to current requirements, then a sale to a party outside has seemed to be the preferred route. Thus, in all the restructuring of the group that has taken place since 1978, only two companies have been sold to their management and in only one has it made the sale public.

The sale is that of the Kings Norton business producing simple cotterpin fasteners and extruded plastic fittings. The buy-out only took place after very careful consideration of the alternatives, and complete closure had appeared a likely possibility. Indeed, the personal regard with which the managing director of the Kings Norton division was held by the main board director responsible for closing the plant probably tipped the balance. The new company, now called KN products (where KN stands for Kings Norton but also is not too dissimilar to the GKN label the products previously carried), does only about 25 per cent of the turnover of the former division but achieves it with less than 10 per cent of the workforce. The flexible use of labour in a non-union environment, a careful assessment of the profitability of the business and a concentration on the basics, coupled with the imaginative and labour-saving use of a computer control system, all contribute to a successful new company.

In this instance, GKN might well have been prepared to retain the company within the corporate framework if it could have performed in this way, but the changes that were possible in resurrecting a last-minute divestment from a projected closure would not have been made from within GKN. The changes would have been too expensive in terms of management time, particularly given the small-scale of division, and too risky in terms of confrontation and 'knock-on' effects amongst the unionised workforce. The deal was completed with a great deal of good will on the part of GKN who were accommodating in the financial arrangements on turnover, the continuation of orders, the release of patterns, etc.

However, the actual process of purchase did illustrate the difficulties of the dual responsibilities of the executives in the company to be bought out in the period up to purchase. The chief executive was trying to prepare for closure in accordance with GKN instructions and then had to declare an interest and simultaneously prepare to purchase. The buy-out team was meticulous in the separation of all its plans for purchase from company time, facilities and resources. For example, it would hire cars to go to financial planning meetings rather than go in its own vehicles which were provided by the company!

In this case also the essential role of the intermediary was seen to good effect. The early 1980s was perhaps not the best time to hawk round a proposition to purchase a West Midlands engineering company, the core product of which was well over 100 years old in concept and design. The company was well advised, knew its business and recognised the need to get a comprehensive business plan and cash-flow forecast together to put to financiers. The highly geared nature of buy-outs means that they need to be able to generate cash to meet the loan repayments, and therefore a detailed two-year cash-flow forecast is a minimum requirement that financial institutions look for.

Good will, personal contact and a product-mix that would not compete with the parent's remaining businesses were the ingredients that made divestment by buy-out of KN products a possibility.

A more conventional divestment through buy-out of a UK subsidiary by its UK parent took place in the case of Smiths Industries sale of Dennis and Robinson which trades as Manhattan Furniture. This is a classic example of the way in which technical development and a changing market place combine to alter the balance of a business to such an extent that previously logical parts of a group become odd and ill-fitting. Dennis and Robinson had originally been purchased by Smiths Industries as part of a strategic decision to fully integrate production in their clock-making division. This subsidiary's line was cabinet making, producing the clock cases into which Smiths mechanisms were fitted, and it was therefore a logical step to bring the company under the Smiths umbrella and integrate its major case supplier. However, as the market for wooden-cased clocks fell away, Dennis and Robinson had to diversify, but the basis of its diversification was from its own expertise base, woodworking, and in no way related to other activities within Smiths. Thus, it moved into kitchen furniture and became a successful manufacturer with a strong regional market, a successful record of ready-assembled sales to the building trade and a profitable track record. The company was never going to be a priority investment area within Smiths, as the group policy was to extend into wider areas of instrumentation and electronics, but it was always useful in so far as it was a cash generator for the rest of the group and required little managerial or investment input. Herein lies the dilemma that led to the buy-out. The local management were happy to be given a free hand, but unhappy to be denied money for reinvestment which usually had greater calls elsewhere. The non-priority of the company within Smiths meant that it would always remain an ill-fitting curiosity. The local management and, in particular, the managing director would have preferred complete independence. Indeed, the managing director approached Smiths with an offer to buy and began to assemble a buy-out team and the necessary finance. The actual purchase was quite drawn out, not so much because it was not a good business or that the price was not right but because in merchant-banking circles kitchen furniture was anything but the 'flavour of the month'! Eventually, with good will on both sides beginning to fade, the deal was completed. Dennis and Robinson became independent and Smiths was able to cash in all at once its interest in the company and reinvest the money internally more in line with its corporate strategy.

The opportunity at Dennis and Robinson arose as the result of a long process of corporate adaptation within Smiths during which time the fringe nature of Dennis and Robinson developed. However, opportunities can arise much more quickly where an acquisition of one group by another, where a particular aspect of the acquired group is the target for the predator, quickly creates corporate misfits which are ripe for sale and therefore ripe for buy-out. The recent (1984) takeover of UDS by Hanson Trust created just such opportunities. UDS was an amalgamation of assorted retailing businesses from general supermarkets to specialist high-street shoe retailers. After the takeover, Hanson Trust, who did not particularly want to be in shoe retailing partly because of its very special nature which involved slow stock turnover, small outlets, and a high volume of capital tied-up in the business, was receptive to overtures from management to buy-out the Timpson's shoe retailers. Indeed, Timpson's, Farmers and John Collier (the clothiers) all attempted to mount buy-outs, with the most spectacularly successful being Timpson's. The team, led by John Timpson, following in the family firm tradition, purchased the company for £44m. and returned it to a private company, which status it had lost in 1973 when an agreed takeover by UDS took place.

The deal was complex involving, as it did, a significant portfolio of retail freeholds, and a number of sale and leaseback arrangements to release cash, but what the case does illustrate is that the opportunity can arise very quickly as a result of corporate moves elsewhere. In this case the inside knowledge of the buy-out team, and the speed with which it could respond and give Hanson Trust the opportunity to recoup a not insubstantial proportion of the sum it had paid for the whole UDS group, was vital to its success. Hanson Trust had owned the company for so short a time that the asymmetry of information worked significantly in the management's favour. A contested buy-out a little later at Farmers failed and the company was sold to an outside buyer, Clarkes.

Opportunities from rationalisation also often occur where the parent is a foreign company and is making a strategic withdrawal from a particular geographical location. A number of UK buy-outs have come from this source, notably from American parents who have experienced the highly geared leveraged-type arrangements in the United States. In these cases the sale to local management is sometimes compounded by courtesy as well as commercialism, though the ease, lack of publicity, and public relations aspects should not be overlooked. It is often the most acceptable way of getting a fair price. One of the most successful of the buy-outs in the UK has come from a foreign parent, though unusually enough from an Australian company. DPCE was bought out from the Australian Datronics Corporation in 1981 and was listed on the UK stock market in 1983. Since listing, it has enjoyed such success that it is one of the market's star performers. The decision of the parent to sell simply reflected the difficulty of controlling just one subsidiary at a distance of 12,000 miles and the need to have resources available to meet commitments elsewhere within the Australian group. The well-placed local management, boosted by the arrival of an entrepreneurially-minded chief executive, was well-placed to assess the true potential of the company and to effect a transfer from under the noses of any other would-be purchasers.

Conclusions

As the brief case studies illustrate, the management buy-out is an extremely useful variant on the conventional divestment and contains great variety in the forms it can take and the source from which it can be effected. It is becoming established as a well-respected option within the range available to corporate strategists when considering adaptation to a changing environment. Though the recession in UK industry has probably accelerated its development and thrown up opportunities, the buy-out is rather more than a simple product of the recession itself. The concept will endure within the UK economy and is already beginning to be picked up in Europe as well. Combining, as it does, the remarriage of ownership and control, the exercise of entrepreneurship and the pursuit of efficiency in an independent framework, it has implications for the whole of UK industry.

References

Alchian, A. and Demsetz, H. (1972) 'Production, information costs, and economic organisation', *American Economic Review*, 62.

Anslow, M. (1984) 'Faster growth for buy-out managers', *Your Business*, July.

Beed, C. (1966) 'The separation of ownership and control', *Journal of Economic Studies*, Vol. 1.

Berle, A. and Means, G. (1932) *The Modern Corporation and Private Property*, New York.

Binks, M.R. and Coyne, J. (1983) *The Birth of Enterprise*, IEA, Hobart Paperback 98, London.

Cantillon, R. (1755) *Essai sur la Nature du Commerce en Général*, Fletcher Gyles, London.

Casson, M. (1982) *The Entrepreneur*, Martin Robertson.

Chiplin, B. and Wright, M. (1980) 'Divestment and structural change in UK industry', *National Westminster Bank Review*, October.

Chiplin, B. and Wright, M. (1983) 'The sale of subsidiaries between company groups: a note', *mimeo*.

Coyne, J. Wright, M. and Lockley, H. (1984) 'Regional aspects of management buy-outs: some evidence', *Regional Studies*, Vol. 16, No. 5.

Curran, J. and Stanworth, J. (1982) 'The small firm in Britain: past, present and future', *European Small Business Journal*, 1.

Fairley, A. (1984) 'Second Marché is walking in the right direction', *Accountancy Age*, June.

Garvin, D.A. (1983) 'Spin-offs and the new firm formation process', *California Management Review*, 2, January.

Hardman, J.P. and Young, M.R. (1983) *Management Buy-Outs*, Accountants Digest, No. 113, Spring.

Hayek, F.A. (1978) 'Competition as a discovery process', in *New Studies in Philosophy, Politics and the History of Ideas*, University of Chicago Press.

Kirzner, I.M. (1979) *Perception, Opportunity and Profit*, University of Chicago Press.

Kirzner, I.M. (1980) 'The primacy of entrepreneurial discovery', in *Prime Mover of Progress: The Entrepreneur in Capitalism and Socialism*, Institute of Economic Affairs, Readings 23.

Littlechild, S. (1977) *The Fallacy of the Mixed Economy*, Institute of Economic Affairs.

Marris, R. (1964) *Economic Theory of Managerial Capitalism*, Macmillan.

Meeks, G. (1977) *Disappointing Marriage – A Study of the Gains from Mergers*, Cambridge University Press.

O'Brien, D.P. (1978) 'Time to turn the tide', *Lloyds Bank Review*, October.

Prais, S.J. (1976) *The Evolution of Giant Firms in Britain*, Cambridge University Press.

Say, J.B. (1854) *A Treatise on Political Economy*, J.B. Lipincott and Company.

Spicer and Pegler (1984) *Management Buy-Outs*, 2nd edition.

Storey, D.J. (1983) *Entrepreneurship and the New Firm*, Croom Helm.

Wallner, N. (1980) *The Leverage Buy-Out Manual*, The Wallner Company, La Jolla, California.

Wright, M. and Coyne, J. (1985) *Management Buy-Outs*, Croom Helm.

Wright, M. and Jarrett, M. (1982) 'New initiatives in the financing of small firms', *National Westminster Bank Review*, August.

7

Divestiture: The Case of AT & T

D.P. O'Brien

Introduction

'Divestiture' is the term used in the context of antitrust policy to refer to both the forced sale of shareholdings in one company which are owned by another company, and the forced breaking up of a single firm. The latter may in turn either represent the sale of parts of a company which are financially linked but not otherwise integrated, or involve the breaking up of a unitary firm; and the firm against which action is taken (by the antitrust authorities) may have reached its present position either through internal growth or through merger. While the American literature distinguishes between 'dissolution', 'divorcement' and 'divestiture',[1] these legal categories do not do a great deal to illuminate the complex possibilities while, as should be clear from the description above, the various possible situations shade into one another. In the circumstances it seems reasonable to use the general term divestiture to cover all forced sales, and this practice will be followed here.

Faced with a difficult problem in competition policy, divestiture may well seem an attractive policy alternative to regulation, as a number of authors have pointed out;[2] and certainly, if the alternative is the sort of haphazard regulation experienced by some industries in Britain, divestiture might well also be attractive to the firms concerned as an alternative.[3] As we shall see, there is provision for divestiture in both British and American legislation; and, as the case study in this chapter will demonstrate, it was at least partially the difficulties of regulation which made divestiture attractive both to the American antitrust authorities and to the company itself in the most sweeping divestiture case in history – that of AT & T.

The chapter begins with an examination of the conceptual economic issues surrounding *divestiture*. The grounds for divestiture may be divided into those which relate to the *structure* of an industry and those which relate to the *conduct* or behaviour of a firm. The means by which the enforced disposal of a subsidiary may be carried out have attracted a great deal of debate in the literature and this issue is addressed below together with the question as to whether divestiture involves penalties for the divestor, the divestee and their shareholders. Turning to actual practice, the British context is considered first, followed by that in the US where divestiture has been a more prevalent feature of antitrust policy. The case of AT & T is then examined in detail.

The Economics of Divestiture

Grounds for Divestiture

There are basically two grounds for divestiture: as a means of attacking a *structure* which is deemed to be unsatisfactory; and as a means of remedying *conduct* by firms in an industry which is anti-competitive in effect and which, it is judged, cannot be dealt with by regulation.

(a) Structure The structural approach, in which a *per se* approach to concentration is adopted, without explicit reference to conduct, has attracted widespread and influential support. It was, in particular, advanced as a desirable course of proceeding by Kaysen and Turner in their influential book, in which they recommended divestiture as part of a strengthening of antitrust policy generally, proposing the use of a special court and implementing both horizontal and vertical divestiture.[4] A number of other economists have supported this approach[5] and it received considerable impetus from

the report of the Neal 'Task Force' in 1968 and the introduction in 1972 and 1973 by Senator P.A. Hart of an Industrial Reorganisation Act.[6] The advocates of a structural approach cite evidence that large firms are not required for static or dynamic optimisation,[7] and point to the possibility of implied conspiracy over prices where the number of firms is small. Indeed, Turner used the term 'shared monopoly' for the situation where close oligopolistic relations enabled implicit collusion to take place.[8] Moreover, empirical work does indicate that conspiracy is most likely where numbers are small and the concentration ratio high.[9]

The structural approach, however, encounters a number of difficulties and has been the subject of sustained attack in the literature over recent years.[10] Indeed, it is arguable that, under the influence of Bain's work, there was a shift from conduct to structure in the emphasis of policy[11] and that, as a result, certain weaknesses in the structural approach became apparent.

The first difficulty is that the structural approach, since it involves market concentration, requires a market to be defined; and it is clear that there are endless possibilities of contesting the market definition used.[12] Secondly, critics have pointed out that unless a concentrated structure is protected by barriers to entry, supernormal profits cannot be maintained in the long term.[13] In turn, it is clear that both the existence and the durability of such barriers can be contested as strongly as the market definition.[14]

It can also be contended that the use of profit data in identifying non-competitive structures is highly misleading. It is fairly easy to argue both that accounting profit data bear little relationship to the economic concept of profit and, secondly, that supernormal profit will become capitalised and thus undetectable.[15] But even if accounting data were to represent economic profit correctly, it would still be open to firms (and their economists) to argue that high profits are due to high efficiency and that any evidence of a statistical relationship between concentration and profitability can be explained by considerations of scale economies and other forms of efficiency.[16]

Furthermore, it is not difficult to argue that structure, on its own, is ambiguous. As Hexter and Snow point out:

> A merger may at the same time increase the share of the market held by the largest firms, but reduce size inequality among those firms.[17]

Moreover, critics argue, the structure approach to policy can lead antitrust authorities towards the wrong targets; industries are selected because they have a structure which is *capable of* divestment rather than because they have a structure which is at an undesirably high level of concentration.[18] Finally, the structure approach, precisely because it is not based upon any observable conduct, puts courts into such difficulties of predicting the outcome of the divestiture order that they become reluctant to order divestiture.[19]

The difficulties facing the structural approach have become much clearer as, in response to criticisms, the goal of efficiency has become explicit rather than implicit.[20] The literature is now much clearer about efficiency as the aim of antitrust policy; and this efficiency is extended beyond technical (engineering) considerations to include transactions efficiency and even efficiency in the use of 'intangible resources' – meaning, in effect, various forms of overheads such as advertising.[21]

Of course, there may be other (and valid) aims of antitrust, such as the constraint of power.[22] But these are not really matters on which the economist has any special expertise; and they do not, therefore, provide a defence of the structuralist approach which satisfies its economic critics.

Indeed, the difficulties with the structural approach have led to root and branch criticisms of the idea of a divestiture programme and even of the existence of a power of divestiture.[23] Critics have argued that there are no sufficient grounds in the literature of economics to support the divestiture programme;[24] that divestiture, coupled with a tough policy on mergers, places emphasis upon preserving *competitors* rather than upon preserving competition;[25] that vertical restrictions do not affect competition;[26] and even that concentration is prima-facie evidence of efficiency.[27] Indeed, one writer has argued that divestiture action in the beer industry has reduced its efficiency compared with efficiency in the manufacture of spirits which has not been affected by divestiture.[28]

Buttressing all this is the thesis that the high profits yielded by a concentrated situation will decline over time, as entry is attracted into an industry, and there is thus no need to use forcible deconcentration. Only in the presence of barriers to entry – the existence of which are increasingly questioned – will this not be the case.[29] Such an approach links neatly with the idea of markets being 'contestable',[30] that is being open to the entry of competitors who will erode market power positions and reduce profits to normal. The doubts over barriers to entry are linked to other doubts over the possibility of 'predatory' pricing.[31] Indeed, one critic has gone so far as to express the view that the possibility of predatory pricing is unimportant 'except in the *unlikely case* in which the intended victim lacks equal access to capital to finance a price war'[32] (my italics).

Given that barriers to entry are held to be of doubtful importance, and that predatory pricing, or its potential, is unlikely to be a source of market power, the critics then move on to arguing that market forces produce the right kind of merger. Reliance is frequently placed upon the well-known analysis by O.E. Williamson of mergers,[33] while paying relatively little attention to the distributional aspects of the Williamson analysis (are supernormal profits distributionally equivalent to increased consumer surplus?) and to Williamson's own stress on the point that economies secured by merger must be real rather than merely pecuniary.[34] Associated with this is an emphasis upon transactions economies within a large organisation, stemming both from the work of Williamson and also from Coase's insight that a firm is much more than a legal entity.[35]

Of course not all these criticisms of the structural approach should be taken at face value. As critics have pointed out, vertical integration creates barriers to entry and, once accomplished, means that dealings are not necessarily based on competitive merit.[36] This is particularly true where entry into a small sector is blocked by large capital requirements for a whole chain.[37] Strategic considerations become important under these circumstances for the firm;[38] in particular, the argument against interfering with vertical mergers (and vertical integration) fails to take account of dominant price leadership. (It may be better to interfere with a vertical merger than to have to regulate thereafter.) One particular problem which can arise in this connection is capture, by one firm, of a common source of supply. Since the development of common sources of supply can be important and has been recognised by economists for the best part of a century – indeed, since Marshall – as a leading form of economies external to the firm and internal to the industry, it follows that allowing such capture is harmful to the development of the industry and that it may indeed produce horizontal concentration (as in the British motor industry).[39] The assets of competitors can be bought cheaply when they are faced with deprivation of their inputs and the problems of attempting to replicate the captured source of supply. Even in less extreme circumstances, vertical integration (and vertical restrictions) remove the incentive to search, which is an important requirement for competition to work in a world of non-perfect information.[40]

Much of the criticism not only assumes, implicitly, perfect information, but also bases itself on a static analysis which could in turn, and if carried to its logical conclusion, be used to justify both cartels and a merger of General Motors, Ford and Chrysler.[41] The efficiency claims made for merged firms could often be made for cartels[42] – and it might be added that, at least in Britain, merged firms have often behaved like cartels. This static, perfect information, approach arises from applying elementary price theory to complex industrial situations. For instance, some writers rely on the Lerner index, despite the cogent criticism of this made by Bauer and others in the 1940s and despite being forced to concede that it cannot deal with limit pricing.[43] Such an approach is, of course, fundamentally misconceived without some notion of *long*-run marginal cost and without reference to the cost of finding marginal cost. Critics have pointed to important dimensions which are missing from such an approach, including entry, product differentiation, oligopoly, and transport costs.[44]

The argument that existing antitrust policy is aimed at preserving competitors rather than at achieving efficiency is itself open to a number of criticisms. Of course it may be preferable to preserve competitors rather than allowing competition to self-destruct through merger, since potential competition can still be important. But there are, in any case, important difficulties with the idea that concentration is prima-facie evidence of efficiency. Not only could such an argument apply equally well to cartels[45] but, on the transactions front, it fails to take account of the fact that large firms typically exhibit managerial diseconomies and communications problems. The position that everything will be put right, in the long run, by entry, fails to take account of the fact that divestiture might work very much more quickly and effectively and also of the fact that the apparent long-run decline of profits in concentrated situations may equally well be due to the development of organisational slack rather than to competitive pressure[46] – the evidence that, in the long run, prices fall in concentrated situations is not strong.[47] Indeed, if entry were the solution to everything, cartels would be no problem since they would promptly be undermined by entry. For those less inclined to accept the insignificance of barriers to entry, divestiture may be a good way of attacking such barriers. (There is some evidence that advertising can be an effective barrier to entry.[48])

The argument that concentration is prima-facie evidence of efficiency also conflicts with the available information on minimum efficient scale and with the fact that evidence for cost savings in mergers is not exactly strong.[49] Indeed, cost curves are not well defined where there is market power,[50] making application of the Williamson analysis of mergers rather difficult. In addition, this also encounters problems because, as Williamson himself stressed, the shape of the time stream of benefits and costs is important and because, as he recognised in response to criticism, it is also necessary to analyse the alternative time stream of benefits and costs from internal expansion.[51]

Faced with these difficulties, especially the engineering evidence over minimum efficient scale, reliance upon 'intangible' economies does not help very much because the welfare implications of such matters as economies of scale in advertising, quantity discounts, and bargaining power in the capital market are hardly unambiguous. In particular, it is important to distinguish between real and pecuniary economies.[52] But in any case we cannot assume that firms are *necessarily* seeking economies if they are growth or sales maximisers.

An attitude of complete complacency where a small group of firms, apparently immune to outside competitive pressure, is enjoying a high level of profits, does not then seem warranted on the grounds that this is prima-facie evidence of efficiency. In this connection it should be noted that those who are totally dismissive of the idea that accounting rates of return have anything at all to do with economic profits have got a very serious difficulty to face. If their position were really valid, then their whole case for the role of profits as resource allocation signals, attracting entry into industries, would also go by the board – for the signals are accounting profits.

(b) Conduct However, there are sufficient problems with the structural approach for other explanations to be sought. An alternative (and more modest) approach is available. Instead of attacking concentrated situations *because they are concentrated*, it is

possible to attack those concentrated situations where *conduct* is found to result in the inefficient allocation of resources, and that conduct is directly traceable to the structure. There is, in the literature of competition policy, a good deal of evidence concerning objectionable practices by which firms have sought to gain, and then exploit, market power; and the links to industry structure are often quite clear.[53] Attacking structure through divestiture, having started from conduct, would then seem reasonable. Such an approach would apply to conglomerates as well as to horizontally and vertically merged firms. There is a strand in the American literature which argues that conglomerate mergers do not matter; but a conglomerate has almost unique scope for predatory pricing over a wide range of fields, and the *potential* for this may deter entry, unless an attack on all its fields simultaneously can be organised.[54] Conduct, therefore, is of central interest: if a conglomerate has a record of predatory pricing, then divestiture rather than regulation may be the appropriate path. Moreover, divestiture could well be more feasible with a conglomerate than with companies horizontally or vertically merged, because conglomerates typically have about them (at least in the UK) an aspect of a holding company rather than of an integrated business. In turn, the very fact of this power becoming established as a penalty for predatory pricing would produce a substantial deterrent.

The Mechanics of Divestiture

Divestiture proceedings, as carried out in practice, have attracted much academic criticism. An important early contribution was Adelman's discussion of the A&P case,[55] even though many of his criticisms were later met by Dirlam and Kahn.[56] While individual cases have necessarily attracted detailed discussion,[57] it is of more interest to note that several wide-ranging reviews of the entire history of divestiture proceedings in the United States have adopted both a critical and a pessimistic tone. A much cited early survey is that by Adams;[58] another recent, and highly effective, critic has been Elzinga, who has found that three-quarters of divestiture decrees were unsuccessful and that the delays have been farcical.[59] Another critic, Posner, reviewing the years 1890–1974, found that divestiture had only been a suitable remedy, in the view of the courts, in a small minority of cases and concluded, after reviewing these cases, that the divestiture measures had been ineffective.[60] There has also been an important general survey by Pfunder, Plaine and Whittemore[61] which was also distinguished by its suggestions, later followed by other writers, for remedying the situation.

Undoubtedly, when we examine the mechanics, there are formidable difficulties. Firstly, there is the question of delay.[62] Due to the reluctance of the courts to penalise firms subject to divestiture orders, and because of the interests of the firms themselves both in delay and in securing the highest possible price, there is a tendency to ask for a price at which no buyer can be found. The divestiture order thus becomes ineffective. Secondly, there is a problem over the choice of assets to be divested.[63] On the one hand, it is necessary to have an economically viable collection of assets to be sold; on the other hand, it may be very difficult to untangle these from an integrated firm and, in addition, the desire to avoid inflicting hardship on a divested firm biases competition policy officials in favour of minimal divestiture. In the case of mergers there is a clear choice between requiring firms to restore the status quo or limiting divestiture to the sale of those assets which offend the requirement of competition. In practice this 'partial divestiture' has proved very unsatisfactory.[64] The assets are not viable on their own.

Thirdly, there is a problem of finding a buyer;[65] there is always the difficulty that the most likely purchaser will be a close competitor in the same line of business. While this does not *necessarily* have an anti-competitive effect, it may well do so. Indeed, such a purchaser can afford to offer a higher price for the assets.

Since firms are usually entrusted by courts with implementing the divestiture themselves, they are in a prime position to obstruct the whole process,[66] particularly as the firm is possessed of information about both the industry and the assets which is not available to outsiders.[67] There are difficult choices to be made over the allocation of overhead staff, and of liquid assets, and concerning the accounting procedures to be used;[68] and in all these the firm opposed to its own divestiture is in the best possible strategic position. Moreover, the matter cannot be resolved by handing divestiture over to antitrust officials. Although Federal Trade Commission surveillance generates large quantities of paper, it seems to be very ineffective;[69] and it is a commonplace in the American literature that there are no incentives to antitrust officials to make divestiture work. Careers are advanced by winning cases, not by formulating good plans for relief.[70]

Despite these difficulties, however, there is no reason in principle why, given a different institutional structure, divestiture should not be possible. While it is perfectly true that unscrambling a financially integrated firm is difficult, the case of buy-outs and other voluntary divestments shows that such unscrambling is perfectly possible.[71] Information is of critical importance here; it is perfectly true that those contemplating a buyout have a peculiar combination of specialised information and incentive which is not available in a divestiture case. But the episode of the 1935 Public Utility Act in the United States shows that divestiture can still work under less uniquely favourable circumstances – a fundamental reorganisation of the gas and electricity supply industries, breaking up large companies, was extraordinarily successful.[72] In the field of competition policy various suggestions have been made for improving the mechanics, including the appointment of a 'divestment trustee'[73] (thus creating an official with an incentive to ensure that the job was done) and random assignment of shares in the different companies created by divestiture to the shareholders, in order to provide an incentive to divest so as to maximise the value of the reconstituted parts.[74] A greater role of administrative, as distinct from judicial, proceedings is also envisaged. There is no doubt that divestiture has been more successful in cases involving consent decrees;[75] and the early use of divestiture power (as a precondition of a merger) is also promising, not least because it provides an incentive for the company involved to cooperate.[76]

Divestiture as a Penalty

While there may be no particular capital market problems of divestiture,[77] it is frequently argued that divestiture necessarily involves penalising shareholders. The argument is usually put thus: if a monopoly has been enjoying its market power,[78] the shareholders will lose by the removal of that power; if they do not lose, then the monopoly was not enjoying its market power. In general the courts have accepted this argument and attempted to avoid penalty;[79] and those writers who envisage that this may be a real problem, but who otherwise favour divestiture, tend to take the view that the courts are over-solicitous, particularly as the courts do not show such solicitude in applying other parts of the antitrust legislation which also affect share values.[80]

However, measurement of the effects of divestiture on stock

prices does not always indicate that shareholders have lost.[81] While this is probably an econometric problem in part – too ready acceptance of a null hypothesis[82] – there are reasons for doubting that the penalty argument is necessarily correct anyway. In practice, it has been observed that parts of a large firm are typically worth more than the whole;[83] and it is perfectly possible for subsidiary parts of a large firm to be run inefficiently, involving welfare losses, and enjoying monopoly through a quiet life, while sheltered behind the entry barriers of an integrated business. Divestiture, by producing search and introducing profit-maximisation incentives, could perfectly well make the shareholders better off than before. The main penalty, and one which has received little attention in the literature,[84] is the *administrative* cost which may be imposed upon a company, absorbing profits and thus penalising shareholders, where a substantial divestiture is involved.

Divestiture in Britain

The power to order divestiture has been available in Britain since the 1965 Monopolies and Mergers Act and it is now enshrined in section 73 (and Schedule 8, part 2) of the 1973 Fair Trading Act. A divestiture order requires positive approval by both Houses of Parliament, and firms affected may petition the House of Lords.[85] The power has, however, rarely been used despite the frequency with which situations which would seem to merit its consideration have been identified by the Monopolies and Mergers Commission (MMC). These include the case of matches, where concentration was associated not with economies of scale but with exclusionary practices[86] – divestiture (not then available in law) was considered here but it was decided that it was impraticable,[87] British Oxygen (the MMC do not seem to have considered divestiture in this case but opted for regulation),[88] and beer.[89] In this latter case, vertical restrictions acted as a substantial barrier to entry but negotiations were left to the Department of Prices and Consumer Protection and, it transpires, very little has happened. In the case of the supply of asbestos, it was recognised that the main firm had set about acquiring its competitors and used vertical integration to squeeze out competition, but divestiture was held to be impracticable as the business had become integrated.[90] In the case of the supply of petrol, the Office of Fair Trading is supposed to keep the matter of vertical restrictions under review,[91] while in the case of rayon the MMC, which recognised that the scale economies argument, even where intangible scale economies were included, provided only a partial basis for Courtalds' position, nevertheless rejected divestiture as less cost-effective than a tariff reduction.[92]

It is particularly interesting, in the light of the disputes discussed in the first part of this essay, that the Commission has frequently identified vertical integration as a potent method of restricting competition. This was true in the case of beer, asbestos, rayon, matches, and industrial gases.[93]

This is perhaps unsurprising, given the very lax nature of British policy.[94] While section 7 of the Clayton Act has brought mergers under control in the United States, the same has not happened in the United Kingdom. If the deeply conservative British attitude to mergers is to continue, a power of divestiture is needed to cope with the problems subsequently manifested. The British approach has been the subject of comment both caustic and startled on the part of American writers. There is no room here to examine the details of the case, but there is little doubt that a number of episodes, especially during the late 1960s and the era of the Industrial Reorganisation Corporation, have left a legacy which makes the existence, and exercise, of a power of divestiture very desirable.[95]

It is rather ironic that while the Commission has been prepared to accept that scale economies could justify the acquisition of competitors,[96] and to have looked to regulation rather than to divestiture,[97] it should on one occasion have recommended divestiture before the power was available.[98] (Needless to say, the recommendation was not implemented.) However, there have been, more recently, signs of an increased willingness to use divestiture, at least under the very limited circumstances where a firm, contemplating merger, has already obtained a substantial shareholding in its intended acquisition. This occurred in the cases of Eurocanadian Shipholdings–Furness, Withy, and of Great Universal Stores–Empire Stores.[99] However, even this, it is understood, is limited by the necessity of requiring divestiture within six months of the shareholding becoming publicly known. Beyond this modest start the MMC seems reluctant to go; even partial divestiture, as a precondition of merger, does not seem to meet with its approval.[100]

Divestiture in the US: The Case of AT & T

The American Background

Divestiture is a longstanding remedy under American antitrust law. It was first introduced by the Sherman (monopolisation) Act of 1890; but it is provisions under the Clayton (merger) Act of 1914 which have been more frequently used.[101] One hundred and fourteen cases of divestiture have covered such industries as oil, tobacco, glucose, gunpowder, photographic equipment, harvesting machinery, aluminium, fruit, broadcasting, shoe machinery, films, and railway coaches.[102] A number of commentaries have discussed these[103] but none seems convinced that the divestiture measures have been particularly successful so far, although there are a number of respects in which this is clearly remediable. While it has not proved too difficult to achieve a measure of divestiture in the cases of industries involving large numbers of producing plants held together by financial control, and in vertical integration cases, the practical difficulties have proved almost insuperable in others.

However, in some cases the courts have gone to very considerable trouble to ensure the best possible conditions for divestiture to work. In the case of the Ford–Autolite divestiture, Ford was not allowed to make spark plugs for ten years; it was required to purchase half its requirements for the next five years from the divested competitor; it was not allowed to sell at less than the wholesale plug price to dealers; and it was not allowed to buy any other manufacturer of spark plugs for ten years.[104] More typically, however, the courts have been careful not to injure the divested firm and this may, as some commentators have suggested, account for the limited success of divestiture. At all events, its limited success to date did little to indicate that the largest company in the world would be broken up. Yet this, as we shall see, is what happened.

AT & T

American antitrust has a strong history of company regulation and AT & T – 'Bell Telephone' – was for a long time a closely regulated company. The regulation became ever more complex with rate control, separation of regulated and unregulated activities, and disputes concerning inter-connection of competitors.[105] The regulations produced their own distortions, including nationwide rate averaging despite the diverse cost of supplying services to America's telephone users.[106] The regulations ultimately became so shackling that they provided AT & T with an incentive to settle with the antitrust authorities through a consent decree; the antitrust authorities for their part had either been captured[107] or (in the case of the Federal Communications Commission) had given up trying to regulate AT & T effectively because of the virtual impossibility of obtaining adequate data.[108]

But the only alternative to regulation was to produce, somehow, an industrial structure which exposed AT & T to competition. This was a daunting task. Measured by assets AT & T, before divestiture, was the world's largest corporation with assets of $155bn,[109] 84 million customers, and employment of almost one million people and an annual revenue of about $65bn. Its assets exceeded the combined total for the three biggest companies (including General Motors) in the Fortune Industrial 500.[110]

AT & T had a long history of resisting regulation. When the regulators allowed limited competition to affect it, it reacted with political lobbying in favour of legislation to strengthen its monopoly position.[111] It used various devices to block the FCC attempts to allow competitors to attach their equipment to its common carrier service, including requiring customers of other firms to use 'interface devices' between the equipment and its own.[112] There are striking parallels between the resistance of AT & T to any liberalisation and the resistance manifested in the United Kingdom by British Telecom. Indeed, it is instructive that divestiture has also been suggested in the case of British Telecom.[113]

AT & T showed classic signs of organisational slack,[114] although this was turned to great public benefit in a way unusual for monopolies with the financing of research and academic publication, resulting in seven Nobel prizes.

Under the framework of regulation, AT & T was encouraged to engage in cross-subsidisation so as to load its monopoly with costs which really belonged in the more competitive equipment sector, thus keeping the rate of monopoly return down to a level acceptable to the regulators.[115] This encouraged it to use cross-subsidisation of equipment as a barrier to entry.[116] There is no economic case for such cross-subsidisation because the cost of providing hand-sets to consumers is independent of the use made of long-distance calls.[117] But AT & T argued in turn that it needed a monopoly of equipment sales in order to obtain large profits on business sales which it could then use to subsidise private domestic consumers.[118] Not surprisingly, this was interpreted as a device to protect its competitive position.

Nevertheless AT & T, as already indicated, was not happy with the regulations experienced. For one thing, it was excluded from certain areas of business such as computers; for another, its dominance hindered its introduction of new equipment. Competitors could claim that the introduction was predatory, and then copy the device during the ensuing delay.[119] Thirdly, the need to maintain spares for the entire nation's telephone system imposed enormous equipment storage costs on AT & T.[120]

Nonetheless, despite these irritants, it is unlikely that AT & T would have agreed to a consent decree had it not been that, from the late 1950s onwards, the FCC began chipping away at its monopoly. For without these erosions, the monopoly was a very strong one. It was a vertical restriction on entry of the most complete sort. The business was integrated from basic research, through equipment manufacture, through local telephone companies, to the long-distance service.

Erosion of this comfortable position began in 1959 when the FCC allowed the use of radio waves for microwave communications. This led to a gradual erosion of the AT & T monopoly in long-distance communication. The equipment monopoly was gradually whittled away from the late 1960s and the FCC introduced an equipment registration programme (note that, in contrast to the British case, equipment registration was not operated by AT & T) so that an important entry barrier was removed. Then the long-distance monopoly began to give way under competition from Microwave Communications, who moved first of all, with FCC approval, into private-line long-distance services and then into ordinary long-distance service. At the same time AT & T was excluded from telecommunications satellites, while from 1972 competitors were allowed into this field.[121] By 1980 a situation had arisen as a result of market forces, technical change, the courts and the FCC, which made divestiture of this once apparently impregnable natural monopoly a possibility. But it has to be said that, whether because of the superiority of regulation to nationalisation[122] or, partly at least, because of the chipping away of the AT & T monopoly, the American telephone system was (and is) the best in the world by a substantial margin. The competitive structure created by divestiture has, then, to offer substantial benefits by way of competitive pressure if the divestiture is to yield benefits, let alone a surplus of benefit over cost.

The new structure, arrived at via a consent decree, under which agreement is reached between the company and the antitrust authorities without a court decision (thus avoiding many of the pitfalls of a purely judicial settlement), involved dividing AT & T into eight separate companies. Twenty-two local telephone companies were spun off from the main company which was left with assets of 'only' $43bn. These 22 companies are reorganised into 7 regional holding companies. The rump of the old AT & T is made up of the long lines, the Western Electric manufacturing company, Bell Laboratories, American Bell (making user equipment as distinct from telephone company equipment which is the province of Western) and AT & T International to deal with overseas sales of equipment. A shareholder with 10 old AT & T shares obtains 10 shares of the new rump of AT & T and 7 shares in addition, one for each of the 7 regional companies. The half million or so AT & T shareholders with less than 10 shares did not receive shares in the regionals but cash instead; a similar share-splitting arrangement occurred in the demerger at Bowater (see Chapter 3).

The companies thus created are still extremely large. The rump of AT & T would still top *Fortune's* list of utilities and the remaining 7 regional companies would occupy places 3 to 9. The scale of the operation is enormous. The 3.2 million shareholders with over 950 million shares have had their holdings reorganised.[123]

The local companies retain their (regulated) local monopolies; long-distance calls and consumer premises equipment are now competitive. AT & T will no longer have a preferred access to the local exchanges, and cross-subsidisation will be minimised.[124] The incentive, which existed under regulation, to cross-subsidise is removed except for AT & T purchases from Western Electric.[125]

The reorganisation is based upon the essential perception that while a local company may be a natural monopoly – though even this is likely to be eroded by further technical advance – long lines and equipment are not.

In return for consenting to all this, AT & T is now to be allowed to compete with IBM in the computer market – thereby perhaps contributing to the solution of American antitrust's other long-standing problem. AT & T had been kept out of the computer market by a 1956 consent decree, and a desire to enter the market is widely judged to have been an incentive to settle with the divestiture consent decree.[126] It should be a powerful competitor, not only because of its size and proven research record but also because the patent licensing compuision which the regulation regime involved for AT & T, which meant that the company effectively supplied technical information to the world, has been removed.[127]

However, AT & T is still subject to a good deal of regulation.[128] It is envisaged that regulation may be necessary because AT & T is still dominant in long-distance calls and the supply of equipment. It has the capacity for predatory pricing. Limit pricing on the basis of economies of scale may yield funds for predation. Whether this is a real danger remains to be seen. It seems unlikely that AT & T would risk further antitrust action. The seven 'local' companies also know that they risk antitrust prosecution if they use the proceeds of their local monopolies to subsidise equipment sales.[129]

Not only does the continuance of limited regulation impose costs on AT & T but there is also the vexed question of the so-called 'access charges'.[130] The access charges are in fact charges levied on both the telephone user and the long-distance line owner and paid to the local company. In the past the long-distance line, owned by AT & T, subsidised the local company – also owned by AT & T – in order to keep the rate of return on long-distance lines to a regulated level. Under the new arrangements this burden will gradually be withdrawn as the access charge paid by the long-distance line owner will be reduced and the burden of paying for the local telephone company will be borne by the local telephone user. In order to impose a gentle transition, however, a substantial part of the burden is initially to fall upon the long lines. At present the bulk of the burden is falling on AT & T which is reported to be paying $17bn. out of a total revenue of $26.4bn. back to local companies. AT & T in fact faces a differentially high access charge – to the extent of 55 per cent higher than other companies. Now the distant day on which the burden will be transferred to local users has been deferred further as a result of political lobbying.[131] In the meantime, AT & T is forced to pay the very substantial cost of implementation of divestiture.[132]

The company is also having to learn to compete in a new world. This, for all its employees, is a new experience.[133] It has also had to learn to engage in increased market search for new selling opportunities and for new uses for existing equipment.[134]

It is difficult to know what outcome to forecast once these transitional phases are passed.[135] On the face of it the new structure of the industry is calculated greatly to intensify competition, particularly since AT & T's competitive conduct is subject to officially imposed handicaps. Several companies – MCI, South Pacific, and ITT – are reported to charge as little as half AT & T's long-distance charges. Rivals are expanding very fast with annual rates of 50 per cent reported. There are 14 rival carriers to AT & T. Local telephone users have a choice of long-distance services and in some areas of activity AT & T has only a minority market share.[136] The company itself reports that it is facing strong competition and that its main competitors are already doing a lot of business with the big telephone users while 70 per cent of microwave transmission routes are owned by its rivals. In addition to this, big companies such as Westinghouse are beginning to build their own communications network.[137] Against all the expectations of those brought up in the British 'natural monopoly' tradition, it does look as if this particular divestiture may work. But this is partly because of fortuitous technical changes – such as the switch from electro-mechanical to electronic operation which reduces minimum efficient scale substantially – which are themselves only recent developments.[138] Nevertheless, the slow rate of introduction of these technical advances in countries other than the United States does indicate that there is nothing inevitable about the outbreak of competition based on new technology in telecommunications; and the divestiture of AT & T remains a remarkably bold step both on the part of the regulatory and antitrust authorities and, let it not be forgotten, on the part of the company.

Conclusion

The AT & T case, coming on top of long-term American experience with divestiture, shows that divestiture itself is a practical possibility even if the AT & T case itself is astonishing in its boldness. It is also clear that capital markets can cope with divestiture, even on the largest scale, and it seems that shareholders by no means necessarily suffer as a result of divestiture.

Moreover, there clearly is a case for the implementation of divestiture under certain circumstances. A number of defects in the root and branch criticism of divestiture have been discussed above. In addition, a number of other issues are implicit in the critical discussion and need emphasis here. In particular, the need for search, both internal and external, is neglected because it relies on a background of models in which perfect information is implicitly assumed.[139] It neglects the interaction between competitive pressure and search which may be vital in securing technical advances. It neglects the importance of vertical integration as a barrier to entry although this is starkly illustrated in the AT & T case. Nevertheless, the Chicago writers have correctly stemmed the advance of the blanket approach to divestiture which was foreshadowed in the Neal Report and embodied in the Hart Bill. Structure on its own is an unsatisfactory point of departure. In the AT & T case itself it was the conduct of the company, engaging in cross-subsidisation, regulatory evasion, and the employment of devices to exclude competitors at every stage of its business, which justified a reorganisation of its structure.

The question remains, however, whether the benefits of divestiture are likely to be greater than the costs, as well as the related question of whether the margin of benefits over costs is greater for this policy than for alternatives. With regard to the first question there are, as already noted, divergent views based upon American experience. Elzinga and Breit think it unlikely that benefits will exceed costs while Turner takes the opposite view and indeed advocates a wide-ranging attack on concentrated situations on purely structural grounds.[140] This seems a difficult position to defend, in the light of the evidence adduced by Elzinga and others. British, as well as American, competition policy already involves regulation of conduct; and it seems reasonable to argue that such regulation would itself work better if divestiture were clearly available as a reserve power which could be used in the event of regulation failing – as it failed in the case of AT & T.[141] A divestiture approach which starts from conduct does at least offer the prospect of net gain. Moreover, in a British context, with a merger policy which has always been remarkably permissive, and which is reported to be slackening further,[142] it seems highly likely that situations in which net benefit would flow from divestiture are to be found. As an American critic has remarked of one particular example of the operation of British merger policy:

> Two firms that equally split ninety per cent of the . . . market were allowed to merge without any substantial showing of efficiency gains or other public benefits.[143]

To put it mildly, even the most vociferous anti-antitrust Chicago critic would be unlikely to consider condoning such a state of affairs. The structure of industry which has been created in Britain in this way makes the retention of a divestiture power all the more necessary since, even without relying upon concentration ratios (and most of the criticisms of concentration ratio data actually boil down to the well-known fact that a point observation provides a lot less information than a (concentration) curve), *conduct* considerations are likely to manifest themselves; and though it is clearly envisaged that conduct may be *regulated* (via the Office of Fair Trading, the Monopolies and Mergers Commission, and the concept of anti-competitive practices), there is no reason why modification of the structure which produces the conduct should be ruled out.

In turn, and given this widely recognised interdependence between merger policy and divestiture,[144] the use of divestiture in Britain should concentrate on undoing mergers rather than upon breaking up companies which have achieved their present position through internal expansion. This, by simplifying divestiture, would not only increase the chance that the benefits would be greater than the costs, but would also help to tilt the balance towards internal expansion as against capturing one's competitors through purchase.

Divestiture would normally aim for restoration of the status quo[145] (rather than for speculative hiving off of those parts of the acquired business which were held to offend against competitive requirements) and it would thus bypass the problems over finding a buyer (since the previously independent company would again be restored to independence) and of asset selection.

Such an approach would thus make the policy available to deal with conglomerates. While conglomerate mergers may, or may not, have adverse effects on small firms in the same industry (and the potential for predatory pricing is always there, albeit having temporarily fallen out of academic fashion), they *do* obscure information and interfere with efficient capital market functioning which they only replace partially with divisional structure. This does not mean that conglomerates should be attacked on structural grounds; only that conglomerate conduct should be as open to inspection, and to the possible remedy of divestiture, as that of other large firms.

The remaining question is whether or not, where benefits of divestiture exceed costs, the margin of benefit over cost is likely to be greater than that obtained by using other remedies. While no general answer to this is possible, it seems likely that a great deal depends upon the institutional structure. If divestiture proceedings become bogged down in legalities – and the British legislation offers even the possibility of appeal to the House of Lords – then it seems likely that other more cost-effective remedies will be found. American experience, in which antitrust is perhaps unduly hampered by legalities,[146] shows that, because of the importance of speed in making divestiture work, a judicial system offering endless possibilities of delay can render the policy nugatory. Elzinga records a case in which:

> In the trial records of that case, pages 11 through 1649 are consumed by pre-trial jockeying for position, correspondence for extensions, pre-trial conferences, re-setting of trial dates, admissibility of evidence questions, etc. These tactics ran out over three years of the judicial clock.[147]

As another commentator has pointed out, adversarial gambits can sink antitrust, and divestiture proceedings are particularly vulnerable.[148] The fact that divestiture proceedings have had much better results in consent cases is not an accident. Though the MMC is frequently accused of delay, its delays are as nothing compared with delays in the judicial process when dealing with the large companies like AT & T and IBM.[149] A primarily administrative approach to divestiture, coupled with appeal to the Restrictive Practices Court, would seem to offer the prospect of relatively speedy and effective remedy.

Moreover, the availability of a divestiture power, and a demonstrated willingness to use such a power, on the basis of conduct derived from structure, would have a salutary effect on the misuse of market power. Not only is it the case that the possibility of competition policy proceedings being taken out is itself salutary, since firms would wish to come to the MMC with clean hands, but there is also the importance of 'demonstration effects'. As the authors of an empirical survey of price fixing conspiracies have observed:

> The demonstration effect of moving for dissolution or divestiture in a price fixing case should not be overlooked.[150]

Such 'demonstration effects' proved powerful in the history of the operation of the 1956 Restrictive Trade Practices Act in Britain; and it seems likely that if divestiture were used seriously in British competition policy, the benefits, once account was taken of those external to a particular case, would far outweigh the costs.

Notes

*I am extremely grateful to Peter Johnson, Steve Littlechild, Valentine Korah, Joel Dirlam and Mike Flemming for helpful comments on an earlier draft of this paper.

1. Elzinga and Breit (1976), pp. 44–45; Wilcox and Shepherd (1975), p. 131n.
2. Blake and Jones (1965a), pp. 377–79; Edwards (1975), p. 344 notes that in the 1920s corporatism led to a weakening of antitrust policy; Greer (1975); O'Connor (1976).
3. In Britain, the experience of the bread industry is instructive in this respect. See Reekie (1978).
4. Kaysen and Turner (1959), especially pp. 46, 48, 93, 114, 124, 126, 141, 268–9.
5. See the responses of Baldwin, Costello, Leonard, Mann, Farmer and White in Baldwin *et al.* (1968); Edwards (1975); *Columbia Law Review* (1973); Samuels (1975).
6. There is a most useful account of this episode in Scherer (1980), p. 542. It should be emphasised, however, that the approach was purely structural; for instance, the Neal Report proposed that in *any* industry with sales of $500m and a four-firm concentration ratio of 70 per cent, divestiture proceedings should be undertaken to reduce individual market shares to a maximum of 12 per cent. See Brozen (1970), p. 279.
7. See the references to Blair and Scherer cited by Elzinga and Breit (1976), p. 104. See also Swann, O'Brien, Mander and Howe (1974), Ch. 3.
8. Turner (1969), p. 1230. However, Turner believed that minimum efficient scale should have priority when considering the restructuring of firms (p. 1216).
9. Hay and Kelley (1974).

10. A nice sample of the present situation can be obtained by reading the contributions of Weiss (1979); Liebeler (1979); Phillips (1979).
11. C.E. Mueller (1968) pp. 88–89.
12. Stocking and W.F. Mueller (1955); Elzinga and Hogarty (1973); Elzinga and Breit (1976), p. 107; Fisher, McGowan and Greenwood (1983), Ch. 3.
13. An excellent survey of the relevant literature is contained in Pautler (1983).
14. Pautler (1983), p. 650.
15. For example, Elzinga and Breit (1976), pp. 103–4, 108; Fisher, McGowan and Greenwood (1983), Ch. 7. For a list of such critics see Pautler (1983), p. 580n. 22.
16. Again Pautler (1983), pp. 615–37, and Scherer (1980), Ch. 9, provide valuable summaries of the debate.
17. Hexter and Snow (1974), p. 402. This article also has a useful discussion of the idea of supplementing concentration ratio data with 'entropy' as a measure of size inequality.
18. Neale and Goyder (1980), p. 404.
19. Neale and Goyder (1980), pp. 452–3.
20. Williamson (1979a), p. 918.
21. Bork and Bowman (1965); but see Blake and Jones (1965a), pp. 395–7.
22. Blake and Jones (1965b), pp. 422–3; Edwards (1975); Samuels (1975), p. 388, is not clear why economies of scale should override the need for competition.
23. The critical literature, excellently surveyed by Pautler (1983), has succeeded in casting sufficient doubt upon a purely structural approach (and in fact the relationship between concentration and profitability was never as clear as some writers, especially lawyers, suggested, particularly in the UK) as to affect seriously its credibility.
24. Whitney (1964).
25. Bork and Bowman (1965), p. 363.
26. *Ibid.* p. 366; Posner (1979).
27. Bork and Bowman (1965), p. 368.
28. Ornstein (1981).
29. See especially Brozen (1970), (1971).
30. See Spence (1983) for a useful summary of the 'contestable markets' literature.
31. See the exchanges between Areeda and Turner (1974–5, 1976) and Scherer (1976 a, b).
32. Posner (1979), p. 927.

33. Williamson (1968a, b); Elzinga and Breit (1976), pp. 100–1. Williamson (1979b) apparently accepts that vertical restrictions are influenced by transactions cost economies.
34. Williamson (1968a), p. 24; it is unfortunate that Williamson's carefully thought-out qualifications have been ignored in much of the subsequent literature.
35. Elzinga and Breit (1976), p. 105; see also Coyne and Wright (1984a) on the question of the need to internalise transactions.
36. Blake and Jones (1965a), p. 389.
37. Blake and Jones (1965b), pp. 441, 462–4. In particular, lenders may consider that risk increases to an unacceptable level if an entire vertical chain has to be duplicated.
38. Williamson (1979a).
39. See Wasserstein (1972–3), p. 678, and references therein.
40. Litman (1980) sees network-owned broadcasting stations as captive outlets which do not search; see also Williamson (1979b) – his reference to 'comparison shopping' implicitly recognises the point about search costs which are increased by vertical restrictions.
41. Blake and Jones (1965b), p. 427.
42. Blake and Jones (1965a), pp. 385, 399.
43. Landes and Posner (1981), especially p. 942; Bauer (1941).
44. Schmalensee (1982); Kaplow (1982); Brennan (1982); Ordover *et al.* (1982).
45. Blake and Jones (1965a), p. 399.
46. Wenders (1971), especially pp. 485, 487.
47. Pautler (1983), pp. 615–624.
48. Bond and Greenberg cited in Pautler (1983), p. 608.
49. Sherman and Tollison (1971); Green Paper (1978).
50. Because of the development of organisational slack. See Elzinga and Breit (1976), p. 103.
51. Williamson (1968b); Ross (1968).
52. Blake and Jones (1965a), pp. 395–7; (1965b), p. 459.
53. See especially Pass and Sparkes (1980).
54. See Besen and Woodbury (1983) for the literature of predatory pricing. See also Schmalensee (1979). On conglomerates more generally see Areeda and Turner (1979) and Arndt (1972) p. 1113.
55. Adelman (1949).
56. Dirlam and Kahn (1953, 1954). See, however, Adelman (1959), especially pp. 526–30.
57. See also Zelenitz (1980) for criticism of another divestiture case. Details of the Ford–Autolite case are in Neale and Goyder (1980), p. 406.

58. Adams (1951).
59. Elzinga (1969); Elzinga and Breit (1976), especially pp. 46, 53. See also Baldwin (1972–3) and Elzinga and Hogarty (1973).
60. Posner (1976), pp. 84–8. Posner notes that in the years 1890–1974 divestiture was ordered in only 24 out of 118 decided monopolisation cases and is satisfied from his examination of the history of these cases that the measure proved ineffective.
61. Pfunder, Plaine and Whittemore (1972) (hereafter PP&W 1972). Baldwin (1972–3), pp. 110, 115, adopts the ideas of a divestment trustee and the giving of priority to the creation of new competitive entities.
62. Elzinga (1969); PP&W (1972), pp. 85ff, 105–6; Posner (1976), p. 88.
63. Elzinga (1969); Elzinga and Breit (1976) p. 51; PP&W (1972), pp. 54–62, 70–2. While such difficulties can certainly be genuine, it is as well to bear in mind the comment that 'Any industrial behemoth can always produce six good reasons why it cannot be split in half', *Economist*, 15 October 1983, p. 35, referring to British Telecom.
64. Elzinga and Breit (1976), p. 53; Elzinga (1969); Martin (1963), p. 350.
65. Elzinga (1969); Elzinga and Breit (1976), pp. 51, 53; PP&W (1972), pp. 38–40, 45–54.
66. Elzinga (1969), pp. 64–5; PP&W, pp. 82–5. The latter note that, of eight cases of non-compliance, six had fair price provisions in the order.
67. On the problem of asymmetric information, see Chiplin and Wright (1983). On the problem in relation to divestiture, see PP&W (1972), pp. 95–7, 107. On viability see Elzinga (1969), p. 45.
68. Elzinga and Breit (1976), p. 52. See also Posner (1976), p. 90.
69. On surveillance see PP&W (1972), pp. 19, 40.
70. Adams (1951), p. 33; Elzinga and Breit (1976), p. 51; Posner (1976), pp. 88–9.
71. On sources of finance, see Coyne and Wright (1982), p. 25; though this relates to buyouts, it is not irrelevant to the question of raising funds for divestiture. The number of buyouts reported in Coyne and Wright (1984b), 650 in 1977–83, also suggests that divestiture is perfectly feasible given the right circumstances. On voluntary divestments, see Chiplin and Wright (1983).
72. See Brodley (1975), pp. 368–9; Wilcox and Shepherd (1975) pp. 401–3.
73. PP&W (1972), pp. 130–3.
74. Baldwin (1972–3).

75. PP&W (1972), p. 112, point out that more than half of all section 7 (Clayton Act) cases which resulted in a divestiture decree were the product of consent. See also Flynn (1968) and Goldberg (1962). On the particular AT&T consent decree, see *Economist*, 16 January 1982, pp. 40–1.
76. The FTC required Texaco to sell two refineries and nearly all of Getty's petrol stations, as the price of agreeing to the takeover of Getty – *Economist*, 17 March 1984, p. 64.
77. Whitehead (1983) explores some of the capital market problems of the sale of British Telecom. See also *Economist*, 21 July 1984, pp. 76–7.
78. Dewey (1955) seems to be the origin of this idea which has been widely repeated by other writers. See also Elzinga and Breit (1976), pp. 48–9.
79. PP&W (1972) p. 96; Neale and Goyder (1980), p. 405.
80. PP&W (1972), p. 130. 'A remedy which causes injury or inconvenience to a defendant should be construed as a penalty only where there is available an equally effective method for obtaining relief which would cause less injury.' See also Adams (1978) for a similarly robust view, and Burns (1983). Note that this is also an issue which arises on demerger.
81. Ellert (1976); Burns (1977).
82. Brown and Warner (1980); Wier (1983); see also Jain (1982).
83. Main (1983), p. 67. 'In the typical breakup, the pieces become worth more on the market than the original whole.'
84. See, however, Elzinga and Breit (1976), pp. 97–9.
85. On the legislative position, see Korah (1975), especially pp. 32–6. The possibilities of judicial delay mean, in effect, that the more powerful the monopoly, and thus the deeper its pocket, the greater the opportunity to enjoy the market power over a long period.
86. Monopolies Commission (1953), pp. 86–89. See also Korah (1975), p. 55.
87. Monopolies Commission (1953), p. 90. Even the minority addendum to the report, signed by both G.C. Allen and Joan Robinson, agreed that divestiture was not practicable.
88. Monopolies Commission (1956), pp. 12–20. See also Korah (1975), p. 54.
89. For comment on this case, see Kintner, Joelson and Griffin (1974), p. 240.
90. Monopolies Commission (1973), pp. 117–119, 124.
91. Monopolies Commission (1979), pp. 54–6.

92. Monopolies Commission (1968), especially pp. 62, 79.
93. Kintner, Joelson and Griffin (1974); Monopolies Commission (1973), especially p. 123; Monopolies Commission (1979), p. 55; Monopolies Commission (1968), p. 84. 'At present, through its control of companies dealing in certain chemicals used in the manufacture of matches . . . BMC is able to secure that its competitors are charged for these materials up to 77 per cent more than the companies of the BMC group.' Monopolies Commission (1953), p. 85, and see also p. 89. 'BOC has a substantial measure of control over the provision of plant and machinery for the production of goods which the monopoly itself sells' – Monopolies Commission (1956), p. 91.
94. Howe (1972). See Colenutt and O'Donnell (1978): in the years 1969–77, 18 mergers were reported on by the MMC and another 23 were referred to it but later abandoned. In that time the merger panel, a small group of senior civil servants, examined more than 1,000 mergers.
95. See in particular Wasserstein (1972–3), pp. 658, 666–7, 671, 673, 675–7. This important article seems, unfortunately, to have received very little attention. See also Kintner, Joelson and Griffin (1974), pp. 244–5.
96. See Korah (1975), p. 55.
97. See Pass and Sparkes (1980), pp. 466–8. See also Monopolies Commission (1956), p. 101; Kintner, Joelson and Griffin (1974), p. 240.
98. Monopolies Commission (1961), pp. 183, 193, 307, 213; see also Korah (1975), p. 55. The case was that of Imperial Tobacco and Gallagher. The case itself may have led to the subsequent legislative change, as Dr V. Korah has pointed out to me.
99. Monopolies Commission (1976), p. 51, (1983) p. 36.
100. Monopolies Commission (1983b), pp. 75, 85.
101. O'Connor (1976), pp. 696–7.
102. Adams (1951) contains a good review of American cases up to 1950. Adams points out that divestiture came to a virtual halt in the US in the years 1927–37.
103. PP&W (1972), pp. 34–7; Hale (1940); Moyer (1979); see also Ornstein (1981); Zelenitz (1980). Kotke (1978) contains a detailed history of a number of cases. The most comprehensive discussion is in Neale and Goyder (1980), especially pp. 396–411.
104. Neale and Goyder (1980), p. 406.
105. Besen and Woodbury (1983), pp. 57–66.
106. *Ibid*, p. 65. See also Mirucki (1984) for tentative support for the Averch–Johnson hypothesis in the case of Canadian Bell.
107. [Stewart] (1977), p. 550.
108. Besen and Woodbury (1983), pp. 46–7; *Economist*, 23 April 1983, p. 17.

109. O'Reilly (1983), p. 62; *Time* (1983).
110. de Jonquieres and Betts (1983).
111. *Business Week* (1976).
112. Besen and Woodbury (1983), pp. 42–4; [Stewart] (1977), pp. 538–40.
113. See *Economist*, 15 October 1983, p. 35.
114. Kahn (1984), p. 25.
115. Besen and Woodbury (1983), pp. 44–6 and n.
116. [Stewart] (1977), pp. 538–50.
117. Kahn (1984). Long-distance calls are of particular relevance here since, with costs falling faster than prices, long-distance revenues have been a major source of subsidy. There is an excellent discussion of cross-subsidisation in Johnson (1982).
118. Besen and Woodbury (1983), p. 43.
119. *Ibid*, p. 65.
120. Uttal (1983), p. 84.
121. Baker and Baker (1983); Besen and Woodbury (1983); [Stewart] (1977).
122. The FCC decisions are, of course, subject to legal appeal – see, for example, Besen and Woodbury (1983), pp. 48–9.
123. O'Reilly (1983); Loomis (1983); Main (1983).
124. See Baker and Baker (1983), pp. 7 ff. for details.
125. de Jonquieres and Betts (1983).
126. Besen and Woodbury (1983), p. 50; *Economist*, 10 December 1983, p. 61; 16 January 1982, p. 83.
127. Bylinsky (1983).
128. Loomis (1983), p. 73; Uttal (1983), p. 82; Besen and Woodbury (1983), pp. 49, 56–66.
129. O'Reilly (1983), p. 65; *Economist*, 5 May 1984, pp. 65–6.
130. *Ibid*. and Loomis (1983), p. 73.
131. Taylor (1983); *Economist*, 5 May 1984, p. 65. For an example of the political opposition to the settlement, see Dingell, Nulty and McCarthy (1984).
132. Main (1983), p. 72.
133. O'Reilly (1983), p. 62; Uttal (1983); Tully (1983).
134. O'Reilly (1983), p. 67.
135. According to *Economist*, 28 May 1983, p. 73, Moody's removed the triple. A credit rating from the divested part of AT&T while Standard and Poor's retained the triple A rating.
136. de Jonquieres (1983); *Economist*, 5 May 1984, p. 65; de Jonquieres and Betts (1983).
137. *Economist*, 5 May 1984, pp. 65–6; Kahn (1984) discusses the question of the distributive effects of lowering long-distance charges.
138. Uttal (1983), p. 82.

139. See also Nelson (1979).
140. Elzinga and Breit (1976); Turner (1969).
141. See Neale and Goyder (1980), p. 455, on the value of antitrust legislation as a reserve power.
142. *Economist*, 7 July 1984, p. 72.
143. Wasserstein (1972–3), p. 671. See also Kintner, Joelson and Griffin (1974), p. 244.
144. Turner (1969), p. 1214; Kaysen and Turner (1959), p. 141.
145. See PP&W (1972), pp. 63–4.
146. See Scherer (1976b) for the implication that US antitrust is unduly hampered by legalism.
147. Elzinga (1969), p. 73. The case was the Crown Zellerbach Case (Case No: 16-TTC).
148. Brodley (1975), p. 366.
149. See Fisher, McGowan and Greenwood (1983). It is instructive to compare the handling of proceedings against IBM in the United States with those by the European Commission – *Economist*, 30 June 1984, pp. 57–8.
150. Hay and Kelley (1974), p. 28.

References

Adams, J.W. (1978) 'Trustbusting and the 'innocent' shareholder: 'compensation' if stock prices fall?', *Antitrust Law and Economics Review*, 10, pp. 51–65.

Adams, W. (1951) 'Dissolution, divorcement, divestiture: the pyrrhic victories of antitrust', *Indiana Law Journal*, 27, pp. 1–37.

Adelman, M.A. (1949) 'The A&P case: a study in applied economic theory', *Quarterly Journal of Economics*, 63, pp. 238–57.

Adelman, M.A. (1959) *A&P. A Study in Price–Cost Behaviour and Public Policy*, Harvard University Press.

Areeda, P. and Turner, D.F. (1974–5) 'Predatory pricing and related practices under Section 2 of the Sherman Act', *Harvard Law Review*, 88, pp. 697–733.

Areeda, P. and Turner, D.F. (1976) 'Scherer on predatory pricing: a reply', *Harvard Law Review*, 89, pp. 891–900.

Areeda, P. and Turner, D.F. (1979) 'Conglomerate mergers: extended interdependence and effects on interindustry competition as grounds for condemnation', *University of Pennsylvania Law Review*, 127, pp. 1082–1103.

Arndt, H. (1972) 'Basic problems of concentration policy', *Antitrust Bulletin*, 17, pp. 1107–1124.

Baker, D.I. and Baker, B.G. (1983) 'Antitrust and communications deregulation', *Antitrust Bulletin*, 28, pp. 1–38.

Baldwin, W.L. *et al.* (1968) 'Priorities in antitrust: some communications', *Antitrust Law and Economics Review*, 2, pp. 11–40.

Baldwin, W.L. (1972–3) 'Selective divestiture by spin-off and lottery: a modest proposal', *Antitrust Law and Economics Review*, 6, pp. 107–19.

Bauer, P.T. (1941) 'A note on monopoly', *Economica*, 8, pp. 194–202.

Besen, S.M. and Woodbury, J.R. (1983) 'Regulation, deregulation, and antitrust in the Telecommunications Industry', *Antitrust Bulletin*, 28, pp. 39–68.

Blake, H.M. and Jones, W.K. (1965a) 'In defense of antitrust', *Columbia Law Review*, 65, pp. 377–400.

Blake, H.M. and Jones, W.K. (1965b) 'Toward a three-dimensional antitrust policy', *Columbia Law Review*, 65, pp. 422–66.

Bork, R.H. and Bowman, W.S. (1965) 'The crisis in antitrust', *Columbia Law Review*, 65, pp. 363–76.

Brennan, T.J. (1982) 'Mistaken elasticities and misleading rules', *Harvard Law Review*, 95, pp. 1849–56.

Brodley, J.F. (1975) 'Industrial deconcentration and legal feasibility: the efficiencies defense', *Journal of Economic Issues*, 9, pp. 365–80.

Brown, S.J. and Warner, J.B. (1980) 'Measuring security price performance', *Journal of Financial Economics*, 8, pp. 205–58.

Brozen, Y. (1970) 'The antitrust task force deconcentration recommendation', *Journal of Law and Economics*, 13, pp. 279–92.

Brozen, Y. (1971) 'Deconcentration reconsidered: Comment', *Journal of Law and Economics*, 14, pp. 489–91.

Burns, M.R. (1977) 'The competitive effects of trust-busting: portfolio analysis', *Journal of Political Economy*, 85, pp. 717–39.

Burns, M.R. (1983) 'An empirical analysis of stockholder injury under S2 of the Sherman Act', *Journal of Industrial Economics*, 31, pp. 333–62.

Business Week (1976) 'AT&T's bold bid to stifle competitors', 15 March, pp. 82–8.

Bylinsky, G. (1983) 'Can Bell Labs keep it up?', *Fortune* 107, No. 3, pp. 90–1.

Chiplin, B. and Wright, D.M. (1983) 'Merger activity and sales of subsidiaries between company groups: a note', University of Nottingham, Dept. of Industrial Economics, mimeo.

Colenutt, D.W. and O'Donnell, P.P. (1978) 'The consistency of Monopolies and Mergers Commission's merger reports', *Antitrust Bulletin*, 23, pp. 51–82.

Columbia Law Review (1973) 'The Industrial Reorganisation Act: antitrust proposal to restructure the American economy' 73 pp. 635–76.

Coyne, J. and Wright, D.M. (1982) 'Buy-outs and British industry', *Lloyds Bank Review*, No. 146, pp. 15–31.

Coyne, J. and Wright, D.M. (1984a) 'Staff buyouts and the privatisation of nationalised industries', University of Nottingham, Dept. of Industrial Economics, Discussion Paper No. 80.
Coyne, J. and Wright, D.M. (1984b) 'Shake-outs that can mean job security', *Guardian*, 17 January 1984.
de Jonquieres, G. (1983) 'We'll talk to anyone who has a better mousetrap', *Financial Times*, 24 January, p. 12.
de Jonquieres, G. and Betts, P. (1983) 'America's communications revolution', *Financial Times*.
Dewey, D.F. (1955) 'Romance and realism in antitrust policy', *Journal of Political Economy*, 63, pp. 93–102.
Dingell, J.E., Nulty, T.E., McCarthy, M. (1984) 'Or a free ride for AT&T', *Challenge*, March–April, pp. 30–33.
Dirlam, J.B. and Kahn, A.E. (1953) 'Integration and dissolution of the A&P Company', *Indiana Law Journal*, 29, pp. 1–27.
Dirlam, J.B. and Kahn, A.E. (1954) *Fair Competition. The Law and Economics of Antitrust Policy*; reprinted in 1970, Greenwood Press.
Economist (1982a) 'Stripping Ma Bell', 16 January, pp. 11–13.
Economist (1982b) 'Breaking up is hard to do?', 16 January, pp. 40–1.
Economist (1982c) 'Can AT&T really beat IBM at its own game?', 16 January, pp. 83–4.
Economist (1983a) 'The escaping giant', 23 April, pp. 16–17.
Economist (1983b) 'Ma Bell goes into labour', 28 May, pp. 73–4.
Economist (1983c) 'Gone with the Bell', 23 July, pp. 36–37.
Economist (1983d) 'Buy a telephone, save money', 3 September, p. 27.
Economist (1983e) 'Big Brother?', 15 October, p. 35.
Economist (1983f) 'Trusting the markets more and the trustbusters less', 10 December, pp. 61–2.
Economist (1984a) 'Nobody here but us chickens', 17 March, p. 64.
Economist (1984b) 'What it was always going to be about', 31 March, p. 69.
Economist (1984c) 'Crackles on America's once Bell-clear telephone lines', 5 May, pp. 65–6.
Economist (1984d) 'A chance for IBM's antitrust knight to lay down his lance', 30 June, pp. 57–8.
Economist (1984e) 'Complaints OFT-times told', 7 July, p. 72.
Economist (1984f) 'Privatisation's progress', 21 July, pp. 76–7.
Edwards, C.D. (1975) 'Policy toward big business: what lessons after forty years', *Journal of Economic Issues*, 9, pp. 343–63.
Ellert, J.C. (1976) 'Mergers, antitrust law enforcement and stockholder returns', *Journal of Finance*, 31, pp. 715–32.
Elzinga, K.G. (1969) 'The antimerger law: pyrrhic victories?', *Journal of Law and Economics*, 12, pp. 43–78.

Elzinga, K.G. and Breit, W. (1976) *The Antitrust Penalties: A Study in Law and Economics*, Yale University Press.

Elzinga, K.G. and Hogarty, T.F. (1973) 'The problem of geographic market delineation in antimerger suits', *Antitrust Bulletin*, 18, pp. 45–81.

Fisher, F.M., McGowan, J.J., and Greenwood, J.E. (1983) *Folded, Spindled, and Mutilated. Economic Analysis and US v. IBM*, MIT Press.

Flynn, J.J. (1968) 'Consent decrees in antitrust enforcement: some thoughts and proposals', *Iowa Law Review*, 53, No. 5, pp. 983–1019.

Goldberg, M.S. (1962) *The Consent Decree: Its Formulation and Use*, Bureau of Business and Economic Research, University of Michigan.

Green Paper (1978) *A Review of Monopolies and Mergers Policy*, Cmnd. 7198.

Greer, D.F. (1975) 'Discussion of the Edwards, Brodley, and Samuels articles', *Journal of Economic Issues*, 9, pp. 395–97.

Hale, G.E. (1940) 'Trust dissolution: "Atomizing" business units of monopolistic size', *Columbia Law Review*, 40, pp. 615–32.

Hay, G.A. and Kelley, D. (1974) 'An empirical survey of price-fixing conspiracies', *Journal of Law and Economics*, 17, pp. 13–38.

Hexter, J.L. and Snow, J.W. (1974) 'Mergers, asymmetry and antitrust', *Antitrust Bulletin*, 19, pp. 401–19.

Howe, M. (1972) 'Rethinking British merger policy', *Antitrust Bulletin*, 17, pp. 283–309.

Jain, P.C. (1982) 'Cross-sectional association between abnormal returns and firm-specific variables', *Journal of Accounting and Economics*, 4, pp. 205–28.

Johnson, L.B. (1982) *Competition and Cross-Subsidisation in the Telephone Industry*, Rand Corporation Report, R-2976-RC.

Kahn, A.E. (1984) 'A needed dose of competition', *Challenge*, March–April, pp. 24–29.

Kaplow, L. (1982) 'The accuracy of traditional market power analysis and a direct adjustment alternative', *Harvard Law Review*, 95, pp. 1817–1848.

Kaysen, C. and Turner, D.F. (1959) *Antitrust Policy: An Economic and Legal Analysis*, Harvard University Press, reprinted 1971.

Kintner, E.W., Joelson, M.R. and Griffin, J.P. (1974) 'Recent developments in the United Kingdom antitrust law', *Antitrust Bulletin*, 19, pp. 217–55.

Korah, V. (1975) *Competition Law of Britain and the Common Market*, Elek.

Kottke, F. (1978) *The Promotion of Price Competition Where Sellers are Few*, D.C. Heath.

Kummer, D.R. (1978) 'Valuation consequences of forced divestiture announcements', *Journal of Economics and Business*, 30, pp. 130–36.

Landes, W.M. and Posner, R.A. (1981) 'Market power in antitrust cases', *Harvard Law Review*, 94, pp. 937–96.

Liebeler, W.J. (1979) 'Comments on Weiss', *University of Pennsylvania Law Review*, 127 (1979), pp. 1141–1150.

Litman, B.R. (1980) 'Measuring divestiture of network-owned television stations: an econometric approach', *Antitrust Bulletin*, 25, pp. 363–67.

Loomis, C.J. (1983) 'Valuing the pieces of eight', *Fortune*, 107, No. 3, pp. 70–8.

Main, J. (1983) 'AT&T's holiday gift to Wall Street', *Fortune*, 28 Nov., pp. 67–72.

Martin, D.D. (1963) 'The Brown Shoe Case and the new antimerger policy', *American Economic Review*, 53, pp. 340–58.

Mirucki, J. (1984) 'A study of the Averch–Johnson hypothesis in the Telecommunications Industry', *Atlantic Economic Journal*, 12, p. 121.

Monopolies Commission (1953) *A Report on the Supply and Export of Matches and the Supply of Match-Making Machinery*, HCP 161.

Monopolies Commission (1956) *A Report on the Supply of Certain Industrial and Medical Gases*, HCP 13.

Monopolies Commission (1961) *A Report on the Supply of Cigarettes and Tobacco Machinery*, HCP 218.

Monopolies Commission (1968) *A Report on the Supply of Man-Made Cellulosic Fibres*, HCP 130.

Monopolies Commission (1969) *A Report on the Supply of Beer*, HCP 216.

Monopolies Commission (1973) *A Report on the Supply of Asbestos and Certain Asbestos Products*, HCP 3.

Monopolies Commission (1976) *Eurocanadian Shippings Limited and Furness, Withy & Company, Limited and Manchester Liners Limited. A Report on the Existing and Proposed Mergers*, Cmnd 639.

Monopolies Commission (1979) *Report on the Supply of Petrol in the United Kingdom by Wholesale*, Cmnd 7433.

Monopolies Commission (1983a) *The Great Universal Stores PLC. A Report on the Existing and Proposed Mergers*, Cmnd 8777.

Monopolies Commission (1983b) *The Sunlight Service Group PLC and Johnson Group Cleaners PLC and Initial PLC and Johnson Group Cleaners PLC. A Report on the Proposed Mergers*, Cmnd 8868.

Moyer, R. (1979) 'Horizontal divestiture in the Petroleum Industry: an analysis', *Antitrust Bulletin*, 24, pp. 535–53.

Mueller, C.E. (1968) 'The new antitrust: a 'structural' approach', *Antitrust Law and Economics Review*, 1, pp. 87–130.

Neale, A.D. and Goyder, D.G. (1980) *The Antitrust Laws of the USA. A Study of Competition Enforced by Law*, 3rd edn, Cambridge University Press.

Nelson, R.R. (1979) 'Comments on a paper by Posner', *University of Pennsylvania Law Review*, 127, pp. 949–952.

O'Connor, K.J. (1976) 'The divestiture remedy in Sherman Act S2 cases', *Harvard Journal on Legislation*, 13, pp. 687–775.

Ordover, J.A., Sykes, A.O. and Willig, R.D. (1982) 'Herfindahl concentration, rivalry and mergers', *Harvard Law Review*, 95, pp. 1857–74.

O'Reilly, B. (1983) 'Ma Bell's kids fight for position', *Fortune*, 107, pp. 62–68.

Ornstein, S.I. (1981) 'Antitrust policy and market forces as determinants of industry structure: case histories in Beer and distilled spirits', *Antitrust Bulletin* 26, pp. 281–313.

Pass, C.L. and Sparkes, J.R. (1980) 'Dominant firms and the public interest: a survey of the reports of the British Monopolies and Mergers Commission', *Antitrust Bulletin* 25 pp. 437–84.

Pautler, P.A. (1983) 'A review of the economic basis for broad-based horizontal-merger policy', *Antitrust Bulletin*, 28, pp. 571–651.

Pfunder, M., Plaine, D. and Whittemore, A. (1972) 'Compliance with divestiture orders under Section 7 of the Clayton Act: an analysis of the relief obtained', *Antitrust Bulletin*, 17, pp. 19–180.

Phillips, A. (1979) 'Comments on Weiss', *University of Pennsylvania Law Review*, 127, pp. 1151–4.

Posner, R.A. (1976) *Antitrust Law: An Economic Perspective*, University of Chicago Press.

Posner, R.A. (1979) 'The Chicago School of antitrust analysis', *University of Pennsylvania Law Review*, 127, pp. 925–948.

PP&W (1972), see Pfunder *et al.*

Reekie, D. (1978) *Give Us This Day . . .*, Hobart Paper 79.

Ross, P. (1968) 'Economies as an antitrust defense: comment', *American Economic Review*, 58 (1968), pp. 1371–2.

Samuels, W.J. (1975) 'The Industrial Reorganisation Bill: the burden of the future', *Journal of Economic Issues*, 9, pp. 381–94.

Scherer, F.M. (1976a) 'Predatory pricing and the Sherman Act: a comment', *Harvard Law Review*, 89, pp. 868–90.

Scherer, F.M. (1976b) 'Some last words on predatory pricing', *Harvard Law Review*, 89, pp. 901–3.

Scherer, F.M. (1980) *Industrial Market Structure and Economic Performance*, 2nd edn., Rand McNally.

Schmalensee, R. (1979) 'On the use of economic models in antitrust: the Realemon Case', *University of Pennsylvania Law Review*, 127, pp. 994–1050.

Schmalensee, R. (1982) 'Another look at market power', *Harvard Law Review*, 95, pp. 1789–1816.
Sherman, R. and Tollison, R. (1971) 'Public policy toward oligopoly: dissolution and scale economies', *Antitrust Law and Economics Review*, 4, pp. 77–90.
Spence, M. (1983) 'Contestable markets and the theory of industry structure: a review article', *Journal of Economic Literature*, 21, pp. 981–90.
[Stewart, D.O.] (1977) 'Competition in the telephone equipment industry: beyond telerent', *Yale Law Journal*, 86, pp. 538–60.
Stocking, G.W. and Mueller, W.F. (1955) 'The Cellophane Case and the new competition', *American Economic Review*, 45, pp. 29–63.
Swann, D., O'Brien, D.P., Maunder, P. and Howe, W.S. (1974) *Competition in British Industry*, George Allen and Unwin.
Taylor, P. (1983) 'Muddied waters over AT&T divestiture', *Financial Times*, 21 October, p. 35.
Time (1983) 'Click! Ma is ringing off', 21 November, pp. 40–48.
Tully, S. (1983) 'The US giant is a pygmy abroad', *Fortune*, 107, No. 3, pp. 86–8.
Turner, D.F. (1969) 'The scope of antitrust and other economic regulatory policies', *Harvard Law Review*, 82, pp. 1207–44.
Uttal, B. (1983) 'Western Electric's cold new world', *Fortune* 107, No. 3, pp. 81–84.
Wasserstein, B. (1972–3) 'British merger policy from an American perspective', *Yale Law Journal*, 82, pp. 656–90.
Weiss, L.W. (1979) 'The structure–conduct–performance paradigm and antitrust', *University of Pennsylvania Law Review*, 127, pp. 1104–40.
Wenders, J.T. (1971) 'Deconcentration reconsidered', *Journal of Law and Economics*, 14, pp. 485–8.
Whitehead, C. (1983) 'Privatising British Telecom: the worst of both worlds?', *Public Money*, 3, No. 2, pp. 43–46.
Whitney, S.N. (1964) 'The economic impact of antitrust: an overview', *Antitrust Bulletin*, 9, pp. 509–33.
Wier, P. (1983) 'The costs of antimerger lawsuits', *Journal of Financial Economics*, 11, pp. 207–24.
Wilcox, C. and Shepherd, W.G. (1975) *Public Policies Toward Business*, 5th edn., Irwin.
Williamson, O.E. (1968a) 'Economies as an antitrust defense: the welfare trade-offs', *American Economic Review*, 58, pp. 18–36.
Williamson, O.E. (1968b) 'Economies as an antitrust defense: correction and reply', *American Economic Review*, 58, pp. 1372–6.
Williamson, O.E. (1979a) 'Symposium on antitrust law and economics', *University of Pennsylvania Law Review*, 127, pp. 918–24.

Williamson, O.E. (1979b) 'Assessing vertical market restrictions: antitrust ramifications of the transaction cost approach', *University of Pennsylvania Law Review*, 127, pp. 953–93.
Zelenitz, A. (1980) 'The attempted promotion of competition in related goods markets: the Ford–Autolite divestiture case', *Antitrust Bulletin*, 25, pp. 103–24.

8

State-to-Private Sector Divestment: The Case of Sealink

Alistair Bruce

Introduction

This chapter is concerned with the divestment of assets from the public to the private sector, one form of the 'privatisation' of state enterprise. As such, it clearly differs from analysis of divestments which occur wholly within the private sector in that it addresses issues beyond the purely corporate strategic and raises wider questions relating to the capabilities and limitations of the private-sector market system and more specifically the relative efficiency of private and public enterprise.

The 'private/public' debate can be considered at a number of levels. It may, fundamentally, be seen as an ideological issue, embracing political, moral and social as well as economic factors. It may be viewed as a more narrowly economic debate, in terms of comparative efficiencies of allocative media. On a more practical level, there are arguments for and against state-to-private sector divestments which owe more to their influence on wider economic policy objectives than to any theoretical considerations. Finally, the actual design and management of this type of divestment raises numerous technical and tactical issues which echo the grander debates.

The core feature of the state-to-private sector divestment, which initiates debate at each level, is the fact that while the objective of the private-enterprise manager may be regarded as the promotion of private returns, the administration of public enterprise generally includes the satisfaction of social and strategic considerations in its objective function.

The first section of this chapter considers the issues involved in the state-to-private sector divestment in four stages. Firstly, the ideological debate is briefly summarised; secondly, the economic arguments relating to relative efficiency and market and state failure are discussed; thirdly, the practical appeal to the policy maker of privatisation through divestment is assessed; and finally, the various technical questions relating to the organisation and implementation of divestment are examined.

The second section considers a recent case of state-to-private sector divestment which illustrates a number of issues introduced in the previous section. The case studied is the sale of the British Railways Board subsidiary, Sealink, to Sea Containers Ltd. in 1984.

Privatisation via Divestment: The Issues

Privatising Divestment: Definitional Note

Before addressing the issues directly, it is necessary to clarify briefly the type of divestment under consideration and in particular to note the limits of its comparability with private-sector divestments.

An important point to note immediately in considering state-to-private sector divestments is that there is a variety of related but distinct activities commonly referred to as 'privatisation' and that a number of these, though exposing public-sector activity to the market system, cannot be regarded as divestments. Heald (1983)[1] provides a fourfold classification of privatisation, three elements of which are not divestment. Thus, this chapter is concerned neither with the privatisation of the *financing* of a service which continues to be produced by the public sector, nor the privatisation of *production* which continues to be state-financed, nor *liberalisation*, involving the removal of statutory monopoly or barriers to competition. None of these represents divestment in the sense of the *sale* of state assets and control of subsequent production by the private sector.

The analogy between this latter type of activity and interfirm private-sector divestment may itself be somewhat limited, however. For example, although the sale of a large state enterprise *in its entirety* may be regarded as the divestment of a particular division of a large and diverse state portfolio (or in a sense a state holding company), the types of consideration governing such a 'divestment' decision are unlikely to provide a close parallel to the private-sector case.

More readily analogous to the private-sector divestment is the type of disposal discussed in the case study, where a *specific area* of a state enterprise's activity clearly appears as distinct from the core of the enterprise's business orientation.

The Ideological Debate

On the ideological level, much of the debate surrounding the relative merits of public and private ownership has centred on legal or moral notions such as liberty and choice. Whilst it is not within the remit of this chapter to consider in detail the more philosophical issues involved,[2] some statement of the case for private, decentralised ownership as part of a system which promotes liberty, individual freedoms and societal welfare is necessary, not least because it has regularly appeared in modified form as the ideological buttress supporting the Conservative Government's programme of privatisation in the UK since 1979.

The basis of the ideological case for private ownership is the notion that individual freedom and choice in economic decision making is suppressed by the existence of collective choice mechanisms which are inefficient as transmitters of public choice to governments. This is compounded by the distortive effect of bureaucracy in both design and implementation of policies based on the public will as articulated. In short, agreement between publicly-made economic policies and any represented individual's private view of the desired decision cannot be guaranteed. Simply, the contention is that liberty is preserved and welfare maximised by the maintenance of the power of the individual to negotiate all contracts voluntarily, by the absence of any coercive arrangements made on his or her behalf by the state, in an appropriate legal and institutional framework.

In terms of the role of the state in the economy, this view implies a minimal public function with intervention limited to the provision of the legal framework essential to the completion of contracts between individuals (most notably the assignment and enforcement of propety rights) and the preservation of the integrity of the state as a whole. These arrangements represent the so-termed 'night-watchman' view of the state.

This view of private enterprise as a necessary condition for individual freedom represents a line of argument reliant, according to Heald (1983),[3] on a particular view of freedom as essentially *negative*. As such it ignores the *positive* freedoms generated by intervention and neglects the infringement of individual freedoms which could exist without penalty were it not for specific measures of intervention regarded as legitimate in liberal capitalist societies.

Linblom (1977)[4] catalogues a set of reasons why the association of the private enterprise market system with individual freedom is inappropriate. These include 'coercion through termination of exchange' and coercion stemming from the dependence of the livelihood of many on the sale of their only asset, labour.

The preceding section represents only the briefest sketch of a vast and complex area of ideological debate on the relative merits of public and private ownership. For our purposes, the important point to note is that despite the contentious nature of the supporting arguments, the connection between private-enterprise market systems and individual freedoms is frequently cited as ideological justification for the erosion of the state's economic role. Of more direct importance in this chapter is the economic debate surrounding the public/private-ownership issue. In the following section, two concepts of efficiency are used to compare the relative performance of state and market. Firstly, the notion that *x-efficiency* is more likely in public than privately-run organisations is considered. Secondly, relative *allocative* efficiencies are assessed and particular attention is paid to those areas where, in the presence of 'market failure', state intervention is regarded as a 'legitimate' course of action in liberal capitalist terms.

Private vs. Public: The Efficiency Debate

Defining Efficiency A major economic impetus for initiating a movement away from public ownership and production is centred on the contention that the public sector is inherently less efficient than the private sector. Frey's (1983)[5] recent contribution catalogues a number of studies of relative efficiency which appear to lend considerable, though not unanimous, support to this view. A significant problem in assessing such private/public comparisons is, however, that the relevant notion of efficiency is itself a matter for contention.

The free market advocate's view of efficiency sees it as associated with the generation of private surplus or the minimisation of producer cost. To others, though, this represents a narrow and over-commercial view of efficiency which neglects important wider social welfare aspects. Because of this, many of the studies which profess to demonstrate the 'superiority' of private over public ownership are regarded as inappropriate to those who hold that the function of the public sector embraces wider considerations, for example some redistributive role or support for commercially unviable activities which generate positive net social benefits. Nevertheless, studies which concentrate on relative private costs enjoy wider support due to the familiarity of using private costs as an efficiency measure and because of the problems associated with identification and assessment of wider, often less tangible and more subjective, social impacts.[6]

Explanation of the private sector's superior efficiency in empirical studies is generally couched in terms of both superior *allocative efficiency* and superior *x-efficiency*. The allocative efficiency argument relies on the Pareto optimality of the perfectly competitive market, which invites two lines of dissent. Briefly, the first relates to the inadequacy of the Paretian framework and in particular the fact that it makes no comment on the distributional characteristics of different attainable Pareto-optimal positions; it therefore remains silent on an issue – income distribution – which has frequently played a major role in the operation of state enterprises. More substantially, the deviation of modern capitalist industrial structure from perfect competition denies the unequivocal supremacy of the market system in practice. The factors which give rise to this deviation are discussed below.

X-efficiency is that attributable to and resulting from the non-coincidence of the goals of individuals or subgroups within an organisation with the declared goals of the organisation. Though initially identified in relation to the capitalist firm, it is generally argued that public enterprises are more sympathetic hosts to x-efficiency for a number of reasons considered briefly below.

X-Efficiency: The Case Against Public Enterprise An argument frequently advanced is that public corporations are less exposed to the incentive for efficiency provided by competition in the private sector. This may have some force where the public corporation concerned enjoys a statutory monopoly, though even in such cases genuine competition may exist. An obvious example here is that of British Rail which, though enjoying monopoly status in the provision of rail services in Great Britain, must compete vigorously with other forms of transport such as road freight haulage and road passenger transport, private and public. Also, of course, the degree of competitive stimulus in private-sector markets is not homogeneous, depending importantly on the structure of the supply side in each case.

A more persuasive explanation of differing efficiencies is the notion that the capitalist firm benefits from an efficiency stimulus provided by the threat of bankruptcy, whereas the public corporation enjoys greater security from the financial backing of the state. The more stringent enforcement of public-sector budgets could be seen as having exerted greater discipline with regard to financial performance in the public sector, however. Indeed, there may be grounds for suggesting that the constraints imposed by government both on internal and external finance have had a more significantly adverse effect on public-sector performance than any inefficiency induced by a complacent attitude to expenditure, in the face of allegedly 'soft' government budgets.

A further explanation for claimed private-sector superiority is the discipline exercised by shareholders (particularly institutional shareholders) on the performance of the managerial team in the private-sector firm. This invites consideration of the comparison between the manager in the firm and the bureaucrat in public enterprise.[7] While the former must satisfy the owners of the firm of his effective contribution to the enterprise (thereby risking sanctions imposed by owners in the event of failure or enjoying benefits from rewards if successful), the public-sector bureaucrat faces neither incentives for efficiency nor the threat of sanctions against underperformance. Accountability in public enterprise lies less with the individual, more with the enterprise as a whole. Added to this, with statutory monopolies, there exists no independent yardstick against which to monitor efficiency. This problem of control loss may also be accentuated by the generally larger size and greater bureaucratic complexity of public-sector enterprises which further frustrates the pursuit of accountability and monitoring of performance.

There is a general consensus that the above varieties of x-inefficiency enjoy greater scope in public enterprises. Brittan (1984) summarises the most important elements thus:

> The difficulties of mimicking competitive performance in the public sector are those of incentive and information. . . . officials, deprived of the possibility of direct financial gain, will secure their benefits in the form of status, security and in-house conditions. Every one of these temptations is present in large-scale private corporations too; but the combination of takeover threat and greater personal involvement, via for instance stock options, acts as a mitigating factor. (Brittan 1984, p. 115)

It is important to note, however, that this alone cannot be regarded as a sufficient argument for privatisation. Other routes to increased public-sector efficiency may be available and, indeed, the 1980 Competition Act would seem to represent one positive response to the perceived problem, with provisions for investigation of nationalised industries.[8]

Allocative Efficiency Having summarised briefly the x-efficiency argument, it is necessary to consider in more detail the practical barriers to the attainment of the allocatively Pareto-optimal position associated with perfect competition. These barriers, elements of 'market failure', may contribute to the argument for the replacement of an imperfect market mechanism with public provision, though they cannot be regarded as a sufficient condition for the adoption of such a policy. Market failure may be remedied by less radical policies, e.g. via the tax system, and in any case there is no guarantee that the state can allocate satisfactorily where the market has failed to do so.

There is a considerable literature[9] on the causes of market failure and frequently the more common examples are cited as areas which are regarded as, in a sense, 'legitimate' for state intervention in the liberal capitalist market systems. In this section, we consider briefly four causes of market failure: monopoly, with a consideration of the phenomenon of natural monopoly; externalities; public goods; and the more nebulous but equally significant factor of imperfect information.

Monopoly Concern with the potential for social welfare losses associated with the achievement and maintenance of private monopoly positions became well-established as a basis for 'legitimate' government intervention throughout the advanced industrial nations after the Second World War. In the UK, this awareness has seen, on the one hand, a succession of regulatory legislation while, on the other, elements of the development of the public sector are attributable to the view that state provision represents a form of monopoly which is able to safeguard social welfare. Recent contributions regarding the losses attributable to the deviation of price from marginal cost under monopoly have assured continuing lively debate. Market-orientated neo-Austrian positions,[10] for example, suggest that private monopoly is an essentially transitory and entirely necessary feature of the competitive process, while it is only *statutory* barriers to entry which are regarded as damaging and durable. On the other hand, the persistence of high levels of profit[11] in heavily concentrated sectors is cited as evidence of the continuing abuse of monopoly positions.

The strongest case for direct state provision in the face of private monopoly has been in industries where the production function is characterised by falling average costs at the level of aggregate national output – in other words, where the range over which economies of scale operate suggests that there is room for only one supplier on grounds of economic efficiency. This phenomenon is often regarded as most prevalent in industries where goods or services are provided via a national network or distribution system, for example railways or telecommunications. In such cases of 'natural monopoly',[12] private control of the supply side has been regarded as both politically and economically unacceptable and nationalisation has provided one type of policy response. The nationalised sector of UK industry, therefore, features elements of natural monopoly, though it is important to stress equally that other elements of the public sector are clearly not in this category. Further parts which were perhaps once natural monopolies should no longer be regarded as such. Brittan (1984)[13] cites the telecommunications industry as one in which technological change has removed certain aspects of the business from natural monopoly status, while other parts remain naturally monopolistic. Advocates of divestment from the public sector argue that non-natural monopoly elements present legitimate targets for denationalisation and that where this leads to 'ordinary' monopoly in the private sector, such an outcome is either transitory and harmless (the Austrian view) or controllable via competition policy.

The practice of earmarking the natural monopoly elements in the public sector and disposing of the remainder raises the important question regarding the *extent* of divestment from individual public-sector concerns. The technical problems of pursuing such a policy are considered below.

Social/private returns disparity In the above section, it was observed that concern at the abuse of private monopoly positions has contributed to the shape of the public sector in the UK. An additional impetus for state control has been the recognition that in the private sector, allocation of resources among activities is organised according to the opportunity for private profit (or, for example, managerial reward) to the neglect of any wider social or economic effects of such activities. More specifically, the private enterprise market system, with its narrow basis of costs and returns, will result in an underallocation of resources to goods and services which yield net social benefits and an overallocation to activities which generate net social loss.

Correction of this misallocation demands the internalisation of these 'externalities', their incorporation into the decision-making process. This is theoretically achievable by a choice of measures. Advocates of the market solution suggest that externalities may be eliminated by the establishment and enforcement of property rights,[14] though the size and complexity of such a system questions its practicality.

A 'middle course' solution involves the correction for neglected external costs and benefits by either regulation or compensating taxes and subsidies, and there are applications of this type of remedy in most advanced economies.

More radically, the presence of externalities may be remedied by the replacement of the imperfect market by the state, which (it is argued) is able to apply a wider social welfare cost and returns assessment to its decision making. In the same way, therefore, that elements of the public sector are natural monopolies, so certain parts serve to provide social or broader economic goods which would not be forthcoming were it left to the private sector operating with a private-returns criterion.

While advocates of divestment may be content to tolerate the continued provision of socially desirable goods and services, their preference would generally be for private-sector provision with public subsidy. Certainly, any direct state provision would be limited to specifically identified areas of social need; any additional direct provision would constitute a target for divestment to the private sector. Again, this type of approach demands a clear classification between types of public provision. As with the natural monopoly issue, the associated technical problems are discussed below.

Public goods Another area where the state has established responsibility for the provision of goods and services in the face of market failure is in the case of public goods, i.e. goods which are characterised by non-excludability. In other words, the consumption of the good by any one individual cannot preclude consumption by any number of others. In a market setting, a likely outcome is the *non-provision* of the commodity as it is in no individual's interest to articulate a demand for the product. Rather, each rational individual's best strategy is to wait for someone else to demand and pay for provision of the good and to participate in consumption at zero charge, or 'free-ride'. Thus, in spite of sizeable *actual* demand, signals are not transmitted, hence not received, and therefore the demand remains unfulfilled. There is, then, a role and responsibility for the state in providing the public good directly, levying taxes to finance this provision.

There is considerable debate over the extent of truly public goods.[15] The most ardently market-orientated would probably suggest that only defence fully fits the definition. In the UK the consensus would probably incorporate a number of additional goods and services, though in the last five years many goods traditionally regarded as public (e.g. health care, education, roads) have been queried and the existence of market alternatives has been cited as support for the removal of state involvement. Advocacy of public withdrawal in areas such as health and education is often based on observation of apparently healthily functioning parallel private provision, though this may involve a dangerously simplified perspective. With health, for example, there is for many people a strong moral objection to the dependence of an individual's health on his or her means to express an effective demand in a market system, while in any case it should be noted that it is not strictly any individual's health which is the public good; rather, the public good is the superior level of public/societal health which results from free provision of health services. In that sense, public health is undeniably a public good. A similar argument could be applied to education.

Information Finally, in considering market failure and consequent alternatives to the market for the allocation of economic resources, the imperfect availability of information should be mentioned. In a perfectly competitive utopia, all relevant information is freely available to all economic agents as a basis for informed, rational decision making. In reality, numerous imperfections occur in the transmission, reception and interpretation of information of all types. These frustrate the design and implementation of appropriate responses by agents in the market. A particular aspect of the information problem which has received wide attention is that of asymmetry[16] across markets which inhibits the making of contracts.

Whilst the problem of imperfect information clearly frustrates real-world market operations, however, its introduction here is designed equally to illustrate the immense and complex informational requirements of any state alternative to the market system. Where, albeit imperfect, information channels are closed by the suspension of the market in favour of the state, the state must develop alternative information sources on which to base decisions. In a democratic framework, the political process may provide a partial answer, though the shortcomings of methods of articulating the public will are well documented,[17] as are the immense computational problems associated with centrally-planned economies.[18]

Whilst imperfect information may be seen to inhibit the achievement of market solutions to the problem of allocation, this must not be interpreted as providing a sound or sufficient case for a state-administered alternative. The information problem presents a challenge to all modes of resource allocation and as such should not be regarded as lending particular weight to either side in the public/private debate.

Efficiency Arguments: Concluding Note The above section has provided a synopsis of the economic arguments most frequently aired in the discussion of the relative efficiencies of the public and private sectors. The arguments regarding market failure are important elements in the debate on whether or not to recommend extension of a programme of privatisation via divestment.

In considering the arguments it is of prime importance to remember, however, that just as privatisation alone cannot guarantee acceptable market solutions, so the existence of elements of market failure does not preclude the existence of state failure under the same circumstances.

'Pragmatic' Motivations for Divestment

One class of motivations thus far neglected in explaining the pursuit of privatising divestment is that where divestment is advocated as an aid to the achievement of other objectives of economic policy, rather than as a result of any ideological or economic commitment to divestment itself.

Consideration of the privatisation programme of the Conservative Administration in the United Kingdom since 1979 has led to suggestions[19] that divestments have been implemented chiefly as a means to effect a reduction in the public sector borrowing requirement (PSBR), thus facilitating the achievement of monetary targets, the central pillar of Conservative economic policy. Additional 'spinoffs' of divestment, such as the weakening of public-sector union power, have been cited as a further incentive.

On the first point, Heald and Steele (1982)[20] identify a twofold attraction to the Government: in the short term a lump-sum gain to the Exchequer resulting from asset sale; in the longer term, release of the Government from the provision of external finance to public corporations. It is argued that the disposal of valuable assets for short-term gain, apart from in many cases providing a relatively trivial return, represents a short-sightedness in discounting benefits which flow from state assets in the longer term. This was especially the case with the divestment of hydrocarbon interests. Furthermore, the notion that divestment from the public sector eases the perceived problem of 'crowding out' is challenged, where the sale of potentially profitable state assets is seen as arguably greater in its diversionary impact on private-sector investment funds.

By contrast, Brittan (1984) largely rejects the idea that easing pressure on the PSBR represents a significant motivation for privatising divestments . . .

> . . . it is ludicrous to suppose that major industrial decisions such as whether to denationalise the telephone system or gas and electricity have been taken mainly to massage the PSBR figure. (Brittan 1984, p. 113)

Both Brittan (1984) and Shackleton (1984), however, point to the unsatisfactory nature of PSBR as an indicator of the state's presence in the economy, noting that the one-off revenue from asset sales may give a false impression of the real level of public spending, leading to a considerable understatement of the public-sector deficit.

So far as the question of public-sector union power is concerned, Heald and Steele (1982) point to the absence of privatisation in the traditionally more militant public-sector areas. They are sceptical as regards any moderating impact of private-sector ownership on pay claims, pointing to the difficulty of modifying long-entrenched bases for expectation of Exchequer-funded increments.

On the other hand, recommendations for greater worker participation in the running of privatised concerns appear to represent a legitimate threat to the influence of unions in such areas. The existence of worker-shareholders, as pioneered with the divestment of the National Freight Corporation, dilutes the reliance of the worker on the union-negotiated wage, leads to two 'classes' of worker (shareowners and non-shareowners) and invests workers with a degree of responsibility in decision making which could erode the credibility of union protests against unpopular decisions.

This section as a whole has considered the main economic arguments surrounding the concept of privatisation via divestment. As such, it has dealt with some of the justifications and motivations for embarking on a particular act, or more generally a programme, of state-to-private sector divestment. What it has not considered is the variety of technical and design problems which relate to policy *implementation* and which demand attention once the principle of such divestment has been accepted. These essentially practical issues are considered below.

The Mechanics of Privatisation via Divestment

There are a number of questions which arise in the mechanics of privatisation, in the design of the technical features of a divestment from public to private sector, which are the subject of considerable debate.

Among the more important technical questions which require attention are how much of a public enterprise should be divested, what is the appropriate mode of sale and, closely linked, what is the appropriate price. Associated with this is the question of which parties should be permitted to participate in purchase and what safeguards need to be made to regulate the purchaser's post-sale conduct (in particular with regard to consumer interests). In addition, how can the fear of trade unions regarding post-sale redundancy and changed conditions of service be tempered to allow a disposal free from industrial relations disruption during or after the sale?

Extent of Divestment In considering the first of these issues – the appropriate degree of divestment from the public sector – the policy maker may, as seen above, be guided by the concept of natural monopoly, regarding any elements which cannot be classified as natural monopolies as legitimate for disposal. This invites comparison with the identification by a private-sector firm of its core and peripheral activities in considering divestment.

Another possible principle would involve the retention of only those elements of public enterprise which, though yielding commercially unsatisfactory returns, could be earmarked as fulfilling a significant social benefit. The application of both natural monopoly and social-benefit criteria as a basis for identifying saleable sectors (each demanding careful categorisation of public-sector services) is likely to prove difficult, however, so that in practice it may be administratively more convenient to dispose of state assets as entities. British Telecom provides an example of an entity, partly natural monopoly and partly not, providing commercially profitable alongside loss-making socially beneficial services, which has been treated as an entity for divestment purposes.

A further question pertinent to the design of a divestment from the public sector is that if the more marketable, commercially successful parts are disposed of, what happens to those elements which remain under public control? Clearly, even if earmarked as socially necessary, there is likely to be political pressure for their abandonment, as the extent of their financial cost to the Exchequer becomes more sharply exposed in the absence of cross-subsidisation opportunities within a larger public sector. This, of course, may hold an appeal to those ideologically opposed to the public sector in general.

Tender vs. Share Issue The mode of sale of state assets is a further issue which has attracted wide attention. Two main routes to disposal dominate the sale of public assets in the UK. Either the state may offer a state asset (or part thereof) as an entity by public tender, issuing an offer for sale and inviting bids for consideration by a specified date, or a state enterprise may be disposed of by the public sale of shares at a fixed price, often with merely some percentage of the value of the company represented by the issue.

An area of considerable debate concerning the appropriate mode of sale has been the valuation of state assets for disposal. In those sales which have been administered via share issue, this has led on a number of occasions to charges of 'handouts' to the private sector by the state on behalf of the general public. In such cases the tender (offer) price per share has fallen considerably below the price following early trading. This was most spectacularly illustrated with the sale of Amersham International,[21] but was also seen in the cases of Cable and Wireless, Jaguar and British Telecom.[22]

Misjudgements in the opposite direction, with overestimated investment demand, may also cause difficulties. The sale of Britoil,[23] for example, aroused very little interest in the market, leaving the state's underwriters with a heavy commitment to meet. Similar fears were initially voiced in connection with the disposal of British Telecom, and a £3 million advertising programme, highlighting the benefits of share ownership, was a feature of the pre-sale period.

Problems of gauging the attractiveness of state flotations are naturally related to the capacity of the market to absorb large issues, and have led to the phasing of the disposals of Britoil and British Telecom.

With the part-admission of private capital into state enterprises, the calculation of an appropriate risk/reward ratio is a further consideration. Such investments could be regarded as involving unusually low levels of commercial risk, but at the same time need to appear sufficiently attractive in terms of expected return to the investor, relative to other types of stock.[24]

As regards that variety of public-asset disposal which can be more strictly regarded as true divestment, where an enterprise or part thereof is offered for sale by public tender, similar problems may arise. What is the acceptable price, for example, for a public enterprise with negative rates of return, which demands considerable capital injection to generate commercially attractive returns, as well as organisational, managerial and motivational overhaul? Such an enterprise may be regarded as highly unattractive at the book value of assets, yet sale at a discount from this figure would be likely to generate hostility.

Finally, given the type of problem outlined above, it is likely that the divesting authority will favour public tender as opposed to private arrangements. Accusations of 'giveaways', though unwelcome under any circumstances, would be regarded as less sinister with public administration of sale.

The New Owner: The Problem of Private Market Power

Closely related to, though ultimately more important than, the mode of divestment is the identity of the purchaser of former state assets and consequent implications for the level and quality of service provided.

Earlier in this chapter note was made of the tendency of the private sector under certain conditions to foster a drift towards monopoly and its attendant social costs and that the divestment of state assets might thus generate concern over the increase of private market power. The extent to which this presents a real problem to the policy maker depends partly, of course, on his/her view of the impact of monopoly, but more practically on the nature of the competitive structure of the industry concerned and on the identity of the purchaser. Clearly, greatest concern is reserved for instances where there is already a high concentration of private ownership in the industry and where leading companies express an interest in buying the state assets offered.

In such a setting, various channels are open to the state as means of mitigating the negative welfare effects of private-market power. These may be pursued at the pre-sale stage, embodied in the terms of sale, or applied post-sale. Pre-sale precautions, essentially pre-emptive regulation, may be exercised by, for example, denying participation in the sale[25] to agents with significant existing interests in the industry or, less severely, insisting on clearance from antitrust authorities prior to acceptance of a bid.

In addition, the sale of public assets may, as with the post-1979 UK privatisation programme, be preceded by vigorous publicity, often aimed at sections of the public not normally attracted to such forms of investment in order to promote a wider spread of ownership. If such a policy succeeds in promoting wider ownership, it offers the added advantage to the advocate of privatisation of inhibiting efforts at renationalisation.

Incorporation of safeguards into the terms of sale of state assets constitutes an additional instrument. Hence, limits on percentage of disposed assets purchasable by any one party may be incorporated into the Offer for Sale. To be effective, such conditions would require to be accompanied by conditions relating to the resale of assets. The sale of assets in Enterprise Oil, the offshore oil branch of the British Gas Corporation, in 1984 illustrated graphically the problems caused by inadequate specification of such terms. In this case, the Government was forced to intervene to block the acquisition of 49 per cent of Enterprise stock by Rio Tinto Zinc and to impose a retrospective limit of 10 per cent on purchase of Enterprise stock. Rio Tinto Zinc complied with the initial order, but subsequently mounted a vigorous drive, involving offering premiums of 10 per cent on market price, to attain a 29.9 per cent holding.[26]

Qualitative, as well as quantitative, terms may be inserted in the Offer for Sale. Hence, as in the sale of British Telecom, safeguards for socially important services may be imposed. It is clearly important, however, that in order to preserve the incentive to bid, any conditions imposed should not be regarded as overrestrictive with regard to the entrepreneurial freedom of the new owner.

Post-sale control of market power may be achieved through either existing antitrust legislation, through specially-created industry-specific regulatory bodies, as with OFTEL in UK telecommunications, or by the active promotion of competition by, for example, liberalisation of previously restrictive legal barriers to entry. Again, telecommunications provides an example in the UK.[27] Significantly in this case, however, the degree of competition has thus far been severely restricted with only one company, Mercury, permitted to compete for the supply of telephone services, a fact highlighting a significant natural monopoly element in telecommunications, that is the existing *network*.

Trade-Union Attitudes

Whilst the last section addressed the importance of accounting for the possible postsale emergence of market power in the design of divestment, a further important consideration for the architect of a divestment is the perceived reaction of trade unions to privatisation via this route. Like consumers, workers in the industry concerned have interests at stake when privatisation is mooted. A consideration for the divesting authority is the impact of any industrial action stemming from opposition to privatisation by trade unions representing workers in the industry concerned. The most serious potential effects result from union threats of non-cooperation with new private owners, which could be expected to materially and negatively influence the scale of participation in the sale, the price secured for divested assets and in the longer run the interests of consumers.

In evaluating such impacts, it is important, of course, to avoid incorporating the simplistic view that trade-union interests necessarily mesh with the interests of the workforce. This need not be the case and indeed developments such as worker-shareholding would tend to promote a divergence of interest, as noted above.

Trade-union opposition to privatisation may be identified at a number of levels. Ideologically, the transfer of state-controlled activity, serving the interests of society as a whole, to a private sector, motivated by the pursuit of private profit, is generally unpalatable to the union movement, a fact endorsed by the adoption of antiprivatisation resolutions by the TUC.

More practically, trade unions may object to privatisation on the grounds that it leads to a reduction of their industrial power and, consequently, their membership's welfare. Thus, for example, the probability of job-shedding rationalisation under commercially conscious private ownership poses a threat. In addition, where the sale of a public asset results in a fragmented ownership in the private sector, the negotiating function of the trade union becomes much more complex and difficult. This was a point forcibly expressed by the NUR (1984)[28] with regard to the sale of BTH hotels to a number of independent hotel groups, some of which had neither experience of nor inclination to cooperate with trade unions.

A further problem, also seen in the BTH case, is that union members in areas with traditionally low membership density, such as hotels, may previously have been in a position to expect support from fellow members in high density areas of the public sector (e.g. elsewhere in the railway system). With the isolated privatisation of the low-density area, the potential for effective solidarity is severely diminished.

Finally, with regard to the British post-1979 model of privatisation by divestment, an important principle has been the Government's encouragement of wider worker participation in ownership of the enterprise. As noted above, this has been viewed with some hostility by the unions, which see the dilution of worker dependence on union representation and the development of conflict between participating and non-participating workers as possible results.

There are, then, a number of areas of union discontent with privatisation which could possibly result in industrial action, threatening either the sale or prospects of future private ownership and which, as a consequence, demand attention by the authorities concerned with an enterprise's smooth absorption into the private sector.

Sealink: Divestment of a BRB Subsidiary

Introduction: The Background

The case of the divestment of Sealink from British Rail is considered in three sections. First, the nature of Sealink's origins, business, assets and recent performance is considered and a brief 'diary' of its disposal in 1984 is provided. This supplies the factual basis for a discussion of the specific issues pertaining to the sale. Attention focuses in particular on the case of privatisation, the form of divestment and design of sale, the issue of market power and the attitude of the trade unions to the divestment. The third section attempts a view of Sealink post-privatisation, though at the time of writing this is necessarily somewhat speculative.

Sealink: Origins, Characteristics and Disposal

The privatisation of Sealink, the shipping and harbours subsidiary of British Rail, was to represent the end of over a century of control and provision of such services and assets by railway companies in the United Kingdom.

Following nationalisation in 1948 and through until 1969, BR's maritime interests were administered according to their location within the standard 'regional' framework of British Railways. After a decade in the seventies as a separate, unified division of BR, the shipping and harbour interests became Sealink UK, a wholly-owned subsidiary of the British Railways Board, in 1979.

In early 1981, immediately prior to the announcement of privatisation in the Transport Act of that year, the basic characteristics of the company and its environment may be described thus. The company controlled 25 ferry routes around the UK, divided organisationally between continental and Channel Island services on the one hand and the remaining coastal shipping services on the other. Shipping assets in mid-1981 comprised 21 passenger/vehicle ferries, 3 train ferries, 1 freight vessel and 4 container ships. These were responsible for the carriage of 18.4 million passengers by 1980, a figure which represented an approximate 35 per cent increase on the 1970 figures. Turnover of the company in 1980 stood at £220.3 million, a sixfold increase in money terms on 1970. Of this figure, £196 million was attributable to shipping services, which nevertheless recorded a loss of £6.4 million in 1980. Sealink's workforce, virtually evenly distributed between onshore and offshore staff, numbered 10,318 in May 1981.

The competitive structure of the industry was investigated by the Monopolics and Mergers Commission Report of 1981. Market shares in the Anglo-Continental passenger market were as shown in Table 1.

Table 8.1

	% market share	
	Accompanied tourist vehicle traffic	*Foot passengers*
Sealink (total)	32	44
(of which Sealink UK)	(14)	(27)
European ferries	39	19
Others	29	47*

Source: Monopolies and Mergers Commission (1981).
Note: *includes P&O = 20 per cent.

In the unitised freight market, the share of Sealink and partners in the roll-on/roll-off sector (approximately 73 per cent of total freight) was 22 per cent compared with European Ferries' 37 per cent. Sealink UK monopolised the train ferry sector (5 per cent of the total market) and held a 24 per cent share in the load-on/load-off sector (22 per cent of total freight market).

The enabling legislation for Sealink's sale was contained in the 1981 Transport Act, passed in July of that year. Part 1, Section 1, paragraphs 1 & 2 and Section 3, paragraphs 1 & 2, provide the most significant clauses (see below).

Part 1
Subsidiary Activities of British Railways Board

1(1) Without prejudice to any powers conferred on them by any other enactment, the Railways Board shall have power to provide for the disposal, in such manner as they think fit, of –

(a) any securities of one of their subsidiaries which are held by the Board or by another of their subsidiaries; or

(b) the whole or any part of the undertaking of, or of any property, rights or liabilities of, any of their subsidiaries.

(2) The Board shall not exercise their powers under subsection (1)(a) above except with the consent of the Secretary of State.

and

3(1) The Secretary of State may, after consultation with the Railways Board, give directions to the Board requiring them –

(a) to exercise their powers under Section 1 of this Act in a specified manner and in relation to a specified subsidiary;

(b) to establish a subsidiary and exercise their powers under Section 7 of the Transport Act 1968 (transfer of property, rights and liabilities to subsidiaries) in a specified manner.

(2) It shall be the duty of the Board (notwithstanding any duty imposed on them by Section 3(1) of the Transport Act 1962) to give effect to any directions given under this section.

(Transport Act 1981)

The series of events surrounding the eventual disposal took place in a five month period between March and July, 1984. The key stages in the divestment may be seen as follows:

Date	
March 1984	Morgan Grenfell & Co Ltd, acting on behalf of the British Railways Board, announced the sale, sent letters to all parties who had already expressed an interest in Sealink and to other prospectively interested parties, explaining the basis on which the sale would proceed. It was made clear that important consideration would be given to any assurances which the prospective purchaser could provide with regard to the future security of Sealink employees and the future conduct of its business. Prospective purchasers who were willing to offer share-ownership facilities to Sealink employees would also be regarded favourably.
April 1984	A 50-page Information Memorandum was prepared and distributed to around a dozen parties who had declared a 'firm-interest'. Among these were: Trafalgar House P&O Ellerman Lines Sea Containers Ltd Common Brothers (Newcastle) and a consortium involving: Sealink's management team National Freight Corporation Globe Investment Trust Charterhouse Japhet James Fisher Target date for the sale was set as the end of June 1984.
May 1984	Further information was made available to those parties still interested. European Ferries and P&O were banned from the sale by the Director General of Fair Trading (15.5.84).[30]

	National Union of Seamen mounted a 48-hour strike against privatisation of Sealink (30/31.5.84).
May/June 1984	Interested parties involved in discussions with BRB, Sealink management, some Sealink unions.
10 June 1984	*Sunday Times* reported deadline slippage for the sale.
24 June 1984	Sea Containers Chairman, James Sherwood, publicly criticised the terms of sale.[31]
6 July 1984	Three sealed bids received for Sealink, from: Sea Containers Common Brothers Sealink Management Consortium
13 July 1984	NUS operated ban on roll-on/roll-off road freight carriage.
18 July 1984	Sea Containers bid of £66m. was accepted.
19 July 1984	*Financial Times* noted that the price is at 'the top end of City expectations' and that 'other bids (were) uncompetitive on financial grounds alone'.

Sealink: Issues in the Divestment

The period following the 1981 Act and prior to the ultimate sale of Sealink in 1984 was characterised by considerable discussion of a number of issues raised by the proposed sale. The most important areas for debate emerged over the strength of the case for divestment, the organisation of the sale, the potential problem of market power resulting from the sale and the issue of the trade-union attitude to privatisation. These are considered in turn below, though the issues are not strictly independent.

The Case for Divestment

In considering the impetus behind the decision to privatise Sealink, one factor presents itself as particularly significant: the set of conclusions resulting from the Monopolies and Mergers Commission Report of 1981. The Report, whilst making a clear recommendation against the takeover of Sealink by European Ferries, identified a number of recent and influential developments which together formed a persuasive argument for a considerable rationalisation. In short, two factors were of major significance. Firstly, the recession brought a sharp halt to a decade of profitable market expansion in the seventies. This was compounded by a considerable expansion of capacity in multipurpose ferries by both existing operators and small-scale new entrants during the decade, but most particularly in the period 1979–81. Further, largely as a result of the above developments, a breakdown in pooling arrangements[32] between Sealink and European Ferries Ltd on the shorthaul cross-Channel ferry routes led to vigorous price competition at the beginning of the eighties. Though this provided a short-term benefit to the consumer, load factors still indicated a considerable excess capacity in the industry in the early 1980s which suggested the need for rationalisation, without the threat of increased concentrations of market power.

Alongside the assessment of the MMC, two essentially practical arguments lent weight to the case for Sealink's divestment. In the first place was the fact that as part of BRB, Sealink's access to investment funds to modernise and upgrade its fleet was limited by the competition for funds within British Rail and by the BRB's own External Financing Limit (EFL). This, coupled to uncertainty regarding the possible effects of a Channel tunnel, stunted investment through the seventies. Ironically, new investment in Anglo–French shorthaul ships was only forthcoming at a time when the market growth of the seventies had ended. The 'St Anselm' and 'St Christopher' entered service in late 1980 and early 1981 respectively and, together with SNCF's new 'Cote d'Azur', added 19 per cent car-carrying capacity and 83 per cent commercial-vehicle-carrying capacity to the fleet of Sealink and partners on the high frequency Dover–Calais route. On average, however, Sealink's fleet, even with these additions, was considerably older than its main competitors'. To a government considering privatisation, these circumstances would doubtless have been considered likely to subdue opposition to sale from Sealink management and possibly also from trade unions.

A further practical consideration facing the Government was the extent to which Sealink, if offered, represented a saleable commodity. To a large degree, this would depend on the mode, timing and extent of sale, discussed below, but it was recognised that given the advertised keen interest of a major rival and the relatively modest scale of the disposal, the embarrassing possibility of the sale attracting no (or unacceptably low) offers was very remote.

On a more philosophical level, the likely consequence of the sale of Sealink appeared to satisfy none of the conditions which would theoretically recommend its retention in the public sector. Clearly, for example, given the structure of the industry, ferry services as a whole did not constitute a natural monopoly and, where there was a threat of increased market power, the authorities had demonstrated urgency in disallowing developments with potentially negative welfare effects. Where the public service element in the provision of ferry services was concerned, this could also presumably be safeguarded via the terms of sale and/or subsequent regulatory vigilance. Unlike many areas of the public sector, ferry services were not publicly owned as a response to some failure of the market system. Rather, they were the relic of a nineteenth-century strategic adventure, and while by the 1980s there were still persuasive arguments for the maintenance of the parent's central business (i.e. railway services) in the public sector, publicly-owned ferries constituted a historical anomaly to advocates of privatisation.

The case for privatisation rested then on a variety of arguments – practical, financial and structural. In spite of this, there was no straightforward path to disposal. Three significant hurdles remained. Each was to attract wide debate in the pre-sale period.

Form of Divestment

As with any divestment from public to private sector, there were a number of options open with regard to the form and execution of sale. Formal statements explaining the ultimately selected procedure are elusive, so that assessment of the issues raised is necessarily tentative. A number of questions relating to aspects of the sale procedure merit particular attention. For example, why was the tender method favoured? Why was Sealink sold as an entity (including, eventually, its harbours) rather than on a route-by-route basis or in separate shipping and harbour deals? What strings were attached to the sale? On what basis was the eventual buyer approved? These issues are considered in turn below.

With regard to the choice of the tender method of sale, available evidence suggests that the main alternative to tender – a share issue – which was considered within BRB, may ultimately have been rejected for three main reasons. Firstly, previous privatising divestments via share issue had been received with widely differing degrees of enthusiasm by investors. The tender method avoided the embarrassment of either considerable oversubscription (as with Amersham) or lack of investor interest (as with Britoil). Secondly, the tender method involved a greater degree of vendor control over the terms of the sale, with the opportunity for negotiations with interested parties prior to tender submission, and over the identity of the purchaser. Thirdly, the BRB had experience of the tender method, having successfully disposed of the former British Transport Hotels properties by tender.[33]

The sale of Sealink's harbour and shipping interests as an entity had not been originally envisaged by BRB. Rather, it was an outcome resulting from pre-tender negotiations with interested parties. The Chairman of Sea Containers had indicated that separate disposal of shipping and harbour interests was an unreasonable method of sale.[34] Given the limited availability of ferry-port facilities for cross-Channel ferries, it seems fair to suggest that there would have been relatively few (and relatively small) tenders for Sealink's ships without the guarantee of harbour access. This factor, coupled with the disincentive for maintenance of the fleet's integrity which separate harbour and shipping sale would have entailed, may have been largely instrumental in the eventual joint sale of the two wings. Sale of Sealink shipping interests on a route-by-route basis[35] had been ruled out at an earlier stage. The view of the BRB was that it would have been difficult to dispose of some of the less profitable routes individually, that breaking the company up would have led to administrative delays,[36] frustrating early disposal, and that the interests of Sealink staff (both those attached to individual routes and central administrative personnel) would be best served by the sale of all routes together.

A particularly contentious feature of the Sealink sale was the fact that the extent of participation in the sale was effectively limited to those organisations (around a dozen) which were provided with a highly confidential dossier on Sealink's assets,[37] performance, etc. Most conspicuously absent from the mailing list were European Ferries, whose blocked bid two years previously apparently still disqualified them in 1984. The non-issue of the memorandum, apart from signalling the vendor's disapproval of the neglected party, clearly prevented the submission of a rationally-based bid by European Ferries.

A further and related notable feature of the sale was the absence of a formal 'Offer For Sale' setting out stipulated terms of disposal. Rather, the selectively-circulated memorandum, as well as offering relevant commercial details, invited genuinely interested parties to seek further information, to be released on a similarly discretionary basis. During this period, in the months prior to disposal, there was vigorous consultation between those most eager to submit bids and the vendor, British Railways Board, and its representatives and some of the unions involved. Much of this was designed to influence the eventual sale terms prior to bid submission. It seems reasonable to suggest that this ostensibly undignified 'haggling' procedure may have been permitted or even encouraged by the vendor to stimulate interest in the sale. As noted above, Sea Containers – the eventual purchasers – were able to engineer the inclusion of Sealink's harbour interests in the package during this period.

The criterion on which ultimate acceptance of the Sea Containers bid was based appears simply to have been the size of offer. Again, in the absence of hard evidence, it seems reasonable to surmise that the pre-bid consultations may have been used to approve the detailed basis for a bid between vendor and potential purchaser, so clearing the way for a relatively straightforward decision on receipt of bids. The matter of the price of sale was not without controversy in itself. The eventual figure of £66 million fell a little short of some estimates earlier in the year and represented a significant discount on book value.[38]

It is important to note that though the announcement of Sea Containers' successful bid may have indicated broad agreement on sale terms between buyer and seller, a significant third group of interests, the trade unions, were not involved in detailed consultation prior to sale and remained sceptical as to the conditions of sale following the announcement. The issue of trade-union attitudes is considered in detail below.

An issue which received considerable publicity throughout the sale procedure was the interest of the Sealink management team, in association with a number of city partners, in buying the company. During most of this period it was fairly widely assumed, certainly in the financial media, that this consortium was favourite to secure the company. This was, of course, a reasonable supposition for a number of reasons. Firstly, Sealink's management enjoyed considerable advantages in terms of familiarity with the company's organisation, business and prospects, allowing a more informed basis for advertising plans for the company's future development and for assembling an appropriate bid. Secondly, it was considered that Sealink's management could make more persuasive claims for maintaining the integrity of the organisation post-privatisation. Thirdly, it was a fact that British Transport Hotels' management had failed to carry through a proposed management buyout of BR's hotel assets in 1981/2 and that the failure was known to have been the source of bitterness and disappointment within British Rail. As a consequence, there was an expectation that the Sealink buyout proposal might enjoy favourable discretionary consideration.

As it was, with the award criterion apparently based squarely on size of bid, the consortium's offer was too small. It should be noted, though, that had the ultimate award been based on wider criteria, it seems by no means certain that the consortium would have been successful. The record of Sealink's management suggested to BRB that it might not be the ideal party to be involved in the running of the divested company, while the attitude of the trade unions to the consortium was, in general, hostile.

Market Power

The issue of private market power maintained a high profile during the pre-sale and sale periods of Sealink's disposal. This was inevitable against the background of the Monopolies and Mergers Commission Report relating to Sealink in 1981 and the already highly concentrated state of the market for ferry services around the UK (see above), a factor made more significant by the substantial barriers to entry embodied in harbour ownership by the main ferry companies.

In this section, three aspects of the market power issue are addressed. Firstly, while the MMC Report noted the scope for and desirability of rationalisation, it also indicated the likely consequences of increased concentration and these are discussed. Secondly, building on the last section, the incorporation of safeguards against market power in the mode of sale is considered. Thirdly, the ramifications of the outcome of sale for the future competitive structure are examined.

Following receipt in March 1981 of a reference from the Department of Trade, the MMC Report of 8th December 1981 provided a thorough examination of the proposed acquisition of Sealink UK Ltd by European Ferries Ltd. Profiles of the companies directly involved were augmented by extensive assessment of the competitive environment in the provision of ferry services and by reporting of the views of those parties both directly and peripherally concerned.

The main conclusions of the Report as they related to the anticipated impact of the merger focused on the perceived effects on efficiency, competition in ferry operations, competition at the ports, market entry possibilities and employment.

Briefly, taking each in turn, it was suggested first that increased efficiency levels in ferry provision would demand some attention to the overcapacity which had developed since 1979. The Report predicted 'a period of consolidation and adjustment in the industry' (Monopolies and Mergers Commission 1981, p. 93), following the intensely competitive phase (1979–81) and noted that the prospects for the achievement of rationalisation without merger were improved by the likely absence of substantial capital expenditure claims on the companies, given the existing overcapacity in the industry. The beneficial impact on the consumer during the competitive period was also noted.

As for the effect on competition in the provision of ferry services, the MMC observed that the merger would lead to market shares in excess of 50 per cent 'in all main sectors' (Monopolies and Mergers Commission 1981, p. 93). This brought the possibility of substantial price increases, particularly if the new company found difficulty in implementing its rationalisation programme, and implied restriction of consumer choice.

European Ferries countered by arguing that rationalisation could obviate the need for price increases and suggested that increased prices would only tend to attract new entry to the market. Further, EFL offered to be bound by regulatory agreement.

Competition at ports would, it was suggested, be severely restricted by merger. Even if EFL were not to take over ownership of ports, right of use of existing Sealink ports could, it had been demonstrated, adversely influence access by potential competitors.

The report also noted that entry conditions in the ferry business had become less favourable since the seventies, a period which had been characterised by market growth, rising real fare levels and a number of new operators. The merger of EFL and Sealink would lead to a company with an increased dominance in key routes and harbour control and it was concluded that 'the entry of a major new competitor would be made very much more difficult' (Monopolies and Mergers Commission 1981, p. 97). The MMC report suggested that it would be difficult to predict the relative effects on employment of rationalisation under merger as against that carried out by individual companies.

As a general conclusion, the Report explained its decision to recommend against the merger as resulting from a combination of the potential effects outlined above, coupled with the difficulty of finding satisfactory arrangements to insure against such adverse implications.

Given the concern relating to the possibility of increased market power associated with Sealink's disposal, it was essential that measures frustrating such developments be built into the mechanics of sale of Sealink in 1984. This was achieved by, firstly, limiting the release of the confidential memorandum (see above) to those potential purchasers who posed no ostensible threat to the market's competitive structure. As noted above, the most significant omission from the list of those circulated was EFL, largely on the basis of the MMC's findings in 1981. Following their exclusion from the circulation list, EFL's initial response was to seek some form of agreement with the BRB which would allow them to submit a bid. BRB's reluctance to become involved in any informal dealing resulted in European Ferries approaching the Office of Fair Trading, with the argument that estimates of 70 per cent market share for a merged EFL/Sealink were considerably exaggerated and that 50 per cent represented a more reasonable figure.

In fact, the second line of screening employed by BRB and their advisers, Morgan Grenfell, was that all prospective bidders should ensure clearance to bid with the Office of Fair Trading prior to tendering. Significantly, two of the main contenders for purchase of Sealink appeared vulnerable to this test: P&O, with around 12 per cent of the passenger market in 1983; and Trafalgar House, itself interested in acquiring P&O in early 1984 as well as, reportedly, EFL. Indeed, P&O was to fall at this hurdle.[39] The identity of the eventual bidders is not officially publicly available, though it is widely known that there were only three: the National Freight/Sealink management consortium, Common Brothers of Newcastle and Sea Containers Ltd.

The ultimate sale outcome, announced on July 18, 1984, involved no direct or immediate threat to competition in the ferry business in that Sea Containers were a company with no prior presence in the area. Nevertheless, there was considerable unease regarding the purchaser's identity from the Labour Party in Opposition and from the trade unions in particular. With regard to the issue of the future competitive structure of ferry services, the main concern was Sea Containers' lack of experience in the business, prompting fears of possible withdrawal in the face of adverse trading results.

Trade-Union Resistance

It was suggested above that, apart from any philosophical antipathy towards state-to-private sector divestment, trade-union resistance to measures of privatisation was in large part associated with the threat of redundancy or new pay, work or pensions conditions following rationalisation by the new ownership. The Sealink case provides an example of strong union concern expressed in an organised campaign of opposition which focused in turn on the issue of privatisation, on the participants in the sale and ultimately on the successful purchaser. This section traces the development of the unions' campaign in some detail, reflecting the importance of a factor which maintained a high profile throughout the sale period.

At the outset of the anti-privatisation campaign, the Joint Committee of Sealink Unions represented the interests of six involved unions: the National Union of Seamen (NUS); the National Union of Railwaymen (NUR); the Amalgamated Union of Engineering Workers (AUEW); the smaller Transport Salaried Staffs' Association (TSSA); Merchant Navy and Airline Officers' Association

(MNAOA); and the Radio and Electronic Officers' Union (REOU); though individually these unions had alerted their memberships to the potential disadvantages of privatisation well before the sale period. For example, in October 1983, the NUR informed its members of the responses provided to the union by Sealink in respect of the expected basis for Sealink's disposal. Briefly, at this time Sealink's Managing Director, L.C. Merryweather, suggested that Sealink would be disposed of as an entity (shipping and harbours together), that BR might retain a 'significant minority shareholding' and that existing pension and travel concession arrangements would continue. The NUR pledged its vigilance in the light of lessons learned following the privatisation of British Transport Hotels (BTH).

The joint union campaign opened early in 1984. The threats identified by the unions in a circulation of members were itemised thus:[40]

— the splitting up of the company
— reduction of jobs as a result of the takeover by a private company
— selling of assets
— reduction of routes that are not profitable
— deterioration in pension arrangements

These specific threats were set beside arguments regarding the public need served by Sealink and the experience of BTH staff following sale of the company.

Shortly after this, a further pamphlet identifying and offering specific criticisms of those prospective purchasers known to be interested in Sealink was circulated.[41] Each party was examined in turn. The most extensive criticism was reserved for the NFC/Sealink management consortium which, it was alleged, was bidding for successful tender at a low price in return for share dispersal amongst the workforce. It was further suggested by the unions that the consortium arrangement would allow only a minority worker interest in control of the company, that the involvement of NFC might threaten rail-linked services and that minority employee involvement in the control of the company could not guarantee the maintenance of existing conditions of employment. The attack on the proposed policy of worker/shareholder expansion also pointed to the potential conflicts of interest which could arise:

> Would those who hold shares accept a dividend payment but deny non-shareholders, and themselves, a pay increase? Would they agree to redundancies for themselves and others just to maintain the dividends paid to NFC, Charterhouse, Rothschild, Globe Investment Trust and James Fisher?
>
> (Joint Committee of Sealink Unions 1984b)

It was further argued that the experience of the 'employee buyout' at NFC represented only a cosmetic form of worker control and that in terms of redundancy, investment and asset-stripping, the NFC record was largely negative from the point of view of the workforce.[42]

Relatively little attention was devoted to the other potential bidders at this time. Trafalgar House and Sea Containers were each identified as companies favouring registration under flags of convenience, to the detriment of UK job prospects, while P&O was depicted as a small and ailing force seeking an opportunity to enhance market share and modernise an aging fleet at a low price.

It was significant that two members of the Joint Committee (TSSA and AUEW) withdrew from the more strident and specific criticisms of the second union circulation.

In the remaining weeks prior to tender submission, the TSSA, accepting the inevitability (as they saw it) of Sealink's disposal, focused its efforts on ensuring the protection of its members' interests by engaging in consultation with potential bidders during the period of negotiation following issue of the confidential memoranda on Sealink. This strategy of TSSA doubtless reflected the 'very unfortunate experiences with owners of former British Transport Hotels who have failed to honour agreements' (Transport Salaried Staff Journal 1948a, p. 1). It resulted in an agreement reached with the eventual purchaser, Sea Containers, extensively and enthusiastically reported in the union's newspaper.[43]

Meanwhile, the National Union of Seamen provided the driving force in the anti-privatisation campaign in the weeks prior to sale. Despite repeated attempts by all interested parties to discuss possible future working arrangements with the NUS, the union refused to talk with any of the prospective bidders. Although the NUS, in its total opposition to privatisation, declared no ranking of the relative attractiveness of bidders, it was particularly ill-disposed towards the consortium for three main reasons: the involvement of what it regarded as poor senior Sealink management; the involvement of the NFC; and the attempts by the consortium to curry favour with NUS membership in the pre-sale period.

As an expression of their continued opposition, the NUS called a 48-hour strike for 30/31 May 1984 which resulted in a 100 per cent response from Sealink membership and significant levels of support from members in European Ferries, P&O, Caledonian Macbrayne and Belfast Car Ferries. Further detailed concern was expressed in an NUS release of 8 June, 1984, which warned of the likelihood of a 25 per cent reduction in Sealink's workforce post-sale and of the introduction of outside caterers on board Sealink ferries.

Additional industrial action, supported by the National Union of Railwaymen, involved a refusal to handle roadborne freight from midnight 13th July, though the impact of this action was somewhat diminished by the wider industrial action called over the perceived threat to the Dock Labour Scheme.

Following the announcement of Sea Containers' successful bid on 18 July 1984, the NUS maintained its hostile posture. The Union's General Secretary, Mr Jim Slater, pledged continued refusal to handle road freight until guarantees regarding jobs and pay were forthcoming. Meanwhile on 18 July, Sea Containers issued a News Release which contained the following warning from James Sherwood, President of Sea Containers Ltd:

> The British taxpayer will no longer pay the bill if Sealink UK loses money. The recent stoppages over privatisation can only hurt the company by causing a lack of confidence in its ability to provide services. I trust the staff will recognise this and impress upon their union leaders the necessity of working together for the common good, which means jobs, better wages and a profitable company in which we can all take pride.
>
> (Sea Containers Ltd 1984, p. 3)

In fact, after talks between the NUS and Sea Containers, the action against freight traffic handling was called off within two days of the sale, and during the following week further discussions resulted in the exchange of assurances between the two sides. This was to represent the beginning of a more cooperative phase in company/union relations, though (as detailed below) misunderstanding regarding the nature of assurances made by the NUS almost sparked off a resumption of industrial action within two weeks of the sale.

Sealink Post-Divestment: Some Observations

Introduction

Assessment of the impact of privatisation in the case of Sealink offers little in the form of firm conclusions at this stage, less than a year after the divestment. It may be instructive, however, to consider certain features of Sealink's business under new ownership and to note changes made thus far. Three aspects, drawing on the issues introduced earlier, are considered briefly: firstly, the organisation and management of Sealink under new ownership; secondly, the level of service provided and prospects for future service development; and finally, the trade-union issue. Interpretation of early developments under new conditions may be enriched by referring to the experience of former British Transport Hotels' properties bought by Sea Containers in 1982.

Management Structure

On confirmation of its successful bid for Sealink, Sea Containers was swift to outline the management structure for the divested company. A two-tier management was designed for Sealink, with a parent company – British Ferries Ltd – responsible for 'planning and monitoring'. The former Chairman of Sealink UK Ltd, J.M.W. Bosworth, was appointed to the Board of British Ferries, which was itself a wholly-owned subsidiary of Sea Containers Ltd.

Beneath this strategic level, the executive membership of the existing Sealink UK Ltd board remained in charge of 'day-to-day operations'. The management team at this level was augmented by a Director of Shipboard Services, responsible for 'quality of passenger experience and increase of on-board sales'.

Effectively, in fact, this arrangement amounted to a three-tier managerial hierarchy: Sea Containers Ltd–British Ferries Ltd–Sealink UK Ltd, a fact remarked upon in the financial media:

> The three-tiered board structure for Sealink looks an improbable arrangement given the energies of Sea Containers' Chairman, Mr James Sherwood, and will surely be changed before long.
>
> (Financial Times, 19.7.84)

A novel feature of the arrangements was the degree of autonomy in everyday decision making to be enjoyed by the Sealink management. A feature of both Sealink and British Transport Hotels was that, as subsidiaries of the British Railways Board, many ostensibly mundane or routine decisions required clearance from the BRB. Managerial freedom to take responsibility for such areas has been cited as a major impact of divestment by hotel management working for Sea Containers in the company's five former BTH hotels.[44] A strong and consistent view was that increased managerial responsibility and consequently enhanced credibility in the eyes of the workforce were important factors in offering prospects for improved performance at hotel level.

Aside from autonomy in tactical, everyday decisions at local level, Sea Containers' new style of management suggests greater scope for increased autonomy in investment decision making by British Ferries, with a greater likelihood of backing from the parent company where prospects warrant it. This would appear to offer considerable scope for development and expansion of a company whose initiatives had previously been stifled by both lack of parent-company (BRB) funds as well as by intense competition for funds within the group.

The evidence from the first few months under Sea Containers' ownership suggests that a rapidly conducted appraisal of Sealink's managerial requirements has been translated into the early design and implementation of a new management structure. Based on the twin planks of a less-constrained financial environment and greater decision-making autonomy at tactical and strategic levels, with consequent benefits for worker and manager motivation, the structure invites a tentatively optimistic view.

Services

On the important issue of services, Sea Containers, through British Ferries, was quick to confirm a commitment to the majority of existing routes. In a detailed breakdown of sectors, the company demonstrated a well-informed basis for development of existing routes. Much of the groundwork for the company's plans had been carried out in a survey of existing services prior to the sale. On confirmation of the successful bid, outline plans were presented in an open letter to Sealink employees.

The following proposals were presented. The already profitable Dover Eastern Docks and Fishguard services were to be developed to improve travel quality and on-board sales volume and, in the former case, to increase market share at the expense of European Ferries and P&O. Development of passenger services from Dover Western Docks was also proposed, with greater emphasis on freight traffic from Folkestone, unprofitable at the time of sale. Harwich's freight handling capacity would be expanded, while existing Harwich–Hook of Holland passenger services would be maintained as a separate profit centre. Newhaven would, it was suggested, require considerable service improvement and the emphasis would be on expanded freight services. The main problem area for British Ferries was identified as the Channel Island services, with losses estimated at £1 million in 1984, but development plans for these services had not, at the time of sale, been finalised.

As to remaining services, Stranraer was earmarked as profitable and secure, as were two of the three Isle of Wight services. New ferries for the unprofitable Portsmouth–Ryde service were anticipated. Plans for the improvement of Holyhead's freight performance would centre on improved container freight facilities, while the emphasis on the profitable Holyhead–Dun Laoghaire passenger service would be on increased quality of service and on-board sales. The Heysham–Isle of Man route could, it was suggested, be pulled into the black by introduction of a new ferry, while the port in general would need to exploit business from the Irish Sea oil and gas development. Finally, plans for the small-scale, profitable Lake Windermere services and unprofitable Tilbury Ferry Service had not been formulated at the time of sale.

In general, the plans laid considerable emphasis on the scope for more effective marketing of the company's services, a neglected area evidenced by the fact that Sealink's first marketing director was only appointed in 1982.

In the months since the sale, British Ferries has begun to translate plans into action, largely through redeployment of vessels, but also via the introduction of new vessels.[46] In late September, 1984, the one-ship Tilbury–Gravesend ferry was offered for sale.[47] The service, which had reportedly made losses for twenty years, was operating at a 25 per cent capacity compared with the early sixties. Further developments in the latter part of 1984 have been the transfer of the Newhaven–Dieppe vessel 'Senlac' to Sealink's French partners (with guaranteed employment for related staff at Portsmouth or Dover); transfer of the 'St David' from the Holyhead–Dun Laoghaire route to the Dover–Ostend route; transfer of 'Antrim Princess' from the Stranraer–Larne to the Heysham–Douglas service; the commissioning of a new, large multipurpose vessel for Stranraer; transfer of the 'Manx Viking' from the Isle of Man to the Weymouth–Cherbourg service; and transfer of the 'Earl William' from Weymouth to the Portsmouth–Channel Island–Cherbourg service. Finally, refurbishment of two vessels for luxury Portsmouth–Channel Islands services was announced, though this raised fears of possible redeployment of one of the vessels to Venice to link with Sea Containers' Venice–Simplon–Orient Express train service.[48]

In general, the plans and early actions of the new company appear to demonstrate an increased awareness of the differing commercial potentials of various routes, with a particular emphasis on the quality of service and on effective marketing to enhance market share. The clearly considerable investment in appraisal of possibilities would tend to indicate a genuine commitment to the maintenance of former Sealink services as a whole, in line with assurances made at the time of sale.

Company–Union Relations

The hostile and active opposition to privatisation by the trade unions was a feature of the period leading up to the sale of Sealink. The immediate post-sale period was also marked by threats of industrial action. These arose from the company's misinterpretation of union statements which terminated the industrial action against roll-on/roll-off freight on July 20, 1984, and confirmed that no further action would be taken over the issue of privatisation, without specific cause. Sea Containers' reading of this assurance was that it constituted a broader 'no-strike' agreement, and advertisements to that effect in the national press[49] almost triggered fresh industrial action.

Apart from this area of misunderstanding, talks between management and unions regarding the future of services, jobs and working conditions both emphasised the need and suggested the basis for cooperation in the interests of the company's development. It was made clear by the company that their plans included the purchase of additional ships, with prospects for associated increased employment, and that employee rights, pension entitlements and privileged travel facilities would be safeguarded. Further local consultation with the unions would continue to form part of the company's decision-making process.

The credibility of company assurances may have been enhanced by the relatively good record of Sea Containers in its dealings with former BTH employees in the company's five former BTH hotels. Since Sea Containers' takeover, employment levels in the hotels had been maintained, wage increases had compared favourably[50] with those offered by employers in other former BTH properties, and former BTH employment conditions had been honoured. This said, the NUR had encountered considerable problems in dealing with some of the new hotel owners who were unused to union representation and unwilling to honour established working practices. In addition, Sea Containers had enjoyed favourable relations with the NUR in its treatment of the union's members employed in Sea Containers' Simplon–Orient Express train service operation.

By November 1984, *The Seaman*, organ of the National Union of Seamen, felt able to report that:

> The overall mood of officials is one of cautious optimism that British Ferries is planning – despite the 'Senlac' axe – to expand services and create extra jobs for British seamen.
>
> (*The Seaman*, November 1984)

At the end of 1984, therefore, it is reasonable to suggest that initial hostility, both to the idea of privatisation and to Sea Containers in particular, has been eroded and that prospects for future company/union cooperation appear reasonably favourable.

As indicated earlier, it would be inappropriate to venture a firm conclusion as to the 'success' or otherwise of the divestment of Sealink. It is probably justifiable to suggest, however, that early signs of a greater financial and managerial freedom offer prospects for the continued integrity of the Sealink group and for the development and improvement of ferry services to the benefit of both consumers and workers.

General Conclusion

It has not been the task of this chapter to present a consistent argument either for or against privatisation via divestment. Rather, it has attempted to highlight some of the issues central to the privatisation debate, whether on an ideological, economic or technical level.

Whatever the individual's view of state-to-private sector divestment, an important lesson to note is that the nature of ownership alone is unlikely to be decisive in determining the performance of an enterprise and that in any attempt at direct comparison of private-sector and public-sector operations, a great deal will depend on additional factors such as, within the enterprise, management structure, accountability and financial constraints, and within the firm's external environment, the strength of competitive forces and the influence of regulatory arrangements.

Notes

1. Heald (1983), p. 299.
2. For a brief discussion of the main elements in this debate, see Heald (1983), pp. 68–77; Lindblom (1977), pp. 72–3. For a fuller statement of the 'market' position, see Friedman, M. and Friedman, R. (1980), pp. 9–37.
3. Heald (1983), pp. 58–84.
4. Lindblom (1977), pp. 45–51.
5. Frey (1983), pp. 114–15. See also Pryke (1982) for a study of British examples.
6. For a discussion of the problem of social cost/benefit evaluation, see Pearce (1971), pp. 51–8; Mishan (1972), pp. 85–111.
7. Jackson (1982), chapters 2–5, provides a comprehensive treatment of theories of managerial and bureaucratic behaviour.
8. See Chiplin and Wright (1982) for a discussion of the contribution of the 1980 Act to regulation of nationalised industries in the UK.
9. See, for example, Lindblom (1977), pp. 76–89; Heald (1983), pp. 94–102.
10. For an Austrian view of the role of monopoly in the competitive process, see Kirzner (1973), pp. 1–29.
11. See, for example, Mueller (1977).
12. For an introduction to the theory of natural monopoly, see Sharkey (1982), pp. 1–28.

13. Brittan (1984), p. 117.
14. For the classic expression of this view, see Coase (1960), pp. 1–44.
15. See, for example, Atkinson and Stiglitz (1980), pp. 482–7.
16. For a statement and empirical test of this proposition, see Akerlof (1970).
17. See, for example, Alt and Chrystal (1983), pp. 149–72.
18. Cave and Hare (1981), pp. 178–90, discuss the problem of information under central planning.
19 & 20. Heald and Steele (1982), pp. 341–4, discuss the Government's motivations for privatisation.
21. Amersham International, sold in February 1982, was 23.6 times oversubscribed. See *Financial Times*, 19.2.82.
22. The *Financial Times* provides extensive coverage of the British Telecom sale throughout October, November and early December, 1984.
23. For a report and commentary on the sale of Britoil see, in particular, *Financial Times*, 20th and 22nd November 1982.
24. For a discussion of this issue, see Committee of Public Accounts (1980–81).
25. See above, pp. 229–31, for a discussion of European Ferries Ltd's exclusion from the Sealink (UK) Ltd sale.
26. For coverage of these events, see *Financial Times*, 28.6.84; 29.6.84; 2.7.84; 3.7.84; 5.7.84 in particular.
27. For details of the liberalisation in the telecommunications industry, see Telecommunications Act (1981).
28. See NUR (1984), pp. 3–5.
29. For full details of assets and activities of Sealink and of the company's market environment, see Monopolies and Mergers Commission (1981).
30. See *Financial Times*, 16.5.84.
31. See *Sunday Times*, 24.6.84.
32. For details of the pooling arrangements, terminated in 1979, see Monopolies and Mergers Commission (1981), pp. 60–2.
33. For an account of the disposal of the former BTH assets, see Bagwell (1984), pp. 48–9.
34. See *Sunday Times*, 24.6.84.
35. See *The Times*, 5.4.84.
36. Ibid.
37. See *Sunday Times*, 8.4.84.
38. The *Financial Times*, 16.5.84, reported that estimates of Sealink's price had exceeded £70m in some cases. On the other hand, an earlier estimate, in the *Sunday Times*, 8.4.84, had predicted a price of 'around £50m'. Immediately following sale, the *Financial Times*,

19.7.84, suggested that 'the £66m sale price lies at the top end of City expectations'. The book value of Sealink's assets at the time of sale was £108m.

39. See *Financial Times*, 16.5.84; also *The Times*, 21.5.84. P&O Ferries were eventually sold to European Ferries Ltd in January, 1985 see *Financial Times*, 8.1.85.
40. See Joint Committee of Sealink Unions (1984a).
41. See Joint Committee of Sealink Unions (1984b).
42. It should be noted here that other evaluations of the NFC experience provide a quite different assessment. See, for example, McLachlan (1983).
43. See Transport Salaried Staff Journal (1984b), pp. 1, 5.
44. Sea Containers Ltd bought, via its Batchshire Ltd subsidiary, five hotels for £7m in 1982.
45. *Sealink News*, 18.7.84.
46. See *Financial Times*, 28.9.84.
47. See *Financial Times*, 18.9.84.
48. See *The Seaman*, November 1984.
49. See *Financial Times*, 30.7.84.
50. See National Union of Hotel and Catering Employees (NUHCE) News, March 1984.

References

Akerlof, G.A. (1970) 'The market for lemons', *Quarterly Journal of Economics*, 84, pp. 488–500.

Alt, J.E. and Chrystal, K.A. (1983) *Political Economics*, Wheatsheaf.

Atkinson, A.B. and Stiglitz, J.E. (1980) *Lectures on Public Economics*, McGraw-Hill.

Bagwell, P. (1984) *End of the Line? The Fate of British Railways under Thatcher*, Verso.

Brittan, S. (1984) 'The politics and economics of privatisation', *Political Quarterly*, 55, pp. 109–28.

Cave, M. and Hare, P. (1981) *Alternative Approaches to Economic Planning*, Macmillan.

Chiplin, B. and Wright, M. (1982) 'Competition policy and state enterprises in the UK', *Antitrust Bulletin*, XXVII, pp. 921–56.

Coase, R. (1960) 'The problem of social cost', *Journal of Law and Economics*, 3, pp. 1–44.

Financial Times, various issues.

Frey, B. (1983) *Democratic Economic Policy*, Martin Robertson.

Friedman, M. and Friedman, R. (1980) *Free to Choose*, Secker and Warburg.

Heald, D. (1983) *Public Expenditure*, Martin Robertson.

Heald, D.A. and Steele, D.R. (1982) 'Privatising public enterprise: an analysis of the Government's case', *Political Quarterly*, 53, pp. 333–49.

HM Treasury (1980/81) Committee of Public Accounts, *Private Finance for Nationalised Industries and Publicly Owned Companies*, HMSO.

Jackson, P.M. (1982) *The Political Economy of Bureaucracy*, Philip Allan.

Joint Committee of Sealink Unions (1984a) *Sealink Privatisation – An Ugly Business.*

Joint Committee of Sealink Unions (1984b) *Sealink Privatisation – It's Getting Uglier.*

Kirzner, I.M. (1973) *Competition and Entrepreneurship*, University of Chicago.

Lindblom, C.E. (1977) *Politics and Markets*, Basic Books.

McLachlan, S. (1983) *The NFC Employee Buyout – The Inside Story*, Macmillan.

Mishan, E.J. (1972) *Elements of Cost–Benefit Analysis*, George Allen and Unwin.

Monopolies and Mergers Commission (1981) *European Ferries Ltd, Sealink UK Ltd. A Report of the Proposed Merger*, HMSO.

Mueller, D. (1977) 'The persistence of profit above the norm', *Economica*, 44, pp. 369–80.

National Union of Hotel and Catering Employees News, various issues.

National Union of Railwaymen (1984) *Privatisation*, Paper presented at POEU Conference.

Pearce, D.W. (1971) *Cost–Benefit Analysis*, Macmillan.

Pryke, R. (1982) 'The comparative performance of public and private enterprise', *Fiscal Studies*, 3, pp. 68–81.

Sealink News, various issues.

Seaman, various issues.

Shackleton, J.R. (1984) 'Privatisation: the case examined', *National Westminster Bank Quarterly Review*, May, pp. 59–73.

Sharkey, W.W. (1982) *The Theory of Natural Monopoly*, Cambridge University Press.

Sunday Times, various issues.

Telecommunications Act (1981), HMSO.

Times, various issues.

Transport Act (1981), HMSO.

Transport Salaried Staff Journal, various issues.

Index